THE PAGEANT OF PAINTING

PIERRE D'ESPEZEL AND FRANÇOIS FOSCA

THE PAGEANT

OF

PAINTING

FROM THE BYZANTINE TO PICASSO

HARRY N. ABRAMS, INC. · PUBLISHERS
NEW YORK

LIBRARY OF CONGRESS CATALOG CARD NUMBER: 67–18982
ALL RIGHTS RESERVED
NO PART OF THE CONTENTS OF THIS BOOK MAY BE REPRODUCED WITHOUT THE
WRITTEN PERMISSION OF THE PUBLISHERS, HARRY N. ABRAMS, INC., NEW YORK
PRINTED IN WEST GERMANY
BOUND IN THE NETHERLANDS

CONTENTS

THE PAGEANT OF PAINTING

I

FROM THE CATACOMBS TO GIOTTO

By the end of the first century A.D., when Christianity began to spread in the Roman Empire, the question arose whether art would be allowed to play as great a part in the new religion as it had in paganism; and if so, what symbolic or narrative subjects would be treated by the artists. The attitude adopted by the Church was thoroughly sensible. Secular art, which served decorative purposes, was not prohibited save when it was excessively luxurious. Such art, however, as abetted idolatry, glorified "false gods," or furthered actions that the Church condemned, was forbidden.

Any religion implies public observance — rites and ceremonies performed in a suitable edifice, involving the use of special utensils and garments. Hence it must appeal to the services of architecture and the applied arts. Furthermore, in order to gratify deep human instincts, religion must translate its abstract dogmas into signs, which are its symbols. It has to place before the eyes of its followers images of the supernatural or human beings to venerate and invoke, and may remind them of the major events of existence.

Early Christianity might conceivably have simplified the forms of worship, as the Reformation did, and have proscribed images. But the Reformation coincided with the invention of printing and the spread of books, at a time when the written word was supplanting the image.

Ulysses and Penelope
Fresco, Pompeii

In the early centuries, however, the majority of Christians were illiterate, and manuscripts were rare and expensive.

Christianity was thus led to make use of the visual arts. This was not the result of a deliberate decision. Actually, opinions were divided. Some Christian authors condemned images on the ground that they might lead to a revival of idolatry. Others tolerated, or even encouraged them. On the whole, the congregations felt the need to see with their own eyes those episodes of the Old and the New Testament which reminded them of the great Christian virtues, and, still more, of the life of the Saviour. Accordingly art passed from the service of paganism to that of the Church. At first it was on a small scale, then on a grander, and finally on a magnificent one, once the Church had been officially recognized and was at last free to develop its own forms of worship, and to celebrate its triumph.

Early Christian art was a composite. Even when dealing with genuinely Christian subjects, both aesthetics and technique were borrowed from paganism. Elements were moreover derived from different regions of the Empire – from the Middle East and Egypt as well as from Rome.

PAINTING IN THE CATACOMBS

The earliest Christian paintings, those found in the Catacombs, reflect this variety. First of all there are decorative motives – garlands of flowers or figures of the Seasons – which are neither pagan nor Christian. Next come pagan mythological subjects which had been given a Christian significance – Orpheus taming the beasts, Cupid and Psyche, Aristaeus carrying a lamb. Then we find the purely Christian symbols – the Cross, the Lamb, the Fish, the Dove, the vine, the orant (a figure in the attitude of prayer with arms out-

spread). Then subjects taken from the Old Testament inspired by prayers for the dead, depicting persons God saved from peril – Noah, Isaac, Jonah. Lastly, scenes from the life of Christ. Just as the Old Testament subjects dealt with God's mercy, those from the New Testament dealt with the miracles, demonstrating the supernatural power and goodness of the Saviour. Thus we have the Marriage-Feast at Cana, the Miracle of the Loaves and Fishes, and the Raising of Lazarus. Other frequently found subjects are the Madonna and Child and the Adoration of the Magi.

It must be admitted that the artistic value of these paintings is very modest. They were commissioned by worshipers not out of artistic motives, but merely to proclaim their faith, and to provide visual images for their worship, and they were painted by artisans. The latter did their best, but that did not make them artists. The remarkable thing, however, in these decorations in the Catacombs, is the confidence they radiate, the serenity and joy. In those galleries full of corpses one cannot find a single funeral picture. Paradise is everywhere, and Hell is conspicuously absent.

THE BEGINNINGS OF BYZANTINE ART

In their pictorial language, the paintings of the Roman Catacombs carry on the tradition of mural decoration, exemplified in the works brought to light at Herculaneum and Pompeii. But in 1931 a Christian baptistery dating from the third century A.D. was discovered in the ruins of Dura-Europos, a small town in Syria. Its walls were covered by roughly painted pictures, whose subjects are not symbolic but narrative. The Christian chapel had been preceded by a temple of the old pagan gods of Palmyra, with paintings dating from the second and third centuries A.D., and a Jewish synagogue from the middle of the third century, decorated with scenes from the Old Testament. The paintings of these three buildings show that a Syrian art existed at that period, an art independent of the Hellenic tradition, and derived from ancient oriental sources. This art did not aim at an ideal beauty, nor did it bother with composition, perspective, or the correct proportions of the human body. It sought to record facts.

That was the soil which nourished Byzantine art. The priests of the pagan temple of Dura are represented in the same conventional manner as Justinian and Theodora amidst their courtiers in the mosaics of San Vitale in Ravenna. Byzantine art was both Christian and oriental. We have become so used to associating Christianity with the West, and the non-Christian religions with the East – Islam, Hinduism, Buddhism, etc. – that it is at first difficult for us to imagine an art that is both Christian and oriental. The fact is, however, that Byzantine civilization, though it claimed to be the heir to Hellenism, differs radically from ancient Greece in every respect, religious, intellectual, political, and artistic. As far as the visual arts are concerned, the influence of classical art is confined to certain manuscript illuminations.

Though Byzantine art underwent a greater evolution than was for a long time believed, it possessed certain characters which it maintained throughout its long history.

To begin with, it was essentially religious.

The Calling of Peter and Andrew
Mosaic, Basilica of San Vitale, Ravenna

Jesus, Mary, and the Apostles (detail)
Mosaic, Santa Maria in Trastevere, Rome

Art was at the service of the Church; the duty of artists was to express in line and color those great truths which the clergy, in spoken and written word, were teaching their flocks. The clergy guided artists and would never have allowed them to depart from its instructions. Consequently Byzantine art was profoundly traditional and impersonal. When it did change, it was not under the influence of great artists – as happened from the Renaissance on – but in passive obedience, either to a collective impulse or to the orders of an iconoclast Emperor.

For Byzantine art was at the service both of the Church and of the Emperor, the latter being regarded as God's representative on earth, a spiritual sovereign no less than a temporal one.

The other major character of Byzantine art lay in the fact that it was an oriental art. It was oriental in preferring color to form, and decoration to representation of reality. The Greeks and Romans were interested above all in form. Accordingly, in architecture as in sculpture, they liked to work in the round. A classical temple, like a classical statue, was composed of volumes, of profiles which bathed in the light. With the Greeks, as with the Romans, color played a secondary part. For centuries Greek vases were confined to three colors: black, red-brown, and white, which in differing shadings of light and dark had to provide the whole range of values: the artist never ventured further to explore the beauties of contrasting colors. And where color was used – whether in architecture, sculpture, painting, or the Roman mosaics – its main function was to bring out the form.

Byzantine art, on the other hand, like the art of other Oriental countries, including those of the Far East, was passionately fond of color, and took infinite pleasure in happy combinations of it. It was rather indifferent to sculpture in the round, preferring bas-relief. The arts the Byzantines most loved were those in which color took first place — mosaics of colored glass, cloisonné enamel, and silks. The drawing, the arrangement of forms, took a second place. And the distortions, the stylizations were dictated by the wish to give full value to colors and to achieve a decorative effect. That is why a painting from Pompeii dating from the first century B.C. is closer to a sixteenth-century Italian fresco than to a Byzantine mosaic of the twelfth century. In a Byzantine picture, whether a mosaic or a fresco, the expression of volume, the relief, is reduced to a minimum, it is simplified and subjected to conventions; the perspective is arbitrary, the third dimension (depth) only feebly suggested. Another indication of how oriental Byzantine civilization was is found in music. Recent research has shown Byzantine music to be derived, not from that of classical Greece, but rather, in fact to a considerable extent, from the religious music of the Syrian churches, derived in turn from the chants of Jewish synagogues. As with painting and mosaics, this music was closely related to the liturgy. According to Dr. Wellesz, author of the *History of Byzantine Music and Hymnography*, every art contributed to the liturgy, and the liturgy was regarded as an emanation of the Supreme Being which man was allowed to perceive through the inspiration of the artist. And he goes on to say that the hymns sung in the churches were echoes of those sung by the angels, just as the icons of the saints were images of their celestial appearance.

MOSAICS, BYZANTINE AND ROMAN

Christian iconography was greatly enriched by Byzantine art. The Church gave the artists their subjects — a story from the Old or New Testament or the lives of the saints, or some allegorical theme which embodied one of the great truths of the Faith. The subjects were never chosen for their pictorial possibilities but for theological reasons.

Byzantine churches were simple buildings, unadorned outside by any sculpture, but covered within by mosaics, often with a gold background which picked up the light. Frescoes were only used as a poor substitute for mosaics.

Roman mosaics were confined to floors and small murals, and they were made of cubes of colored marble, which afforded only a small range and little brilliance. The Byzantines preferred cubes of colored glass, which gave them a rich range of color of every intensity. They also used colorless glass backed by gold leaf or silver.

The Story of St. Stephen: St. Stephen Accused by the Jews
Saint-Germain, Auxerre, France

Examining a Byzantine mosaic done by expert craftsmen, we find the shaded parts (folds of drapery, for instance) differently colored from those that catch the light. In green drapery the shadows are yellow-green, the outer folds blue-green. The Byzantines pushed this technique so far, indeed, that in some of their mosaics the flesh tints are pink with the shaded part green. In a painting at Pompeii, on the other hand, the flesh is pink with brown shading.

If we emphasize this use of color it is because, centuries later, it played a major role in modern painting. Forgotten for hundreds of years, it was taken up again by the Venetians of the sixteenth century (particularly by Veronese) and by the tapestry-workers of the seventeenth and eighteenth. Following a new period of neglect, it was rehabilitated by Delacroix, the Impressionists, and Cézanne. It is a method particularly appropriate to mural decoration, for, suggesting rather than stressing relief, it does not break up the surface of the wall.

Byzantine iconography, which was later to inspire the iconography of the West, was a product of Palestine, the country in which Christ had lived, and Syria. The curlyheaded, beardless Christ, which had been the type favored in Italy, now gave way to the bearded Christ with an emaciated face and long hair parted in the middle, a perfect oriental type which was thereafter to be adopted throughout Christendom.

The mosaics and frescoes in the churches were executed in accordance with instructions of the clergy. Figures and scenes were arranged in a characteristic pattern. At the summit of the cupola was a gigantic Christ, the All-Powerful or *Pantocrator*, while the four Evangelists occupied the pendentives, and the Holy Virgin or *Panhagia* the semidome of the apse. The twelve great festivals of the Church were placed, not in chronological order, but according to a theological one.

Very few examples are left of the secular mosaics which decorated palaces, but it is possible to form an idea of them from those that were made by the Byzantine craftsmen called to Damascus in 715 to work at the Great Mosque there. They depicted imaginary buildings and trees treated in a highly decorative style.

The earliest mosaics in Rome (those of Santa Costanza, 324–326, and Santa Pudenziana, 384–389) have nothing Byzantine about them; they reflect the classical spirit. But in the fifth century, with the arrival in Italy of Greek craftsmen, refugees from the iconoclasts, Byzantine characteristics began to appear, as may be seen in the chancel arch of Santa Maria Maggiore and still more clearly in Santi Cosma e Damiano. This Byzantine influence persisted through the following centuries, the principal examples being the mosaics of Sant' Agnese fuori le Mura, Santa Maria in Domnica, Santa Prassede, and Santa Cecilia and Santa Maria in Trastevere.

In a general history of painting it is impossible to review all the mosaics of Italy and Eastern Europe. All we can do is to mention those of Ravenna, Venice, Sicily, and those of Constantinople, Salonika, Nicala, and Daphni.

As we have seen, the Byzantines resorted to frescoes when they were unable to bear the cost of mosaics. The Byzantines did not paint them on fresh plaster, as the Italians did from the thirteenth century onwards. They painted with a similar material, with a foundation of chalk, but applied it after the plaster was dry.

In Italy such frescoes, painted in a thoroughly Byzantine manner, may be found in Rome in the Church of Santa Maria Antiqua (eighth-ninth centuries), at San Angelo in Formis near Capua

(1056–1086), and at Castelseprio in Lombardy. Those at Castelseprio are variously dated by the authorities between the seventh and tenth centuries.

THE CONTRIBUTION OF THE BARBARIANS

For five hundred years, from the beginning of the fourth century to the end of the eighth, successive floods of Barbarians swept over the Western Roman Empire. Peace and prosperity were at an end; activity came to a halt. As far as art was concerned, this state of affairs had several consequences. Few works of art were commissioned, and technical knowledge and skill were lost. Moreover this movement of peoples in the West meant that where formerly a Graeco-Roman tradition had prevailed there was now a new spirit and new traditions brought in from elsewhere. The taste of the newcomers was not founded on that of the people they subdued: for the most part they imposed their own.

The art which appeared in the Carolingian revival of the Western Empire – and it was the same in Rome – was highly composite. It contained in fact the most heterogeneous elements. Mixed with Barbarian art was an indigenous element belonging to a period prior to Gallo-Roman art and the art of the steppes. Added to this was the influence of Byzantine works which were constantly imported from the East by Greeks and Syrians, many of whom now lived in the West – monks, priests, and merchants, to say nothing of pilgrims back from the Holy Land. Still another element was Irish art, represented by the manuscripts illuminated by missionary monks from Ireland. Nor had the memory of classical days been obliterated, for many ancient monuments were still standing.

We know from the early chroniclers that the churches built in the West between the fourth and seventh centuries were richly decorated with embroidered hangings and mosaics with a gold background. Moreover we possess illuminated manuscripts with highly complicated interlaced motives, in which the human body is distorted into a decorative pattern. Some of the decorative works done between the eighth and eleventh centuries have survived. The most important of them are the mural paintings at St. John's, Münster, Switzerland, believed to date from between 780 and 840; in France the mosaic of Germigny-les-Prés dating from the beginning of the eleventh century, and the mural paintings at Saint-Germain d'Auxerre (about 859). In Spain we find only the mural decorations at San Quirce de Pedret in Catalonia, which are so unskilled as to be of merely archaeological interest.

MURAL PAINTINGS IN FRANCE AND GERMANY

From the eleventh century to the beginning of the thirteenth numerous frescoes were painted on the walls and vaults of the Romanesque churches of Western Europe. The walls were interrupted by few windows, and narrow ones at that, and thus, like the vaults, offered ample space for the painter. Except in Italy, mosaic work appears to have been dropped during this period.

Whether painted in France, Germany, Switzerland, or Spain, these Romanesque frescoes show certain general features: the use of flat colors and outlines in black or brown to emphasize the drawing, which is always in continuous lines, sometimes very distorted, and an ignorance of perspective, both linear and aerial. Admittedly these frescoes vary greatly in quality. Some were painted by true artists, others by mere artisans, repeating the lessons they had learned, to which they added nothing. But all, the bad as well as the good, have one merit: treated in very broad terms, with little detail, they were excellently conceived wall paintings. If one takes, for instance, a fifteen-inch figure from the church at Tavant (France) and projects it onto a screen, tripling the dimensions, one does not in the least get the impression one is looking at an enlarged vignette.

In some of these works – those, for instance, at Berzé-la-Ville and Puy, in France – painted on dark blue and green backgrounds, Byzantine influence prevails. The rigidly immobile figures are clothed in sumptuous vestments, draped in complicated folds, and the coloring is heavy. The artist gives the impression of being anxious to rival the work done in enamel or mosaic, getting his effects by his brilliant rich colors. This Byzantine influence is so striking in the frescoes of San Clemente Tahull in Catalonia (early twelfth century) and again in the frontal of the Cathedral at Seo de Urgel (mid-twelfth century) that one cannot help suspecting that their painter came fully trained from abroad.

Nor is Byzantine influence any less dominant in the frescoes done in Germany, those for instance of the Benedictine abbey on the Island of Reichenau on Lake Constance, those of St. George at Oberzell dating from the tenth century and those of St. Peter at Unterzell from the eleventh. The unknown artists painted the Last Judgment, various episodes from the Old Testament, and the miracles of Christ. Unfortunately little is left of them. Others have totally disappeared – those at Ingelheim, Aix-la-Chapelle, the Cathedral at Mainz, and Schloss Merseburg in Saxony, these last being of secular subjects.

The Last Judgment was also the subject of the late eleventh-century mural paintings in the church at Burgfelden in Württemberg. We find in them all the conventions of Byzantine art, including

Lust · Church of Tavant, France

its hieraticism, though we find at the same time a timid attempt to give the scenes more life and more expression.

The ceiling of the church of Zillis (Grisons, Switzerland), which dates from the middle of the thirteenth century, though still clearly Romanesque in style, is composed of small wooden panels with scenes from the life of Christ, angels, fantastic animals, and allegorical figures. The continuous black outline around the figures has led people to think that these paintings, which are in a lively, popular style, were done by a worker in stained glass.

Unlike the bulk of Romanesque fresco-painters, the unknown artist who painted the walls and domes of the church of Saint-Savin-sur-Gartempe in France is little indebted to the Byzantines. A distant forerunner of Giotto and Raphael, he wanted to depict life in movement, he wanted his versions of the Bible stories to be clear and simple. The frescoes in the church of Nohant-Vicq recall those of Saint-Savin by their simplicity and their feeling for action, though Byzantine influence is still apparent in the frame, whose motives are borrowed from illuminations. The attempt to get free of hieraticism and to visualize scenes as they might have happened appears in other paintings at Tahull in Catalonia, one of which shows David and Goliath, another, Lazarus in the parable of the rich man, with a dog licking his sores.

But the great Romanesque painter was the one who painted the crypt of the church of Tavant. Having painted patches on the wall, each in one color —yellow, brick-red, pink, straw—he proceeded to draw freely with strong incisive lines in red ocher. The lines do not contain the form; very expressively they suggest it. The art we have here is rough, vigorous, and distorted. Its swift and passionate drawing recalls that of some Chinese painters, and even of Toulouse-Lautrec in his posters.

The German mural paintings mentioned above were followed by other works of note, dating from between the mid-twelfth and mid-thirteenth centuries. Byzantine influence is maintained in the restored frescoes of the church of the Benedictine monastery of Prüfening near Ratisbon, which date from 1150 to 1170. There are other frescoes in Western Germany, similarly restored, which are very difficult to judge; but we can clearly see a tentative effort to throw off the Byzantine yoke in the figures of the saints and prophets in the Convent of Nonnberg at Salzburg about 1125. In a group of figures in the collegiate church at Gurk in Carinthia, the Madonna appears among women symbolizing the virtues. These paintings, still in good condition, date from 1254–1279.

The fact that mural painting in France and Germany was much less abundant in Gothic than in Romanesque times has been accounted for by the tendency of Gothic architects to make churches a skeleton of stonework, supplanting walls by stained-glass windows so that there was little space left for frescoes. The theory is not unsound, but it does not give adequate importance to the Gothic passion for stained glass for its own sake. In love with color – at its most

The Death of a Martyr · Saint-Savin-sur-Gartempe, France

intense – the men of those days pounced on stained glass as soon as it was invented, preferring its deep and vivid colors transpierced by light, glistening like jewels, to the flat and relatively dull colors of the fresco.

THE FIRST "PICTURES"

From the tenth to the fourteenth century the Emperors were busy building up the Holy Roman Empire, obtaining a foothold in Italy, and getting themselves crowned in Rome. But they ran into three obstacles – the Popes who were seeking to increase the authority of the Church, the city republics in which the spirit of independence ran high, and the feudal barons – three forces which determined the future course of Italian art.

In the twelfth and thirteenth centuries the influence of Byzantine art was still powerful. As many mosaics as frescoes were done in Italy, and the mosaic was an eminently Byzantine medium. But as early as the thirteenth century signs of liberation and rejuvenation had appeared. An attempt has been made to attribute this rejuvenation largely to the religious movement started by St. Francis of Assisi and the Franciscan order founded by him. According to this theory, it was his preaching, his love of humanity and of nature that induced artists to treat religious subjects with greater veracity and greater sensibility. To this it has been objected that Franciscan teaching could hardly have had much influence on the arts, any more than that of the Dominicans, since these two orders made a point of having their churches small and devoid of luxury. Nor must it be forgotten that the tendency toward dramatic or emotional treatment of certain religious subjects had already appeared in French sculpture, which was not unknown to Italian artists.

The four centers in which the first signs of a revival of painting appeared were Lucca, Pisa, Florence, and Rome.

Painting was now to leave the wall, and, with that, the "picture" was born.

During the first half of the thirteenth century, large crucifixes were painted on wooden panels or sheets of leather at Pisa and Lucca, to be placed in the chancel arch, over the high altar. Surrounding the body of Our Lord were little scenes taken from the Gospels or the Lives of the Saints.

Many of these cruxifixes are anonymous, but we know of one family, Berlinghieri, which, as was usual at that time, gave its name to a workshop where painted panels were produced. No doubt hieraticism is still the dominant note in these panels painted on a gold ground, and the perspective is crude. But the big panel by Bonaventura Berlinghieri in the church of San Francesco at Pescia is not lacking in either liveliness or grandeur. At the bottom is St. Francis, standing stiffly in his long homespun robe. His right hand is held up in blessing, while in the other he holds a book, exactly like the Saviour in Glory of Romanesque churches. To the right and left, little scenes illustrate the chief events of the saint's life. Both coloring and drawing are conventional; the red and green buildings, far from having any depth, seem to be made of painted canvas; and the birds, to whom the saint is speaking, are perched sideways, exactly alike, on branches of trees that look like underwater plants.

Similar tendencies may be found in the works of Giunta Pisano of Pisa, who did much of his work at Assisi, in those of the unknown artist referred to as the Master of the Magdalen (whose *St. Mary Magdalen* in the Accademia at Florence is conceived and painted much like Berlinghieri's *St. Francis*), and in that of Margheritone d'Arezzo. The latter's *St. Francis* in the Pinacoteca in Siena is in

BERLINGHIERI
The Crucifixion and Scenes of the Passion
Uffizi, Florence

the same posture as in the Berlinghieri panel. The artist tried to cast off some of the hieraticism, but if the figure is more vivid, it has lost the severe grandeur that characterized the Berlinghieri.

The frescoes of the Basilica of St. Francis at Assisi must be mentioned here, because the most famous painters of the late thirteenth and early fourteenth centuries worked on them. Founded in 1228 by Pope Gregory IX, the Basilica was not consecrated until 1253, but in 1250 the remains of St. Francis, the *Poverello,* had been buried in the crypt of the Lower Church.

It has been very difficult to determine the chronology of the frescoes of the two churches, upper and lower, and their painters, because of the numerous restorations. The frescoes of the transept and apse of the Upper Church and *The Madonna with St. Francis* in the Lower Church are attributed to the Florentine Cimabue who, helped by the Roman Torriti, started working on them in 1277. The remaining frescoes are still under discussion, though it is certain that Giotto had a hand (about 1226) in the frescoes depicting the life of St. Francis in the Upper Church.

CIMABUE

According to Vasari, it was Cenno di Peppe Cimabue who "cast the first light on the art of painting." Dante, who mentions him in Canto XI of the Purgatory, says he was the most famous painter of his day before Giotto. And the fourteenth-century historian, Villani, tells us that it was with him that painting began to take stock of nature. But Vasari, Dante, and Villani were all, like Cimabue, Florentines. In fact, as we shall see presently, the first painter to begin to cast off the Byzantine yoke was a Roman, Pietro Cavallini.

We do not know much of either the life or the career of Cimabue, who was born in Florence in 1240 and died soon after 1302. He went to Rome in 1272,

BERLINGHIERI
Scene from the Life of St. Francis
San Francesco, Pescia

and he may well have known Cavallini there. In 1301 he was working in Pisa, and was in Florence from 1302 to 1303. The principal works attributed to him —though some are disputed— are the *Crucifix* at the Church of San Domenico at Arezzo, the *Madonna* at the Uffizi, Florence, another almost identical *Madonna* at the Louvre, and a *St. John* in mosaic in the Cathedral of Pisa. In these paintings, as in the mosaic, the fetters of Byzantine tradition are still apparent in the static attitudes of the figures, the parallelism of the folds of the angel's robes, and the way clothing is touched up with gold, a relic of the outline plates of Byzantine cloisonné enamel. The anatomy of the body in the Arezzo *Crucifix* and the schematic relief of the head are thoroughly Byzantine. But in the two *Madonnas,* particularly in the face of the Virgin, the angels, and the four small figures at the bottom of the Louvre picture, we sense a desire to do without the outline, which limits and encloses, and to express volume through modeling.

There remains the fresco of the Lower Church at Assisi, which shows the Madonna enthroned, surrounded by angels and accompanied by St. Francis. No doubt the composition is very reminiscent of the Madonnas of the Uffizi and the Louvre, but the Virgin here has been restored. As for St. Francis, his emaciated face is very expressive, but no painter of the thirteenth century ever painted a face in this way, rendering the eyes, nose, mouth, and the thin beard by such light touches. This St. Francis has surely been restored too, though by a talented artist.

PIETRO CAVALLINI

For a long time Pietro Cavallini was only known by his mosaics, executed in Rome in the last third of the thirteenth century. His mosaics in Santa Maria in Trastevere are not without their merits, but they remain strongly influenced by Byzantine traditions.

The discovery in 1899–1900 of his frescoes in Santa Cecilia in Trastevere revealed a very great artist, who, besides rejecting the conventions of Byzantine art, turned, and was the first to turn, towards classical sculpture, seeking its lessons. Incidentally, he had occasion to work in collaboration with the sculptor and architect Arnolfo di Cambio, from which he may well have profited.

Unfortunately only fragments are left of the Santa Cecilia frescoes which depicted *The Last Judgment.* They show Christ enthroned among angels with many-colored wings, St. John the Baptist, and the Apostles. Here we have got well beyond Cimabue's hieratic stiffness and

his timid efforts at relief; the drapery no longer consists of carefully arranged regular folds touched up by gold. The figures and their clothing are composed of volumes that have wonderful breadth and solidity. The saints are no longer stock figures, like the "First Old Man" or "Second Young Man" of the stage, but genuine individuals with characters of their own. And the unforgettable face of Christ, grave and gentle, is utterly unlike the stern, haggard Byzantine *Pantocrator* sitting in judgment.

It is most unfortunate that so few examples of Cavallini's work have come down to us, for he was a painter of the first rank, who stands at the head of a

PIETRO CAVALLINI
An Apostle (detail of *The Last Judgment*)
Santa Cecilia in Trastevere, Rome

long list shortly to be followed by the names of Giotto and Masaccio.

GIOTTO

The name of this great Italian painter is the diminutive of his Christian name,

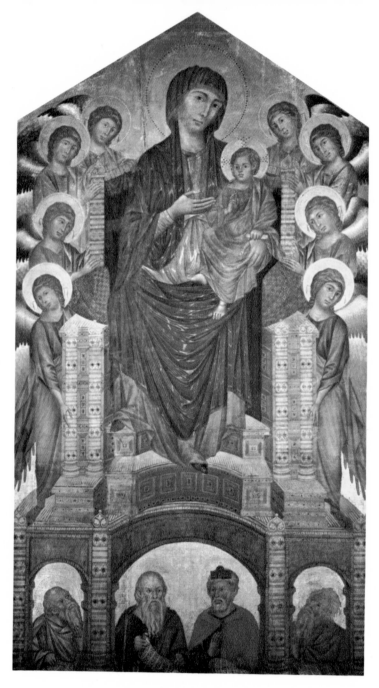

CIMABUE · *Madonna and Child with Angels*
Uffizi, Florence

GIOTTO · *The Lamentation*
Arena Chapel, Padua

which must have been Angiolotto or Ambrogiotto. The family name was Bondone. He was born in 1267 at Colle di Vespignano, a village in the Mugello region, near Florence. At the age of thirteen he was apprenticed to Cimabue, for whom he had, as was usual at the time, to run errands, sweep out the studio, and grind colors. He must have been still under thirty when he arrived at Rome, where he worked at Santa Maria Maggiore. From Rome, he went to Assisi, where, with his pupils, he worked in the Upper Church of the Basilica of St. Francis, painting scenes from the Old Testament. Two years later, still in the Upper Church, he painted episodes from the life of St. Francis. From then on, he led the life of a wandering artist. Traveling with his team of pupils, he worked in Rome, Florence, Pisa, Padua, Assisi, Verona, Ferrara, Naples, Lucca, and Milan. At an unknown date he married Ciuta di Lapo

23

del Pela, who bore him eight children. One of his sons was a painter, another a priest, and one of his daughters became a nun. In 1312, in Florence, he joined the corporation of physicians and apothecaries, which admitted painters too. In his time and after, he was venerated as a great master. Dante, Petrarch, Boccaccio, Villani, Ghiberti, Politian, and later on Leonardo da Vinci and Vasari heaped praises on him. He died in Florence on January 8, 1337, at the age of seventy. The major collection of frescoes by Giotto are those in the Upper Church at Assisi, the scenes from the Life of Christ in the Scrovegni chapel at Padua, and the scenes from the life of St. Francis in the Bardi Chapel of Santa Croce, and the scenes from the lives of St. John the Baptist and St. John the Evangelist in the Peruzzi Chapel, in Florence.

Many other frescoes done by him have been lost, and it is particularly regrettable that we no longer possess those of the Palace of the Kings of Naples at Castelnuovo, and those of the Visconti Palace in Milan in which he portrayed famous characters from the Bible and classical antiquity.

But it must not be forgotten that he also painted a few easel pictures and produced the drawings from which were carved the bas-reliefs of the campanile of the Church of Santa Reparata in Florence, which later became the Cathedral.

Giotto's painting certainly developed during the forty odd years of his career, but his work is sufficiently homogeneous to be considered as a whole without spending too much time on details.

When his paintings are compared with those of his immediate predecessors, one is not surprised that his contemporaries were lost in wonderment, thinking that now, for the first time, the painted figure had become lifelike.

In Giotto's frescoes and panels the By-

zantine formulas have completely disappeared, and with them the gold backgrounds. His figures stand firmly on the ground. The dryness and narrowness have gone; the volumes are broad and simple; all unnecessary detail is eliminated.

But Giotto takes his inspiration from reality only in the case of the human figure; the scenery behind them is summarily executed as though it was of secondary importance. His buildings, with their arbitrary perspective, his mountains,

GIOTTO
The Stigmatization of St. Francis
Louvre, Paris

24

DUCCIO · *The Calling of Peter and Andrew*
National Gallery of Art, Washington

rocks, and trees, are allusions to, rather than representations of, reality. He is only interested in man and what he is doing, and what he is interested in he depicts with both grandeur and simplicity. He keeps to the subject, in fact we might say, borrowing from the courts of law, the subject, the whole subject, and nothing but the subject. All unnecessary frills are excluded, though where the subject requires it he can be picturesque enough.

Thus at Assisi we have the back view of the darkly-clad figure receiving the stigmata, the flagellation of Christ by a Negro at Padua, the Sultan and the Orientals in the Bardi Chapel of Santa Croce. He does not even spurn humor. There is a caustic touch in the treatment of the pot-bellied innkeeper in *The Wedding at Cana.* Indeed the chroniclers depict Giotto as a gay companion, always ready for a practical joke.

In his work there is no trace of the gentle sweetness we find in the Sienese School, and the dramatic scenes are devoid of gesticulation, vehemence, or strained expressions. His eloquence is always controlled. He obtains intense expression by very simple means without emphasis. Take for instance his *Massacre of the Innocents* and his *Raising of Lazarus*. And what could be more moving than the faces of Christ and Judas in *The Kiss of Judas* or the Virgin's in *The Nativity*?

Giotto seems to know exactly what he has to say, and he says it simply, forcibly, and with remarkable mastery.

Giotto could never have undertaken the many sets of frescoes he did, had it not been for his pupils, who helped him as they learned their craft. Some have remained nameless, like the very gifted one who painted the frescoes of Chastity, Poverty, and Obedience, and the one of St. Francis in Glory in the Lower Church at Assisi. For a long time they were believed to be by Giotto, but they are now rightly attributed to another hand, for they lack Giotto's power and restraint. They are full of color effects and picturesque or anecdotal detail which the master would have disdained.

Thanks to contemporary writers, we know the names of several of Giotto's pupils, but it is often very difficult to identify their work. Though they learned a great deal from their master, none of them developed a sufficiently strong personality of his own. The works attributed to Taddeo Gaddi and Bernardo Daddi, for instance, are no more than meritorious echoes of Giotto's art. The most gifted seems to have been a painter not yet satisfactorily identified whom art-historians have called Maso di Banco or Giottino. His frescoes of the life of St. Sylvester at Santa Croce in Florence have picturesque qualities that cannot be denied.

THE SIENESE SCHOOL

While Giotto, the Florentine, was giving new life to painting and exercising his genius in many parts of Italy, another school of painting was intensely active in Siena, a school composed of painters of similar tendencies, which lasted in all for a hundred and fifty years.

The first of these painters was Duccio di Buoninsegna (1260–1318). Unlike Giotto, he never broke away from Byzantine tradition. His great work was the *Maestà* in the Cathedral of Siena, whose two painted surfaces were later divided. The enthroned Madonna and Child are surrounded by saints and angels. It is a large icon with gold ground and highlights, in an ornate frame which the artist has attempted to endow with the richness and brilliance of an enamel or mosaic in order to produce, not merely a picture, but a precious *objet d'art*. It is only in the small panels on the other side that Duccio tries to escape somewhat from Byzantine hieraticism and to infuse his scenes with more life.

The hieraticism, the same gold background and gilded ornaments and vivid colors can be seen in the panels of Simone Martini (1284–1344), particularly in his *Madonna and Child* painted for the Palazzo Pubblico in Siena and his *Annunciation* in the Uffizi, Florence, in which he was helped by his brother-in-law Lippo Memmi. Looking at the latter painting, one is so facinated by the fairy-like appearance of the archangel wreathed with foliage that one is inclined to ignore the humble, shy expression of the Virgin.

In his frescoes, on the other hand, Simone Martini does succeed in breaking away from Byzantine conventions, and takes his inspiration from the life around him. In the church of St. Francis of Assisi, for instance, he has obviously enjoyed in-

AMBROGIO LORENZETTI · *A City*
Pinacoteca, Siena

troducing two jugglers in picturesque
clothes (one playing a double flute, the
other a rebec) into the fresco in which
the Saint is dubbed a knight.

Simone Martini lived the last five years
of his life in Avignon. He was intimate
with Petrarch, by whom he was held in
high regard. But we know nothing of his
activities at Avignon, which was at that
time the seat of the papacy.

Pietro Lorenzetti (1305–1348) and his
brother Ambrogio (1319–1348) were both
painters, and both died in the same year
of the plague. Pietro Lorenzetti's most
important work is the set of frescoes in
the Lower Church at Assisi. In them we
can detect a personal note absent from
his predecessors, greater freedom in treatment, and a sense of drama which make

his *Descent from the Cross* one of the
most remarkable works of the century.

Ambrogio Lorenzetti, too, painted Madonnas and saints in vivid colors on gold
backgrounds without departing from
tradition. But he also painted frescoes in
the Palazzo Pubblico in Siena, which
show him in a totally different light, the
*Allegories of Good and Evil Govern-
ments.* In these frescoes allegory is mixed
with a faithful portrayal of reality, and
reality seems to have a greater hold on
the painter than fable. The scenes of the
country around Siena (painted under a
dark and completely conventional sky)
are liberally interpreted by Ambrogio,
but the rolling hills, the castles, and the
peasants at work in the fields are nevertheless recognizable. In depicting the life

27

of the city, he showed himself an excellent observer, and it is with obvious pleasure that he painted gentlemen riding off to hunt, peasants coming to market, and girls dancing in the little square.

The painters who followed — Andrea Vanni, Bartolo di Maestro, and others — had not sufficient individuality to be mentioned here. With them the Sienese School came to an end. During the time it flourished, it not only produced some fine works of art, but its influence was felt throughout Italy, the Provence region of southern France, Germany, Poland, and Spain.

EARLY PAINTING IN FRANCE

If France in the fourteenth century got her illuminations, tapestries, and stained glass from abroad, it was not so with painting. Admittedly much of the work of this period has been lost, but the

SIMONE MARTINI · *The Annunciation* (center panel)
Uffizi, Florence

surviving fragments of frescoes disclose native talent no less than foreign influences. The sense of form and grandeur which distinguished Romanesque painting had disappeared. Because of their complexity, and excessive pursuit of refinement and elegance, these works must be regarded as enlarged illuminations rather than as mural paintings.

As for paintings on wood, we must, to deal with the subject chronologically, begin with the Barnabas altarpiece – the *Madonna Nursing her Child between St. Peter and St. Paul.* There has been much discussion as to whether this work is of English or French origin, but the experts agree that it dates from the thirteenth century.

The *Portrait of Jean le Bon, King of France,* in the Louvre, which dates from about 1360, is famous as one of the rare paintings of that time that have survived. It is undoubtedly a document rather than a work of art. Also preserved is what is known as *The Narbonne Parament,* the front panel from an altar, done with pen and ink wash on gray silk. Scenes of the passion are depicted with the kneeling figures of King Charles V and his wife; the drawing, thin and angular, is very calligraphic in style. The so-called *Wilton Diptych* in the National Gallery, London, shows King Richard II and his three patron saints kneeling before the Madonna, who is surrounded by angels. This work, dating from 1396, is unquestionably charming, but is still very much of an illumination. Other panels have come down to us, scattered among various museums and private collections, but though their historical value is undeniable, their artistic value is small. For that we must wait till the following century, when French painting had felt the impact of Flemish and Italian work.

Between 1343 and 1347 Pope Clement VI summoned the Sienese painter Matteo Giovanetti, called di Viterbo, to Avignon

SCHOOL OF PARIS
Portrait of Jean le Bon, King of France
Louvre, Paris

to decorate the Papal Palace. The frescoes he and his pupils painted of religious subjects are definitely Italian in character, while the hunting and fishing scenes are astonishingly reminiscent of French and Flemish tapestries. The same is true of the hunting and love scenes in the frescoes painted in a house at Sorgues, probably about 1365.

THE RISE OF GERMAN PAINTING

The first half of the thirteenth century had been an extremely brilliant period for the German Empire, but the second half saw that brilliance vanish. At the same time the burghers, who were becoming rich and conscious of their importance, began to play a part as patrons of the arts. During the whole of that century we may observe more or less pronounced efforts on the part of artists to free themselves from Byzantine influence.

Soest in Westphalia was the center from which this influence was spread over all North Germany. The most typical example is the mural decoration of the Marienkirche in Dortmund which was planned as if for a Byzantine church. The Tree of Jesse, on the other hand, painted on the ceiling of St. Michael's, Hildesheim, brings to mind the stained-glass window of a cathedral.

At Cologne the paintings on the baptismal founts in St. Gereon's and St. Cunibert's are freer and more lively in style, perhaps reflecting French influence.

The first panel paintings are of Westphalian and Lower Saxon origin. They were used for the decoration of altars. The custom had been to decorate the front of the altar with repoussé work in precious or other metals inlaid with enamel, but eventually such metal work was replaced by less expensive paintings on a gilt background. Stucco ornaments in relief were also gilded. Over the altar stood an altarpiece with side panels which could be closed over the central one. In the thirteenth century altar frontals *(antependia)* and altarpieces were produced at Soest and Quedlinburg in Lower Saxony. The most remarkable is the *antependium* of the Wiesen-Kirche (St. Mary of the Meadow) at Soest, now in Berlin. It is in three parts, the Trinity in the middle, the Madonna on the left, and St. John the Evangelist on the right. The figures are still rather stiff and their clothing falls in many angular folds, but the painter has nevertheless thrown off Byzantine traditions and given a personal note to his work.

FRENCH SCHOOL · *The Narbonne Parament*

The revolt against Byzantine conventions gathered momentum in the fourteenth century, as we see from the decorations on the choir screen of the Cathedral of Cologne, dating from the first quarter of that century, and in those of the Mino-riten-Kirche, which are painted with intense feeling. The same features are found in northern Germany, in the mural paintings of Lübeck, Marienburg, and Wismar, while in the south, at Constance and in the Tyrol, we can detect the influence of English and French illumination.

In the panel paintings the influence of illuminations is strongly marked. They are highly expressive, even though the form is still thin and calligraphic. Among the works most worthy of attention we may mention the Bebenhausen altarpiece in the Museum of Fine Arts at Stuttgart and the altarpiece at Klosterneuburg which dates from about 1325.

Charles IV of Luxemburg, elected Em-peror in 1347, made Prague an artistic center, and for some years painters were very active there. The nine panels found in the abbey at Vyssi Brod in southern Bohemia, which date from about 1350, are thought by some authorities to show the influence of the Siena School.

The same features are found in the panels of the Master of Trébon now in the Prague National Gallery, which are believed to date from about 1390. The elongated and emaciated figures look like spirits of some sort.

A certain number of paintings of the Madonna and Child, highly reminiscent of Byzantine icons, were produced in Bohemia toward the end of the fourteenth century. Such works were common in countries with a Slav majority, such as East Prussia and Silesia. A similar style crops up in the work of the Nuremberg School, which was to flourish so brilliantly in the following century. On the other hand, a definite Italian influence is

Louvre, Paris

BOHEMIAN MASTER · *The Madonna of Glatz*
State Museums, Berlin-Dahlem

found in the beautiful triple altar from the Franciscan Church at Bamberg, now in the Bavarian National Museum at Munich.

The same Italian influence predominates in the wall paintings of South Tyrol illustrating scenes of secular life. We find it in some Austrian works, like Altmühldorf's *Crucifixion* (painted about 1420 and inspired by Giotto), but in other paintings the Bohemian style is maintained.

In Spain, Catalonia, grown rich by commerce, was the region of the greatest activity in the second half of the fourteenth century. But is was still too early for original talent to emerge. Ferrer Bassa, born probably 1285–1290, died 1348, is only an awkward and timid imitator of Simone Martini and the Lorenzettis. The same can be said of the Serra brothers, of whom Jaime was born in 1395 and Pedro lived from 1343 to 1403.

On the other hand, in the last years of the fourteenth century and in the early fifteenth very interesting work was being done in the northern provinces of France and in the County of Flanders and Dukedom of Burgundy, then united. The artists involved were as much occupied by illustration as by painting. Whereas for the last century and a half illumination of manuscripts was a painters' sideline, we have the feeling that at this time and in this area artists were primarily illuminators. And when they left their parchment to paint on panels, their style remained that of illuminators.

Among the artists who worked for the Duc de Berry, a passionate lover of beautiful books, was Jacquemart de Hesdin (active c. 1384) and Pol, Hennequin, and Herman of Limburg, whose work we hear of in 1402 and 1416. The illuminations they did for *Les Très Riches Heures du Duc de Berry* are justly famous for

MALOUEL · *Pietà*
Louvre, Paris

bring down his heavy ax on the martyr's neck is depicted with great power, and the faces of the spectators are painted with merciless truth.

ITALY ON THE EVE OF THE QUATTROCENTO

In northern Italy on the eve of the fifteenth century provincial schools were in existence which had been inspired by Giotto and the Sienese painters. They also followed what was going on in the Franco-Flemish and German schools as they gradually developed a style of their own. Venetia was the area in which the most characteristic talents cropped up. At Verona and Padua were Altichiero, who worked between 1369 and 1384, and his collaborator Avanzo (c. 1350–c. 1400). Their manner of grouping figures bears witness to their having studied the

their sense of light and of landscape and for their delightful portrayals of peasants at work and lords and ladies at play. An isolated figure is the unknown artist with a powerful and original talent, who illustrated the *Heures de Rohon* in the middle of the fifteenth century.

The same qualities cannot be attributed to the little panels with gold backgrounds done by Melchior Broederlam, Jean Malouel, and Henri Bellechose. Broederlam, a native of Ypres who worked at the end of the fourteenth century, painted delicate pictures of tender sensibility. Malouel, who died in 1415, has a *Pietà* in the Louvre whose forms are lacking in strength, and he collaborated with Bellechose in a picture commissioned in 1398 by Philip the Bold, Duke of Normandy. Above Christ on the Cross are God the Father and the Holy Ghost while on the right and left are two scenes, the martyrdom of St. Denis, and Christ appearing to the Saint in prison. There is admittedly a good deal of awkwardness in the painting, and the sizes of the various figures seem to be haphazard, but the executioner about to

BROEDERLAM
The Flight into Egypt
Musée Magnin, Dijon

FRENCH SCHOOL
The Last Communion and Martyrdom of St. Dionysius
Louvre, Paris

Giottos of the Scrovegni Chapel. In Venice the style that has been called "International Gothic," mixed with the still tenacious Byzantine conventions, is found in Jacobello del Fiore, who died in 1439, and in the even more tradition-bound Michele Giambono, who died in 1462.

A pupil of Altichiero's, Stephano da Zevio (early fifteenth century) has left us some panels whose gracefulness verges

on mannerism but which are extremely decorative. An illuminator much more than a painter, Gentile da Fabriano (1360–1427) has left us works characterized by charming colors touched up with gold.

The most remarkable of these artists is undoubtedly Antonio di Puccio di Cerreto (c. 1395–1450), known by the name of Pisanello, taken from his birthplace. He was a medalist of genius, a marvelous draftsman, and a painter with a very individual style. Unfortunately, few of his paintings have survived. Not so with his drawings; an admirable collection of them may be seen at the Louvre. His birds and animals are particularly striking. Whether they are familar or exotic – we find a goldfinch as well as a cheetah – they are drawn with great mastery. He was an equally acute observer of his contemporaries. His fondness for animals is shown in his frescoes at Sant'Anastasia and San Fermo at Verona. In the former, a fresco of *St. George and the Dragon*, the saint, on a powerful palfrey, his dogs, and the princess he is rescuing, are placed in front of a town of fantastic architecture. In the one of San Fermo, the archangel Gabriel is swooping down

GENTILE DA FABRIANO
The Presentation in the Temple
Louvre, Paris

ANTONIO PISANELLO
A Princess of the Este Family
Louvre, Paris

on huge wings with the Annunciation to the Virgin, and the painter has not been able to resist the temptation to add a small dog and some pigeons.

His portrait of a princess of the Este family—a simple profile against a background of flowering shrubs with butterflies—is rigorously exact and exquisitely done.

II

THE FIFTEENTH CENTURY

Many attempts have been made to analyze the causes of the great artistic movement we call the Renaissance, which, as far as Italy was concerned, began in the fifteenth century. But historians have too often forgotten that the Quattrocento artists, far from being intellectuals, were really artisans with scant education, so that a transformation of their art must have taken place for artistic reasons in the first place, other causes – such as philosophical or economic ones – being incidental.

Emphasis has been laid on the fact that by the fifteenth century the Italian bourgeoisie had, with their wealth, acquired a new importance and that the commercial and industrial towns were overflowing with money. But if wealth attracts artists, hungry for commissions, it does not bestow the gift of art. Great painters do not spring up just because there is money about; if they did, they would have abounded in wealthy nineteenth-century England.

Emphasis has also been laid on the influence of the humanists, themselves influenced by the literature of Greece and Rome and by Platonic philosophy. As a matter of fact, the ideas spread by those generally regarded as representative of the new mentality – Nicolaus of Cusa, Pico de la Mirandola, Marsilio Ficino, Erasmus – were totally unknown to the painters of the Quattrocento, whose minds were focused on artistic problems. Besides, the Italian humanists, imbued with the classical prejudice that manual work was fit only for slaves, had often nothing but contempt for artists.

There remains the fascination the relics of classical art might have exerted on artists. But on this point we must make a sharp distinction between architects and sculptors on the one hand and painters on the other. The architects and sculptors could not fail to be aware of the buildings, statues, and bas-reliefs that had come down to them from the past. They took them in, without surrendering to them. They never imitated the Greeks slavishly, but gave first place to the study of nature.

The painters, for their part, had little in the way of models to guide them – just a few insignificant fragments of classical painting. The Roman buildings had no direct lesson for them. It is in fact obvious that it could not have been from ancient statues or the bas-reliefs on sarcophagi that they derived their inspiration when they arrived at that subtle, faithful rendering of forms, or, like Botticelli, at that fluid, graceful version of the human body. The way in which Botticelli—or Castagno or Piero della Francesca—conceives and draws the human form shows no trace whatever of the influence of classical sculpture. The naked human body as depicted by a fifteenth-century Italian painter is very different from the human body as rendered in stone by the classical sculptor. Man as painted by the *quattrocentisti* has often a very small waist, an attribute which suited the fashion of the day, and short muscles rather than long ones—two features unknown to classical sculpture. As for woman, she was far from having the proportions of classical statues. She had, as can be seen in Botticelli's *Spring* and *Birth of Venus*, a long slender body, sloping shoulders, little bust, and a rounded stomach, and, as with the men, these characteristics were accentuated by the fashion in clothes.

What the *quattrocentisti* borrowed from antiquity were the edifices they put so often into the background of their paintings or frescoes, or an occasional detail like the sarcophagus in Ghirlandaio's *Adoration of the Shepherds*. When they treated classical subjects, as Botticelli did in his *Birth of Venus*, his *Pallas*, his *Calumny*, as Benozzo Gozzoli did in his *Abduction of Helen*, or as Pinturicchio did in *The Return of Ulysses to Penelope,* they did so without the slightest trace of classical influence. Mantegna, a passionate lover of ancient Rome, was the only exception.

THE BEGINNING OF THE RENAISSANCE

If we want to come to grips with the real causes of the Renaissance we have to put in the forefront the fact that the Italian of the fifteenth century, like his descendant of the twentieth, is naturally responsive to physical beauty, whether it is that of a human body, a horse, a flower, or a fruit. This characteristic, added to the very strong local patriotism current at that time, exerted a profound influence on the way in which painting

FRA ANGELICO · *Christ in Glory at the Gate of Heaven*
National Gallery, London

was understood in Italy in the fifteenth and subsequent centuries.

Another thing that must be kept in mind is the fact that the *quattrocentisti* – many of whom had started as goldsmiths and were sculptors and architects as well – were artisans of humble stock. As far as education was concerned, they could read, write, and count, and that was about all. As for culture they knew plenty of proverbs, legends, funny stories, episodes from the lives of the saints, and prayers. Their knowledge of the Bible was nothing like a theologian's, and of mythology nothing like a humanist's. They made no difference between the Roman gods and heroes, who for centuries had played a part in Italian folklore, and the heroes of the *chansons de gestes*. At the age of nine or ten they entered a master's workshop to learn their trade by seeing how it was done. They did not think of themselves as superior to blacksmiths, carpenters, or cobblers. They were as ready to paint a wedding chest, a standard, or a peasant's basket as a picture or a fresco. They were of modest means. When given a big job to do, such as the decoration of a chapel or a cloister, they were paid by the month or by the area covered. When they set out to depict a scene from the Bible or the life of a saint, they put into it the things they saw about them – people, rocks, animals, olive trees, or cypresses. All they saw was grist to their mill, and they were prompt to reproduce it. They did not work for a restricted circle of connoisseurs, but for the people as a whole. All the world saw their work in the churches and public edifices, and took an interest in it.

The impetus Giotto had given to painting was renewed and spurred on in the following century by a whole troop of Florentine artists, whose example was soon followed in other parts of Italy. To Giotto's legacy two new elements of the greatest importance were added – an unceasing, passionate study of nature, particularly of the human body, and a knowledge of the laws of perspective.

The study of human anatomy made enormous progress in the fifteenth century. Everywhere we can see how eager artists were to reproduce the human form and its musculature – in Masolino's *Baptism of Christ* in the Baptistery of Castiglione d'Olona, for instance, or Signorelli's many paintings and frescoes.

Perspective was rediscovered by the architect Brunelleschi and treatises on it were written by Leon Battista Alberti (1435) and by Piero della Francesca. Giotto went no further than a rudimentary and conventional perspective. Buildings in his frescoes are greatly reduced in size, a church having the dimensions of a summer-house. It is the same in the works of Fra Angelico and in the scenes from the life of St. Stephen in the Vatican painted in the middle of the century. In two scenes from the life of St. Lawrence, on the other hand, though painted at the same time and place, we find two church interiors given in correct perspective. Brunelleschi taught the laws of perspective to Masaccio, who applied them correctly. They were also studied assiduously by Uccello, Andrea del Castagno, and many others. There is no doubt whatever that many of the architectural backgrounds of paintings and frescoes were not there for the sake of the subject treated, but to demonstrate the artist's mastery of this new science.

Florentine and Umbrian artists readily took to linear perspective, as it enabled them to draw their scenes in a more lifelike manner. They took less interest in what is called aerial perspective, the art of portraying distance by different shades of color. For them form took precedence over all the rest. Florentine drawings are scrupulously exact, though without falling into dry meticulousness. There is every reason to think that this preoccupation with form is due to the fact that so many of the artists started as goldsmiths and sculptors.

Lastly, one of the great aims of the painters of that time was to depict human beauty. When a *quattrocentisto* set out to treat a subject, he wanted everyone in it–Christ, the Madonna, saints, and angels–to be as beautiful as possible in both face and figure, except when the subject specifically demanded it, as with St. John the Baptist in the desert or the penitent Magdalen. So far did they carry this love of physical beauty that in scenes of the Nativity they never painted the new-born Christ realistically–that would not have been beautiful enough– but as a child of at least one year old.

Florence was the great center from which the new painting spread throughout Italy, reaching even to Venice.

At the beginning of his career, the Dominican monk Fra Angelico (1387–1455) may seem at first sight a mere follower of Lorenzo Monaco (c. 1370–1456), a Camaldolite friar who also painted pictures of gentle piety, in vermilions and ultramarines enhanced with gold. But Fra Angelico was really of quite another order of talent; in fact, it is no exaggeration to say there is no one to whom he can be compared. He is unique. Throughout his long life he was an exemplary monk, unfailing in piety and obedience. But, monk and mystic though he was, he was well able to keep pace with the progress that was going on in painting outside the cloister. To be absorbed in God did not prevent his looking at and admiring the world God had created, or studying the works of his contemporaries. In his daily works, those at Cortona and Perugia, for instance, the *Madonna della Stella* panel now in the Convent of San Marco at Florence, or the *Christ Glorified in the Court of Heaven* in the National Gallery, London, he is still not much more than a minia-

turist. Little by little he learned to draw his inspiration from nature, and with that his painting became stronger and richer. His greatest work was the frescoes he and his pupils did at the Convent of San Marco. With their simplicity, their freshness, and their wonderful luminous quality, these frescoes rank among the most moving examples of Christian art. Finally, in the last years

MASOLINO DA PANICALE · *Adam and Eve*
Santa Maria del Carmine, Florence

TOMMASO MASACCIO
Adam and Eve Expelled from Paradise
Santa Maria del Carmine, Florence

of his life, Fra Angelico painted some scenes from the lives of St. Stephen and St. Lawrence on the walls of the private chapel of Pope Nicolas V. They show that he was still a remarkable observer, and that his sense of form had become ampler.

To Masolino da Panicale (1383–1447) we owe the very interesting frescoes in the Carmine at Florence and others at Castiglione d'Olona in Lombardy. His pupil, Masaccio (1401–1428), was one of those meteoric artists who in a few years reveal prodigious gifts and then die. Incidentally he is a somewhat isolated figure in the Florentine painting of his day. While all those who came after him were given to outlining their forms

sharply, insisting on the two-dimensional aspect and using bright colors, Masaccio was more interested in volume than the silhouette. He builds up the human body in blocks, like a sculptor modeling in clay. And with little feeling for freshness of color, he uses heavy opaque pigments. From his earliest works on, *The Madonna and Child with St. Anne* in the Uffizi and the polyptych altarpiece at Pisa, down to the frescoes in the Brancacci chapel of the Church of the Carmine in Florence, he painted massive figures eliminating all detail that might interfere with the form. He is moreover indifferent to human beauty. His work is admirable in its simplicity, breadth, and grandeur. According to his contempo-

PAOLO UCCELLO · *The Battle of San Romano*
Uffizi, Florence

ANDREA DEL CASTAGNO · *St. John the Baptist*
Santa Croce, Florence

raries, his frescoes in the Brancacci chapel were studied by his juniors, but the lessons they contained were not really understood before Michelangelo and Raphael. Paolo Uccello (1397–1475) was famous for his love of perspective, to discuss which he would wake his wife up in the middle of the night. He painted scenes from Genesis in the frescoes in the Green Cloisters of Santa Maria Novella. They are done in *terra verde* and their style is restrained and even severe. In perspective, Uccello saw not only a means of painting nature more faithfully, but of producing new plastic effects by the skillful arrangement of volumes in space. He has also left us three very decorative battle scenes and a sequence of small pictures of great originality, such as the *Battle of San Romano* in the Uffizi. The work of Andrea del Castagno (1423–1457) as we see it in the frescoes in the Cenacola di Sant'Apollonia and in the Santissima Annunciata (both in Florence) shows close affinity with Uccello, though Castagno's style is more incisive. He was

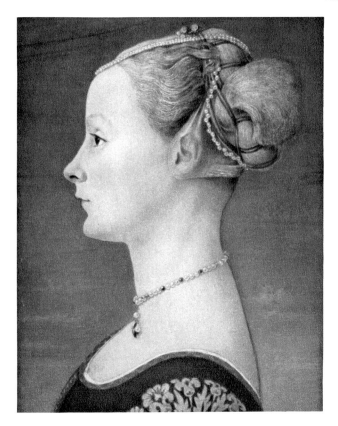

ANTONIO POLLAIUOLO · *Portrait of a Noble Lady*
Poldi-Pezzoli Museum, Milan

a strict, trained draftsman. For him, too, the chief problem was the arrangement of forms in three-dimensional space.

To these painters may be added the Pollaiuolo brothers, Antonio (1432–1498) and Piero (1443–1496), who were sculptors as much as painters. Their drawing is nervous, often intensely so, in their endeavor to depict the human body in movement.

Uccello, Castagno, and the Pollaiuolo brothers, like Masaccio, made no attempt to endow their figures with charm, beauty, or gracefulness. Not so the artists of the next generation, Gozzoli, the Lippis, Verrocchio, Botticelli, and Ghirlandaio.

Benozzo Gozzoli (1420–1497), a pupil of Fra Angelico, was unsurpassed as a story-teller. Of inexhaustible imagination, he was a fresco painter of great resource. Caring little for the fundamental problems of form, color, or expression, he set out to please and amuse, and gave full rein to his taste for the picturesque, for youth and beauty, for gay costumes, and

BENOZZO GOZZOLI · *Madonna and Child with Two Saints*
Palace of Fine Arts, Barcelona

for the landscape of his native Tuscany. Accordingly his frescoes–those in the Riccardi Chapel in Florence where the Medici are portrayed along with other notabilities of the day, and those at San Gemignano and the Campo Santo in Pisa—are enchanting in their diversity.

Those who commissioned Florentine painters to decorate their chapels saw to it that they themselves, their families, and their friends were included among the religious figures portrayed. Thanks to the custom, Domenico Ghirlandaio (1449–1494) became a chronicler of the Florentine society of his day. In his frescoes at Santa Maria Novella and at San Gemignano he used the Florence he knew as a background for Biblical subjects and the life of Santa Fina, giving us not only

portraits of his contemporaries but exact pictures of the interiors they lived in. A fresco painter of perfect mastery, he took pleasure in recording all he saw.

In contrast to Fra Angelico, the Carmelite Fra Filippo Lippi (1406–1469) was far from being a model monk. As for his painting, we can appreciate his sense of feminine gracefulness, but his form is lacking in amplitude, in fact, there is something cramped about it. He is at his best in the frescoes in the Prato Cathedral, the coloring of which is tender and subtle.

His son Filippino (1457–1504) was a pupil of Botticelli. He completed the painting of the Brancacci Chapel, begun by Masaccio. Later, in Rome and Florence, he painted pictures and frescoes,

DOMENICO GHIRLANDAIO · *The Visitation*
Santa Maria Novella, Florence

FRA FILIPPO LIPPI · *Madonna and Child*
Uffizi, Florence

in which he gradually slipped into an unfortunate taste for complication.

To our eyes and to those of most of our contemporaries Sandro Botticelli (1445–1510) and Fra Angelico are the two most representative painters of the Quattrocento—Fra Angelico of the first half of the century, Botticelli of the second. Though practically contemporary with Leonardo da Vinci, Botticelli belonged to a different stylistic period. He had been a pupil of Fra Lippo Lippi and must have collaborated with him. Then he worked with Antonio Pollaiuolo, whose lessons warned him away from facility and helped him to find the style that was to dominate his work. This influence was, however, more of form than of inspiration. He always kept a streak of melancholy, and a slightly uneasy calm

BOTTICELLI · *Portrait of an Unknown Man*
Uffizi, Florence

is stamped on all the female faces he painted, both in his religious and mythological works. No one could deny he had a highly individual feeling for physical beauty, for a cast of feature that is still to be found today in many a Florentine woman, and for a somewhat languid gracefulness in the lines of the body. With that vision in his mind he created a type of feminine beauty very much his own, a creature of dancing gait and slightly thin-blooded charm, and he produced it again and again – to render the Madonna and the angels, as well as Venus and the three Graces. In his *Primavera* and in *The Birth of Venus* classical themes are treated in a delightful way, but in a spirit far removed from paganism. He left relatively few frescoes; those from the Villa Memmi, now in the Louvre, show him highly proficient, but those in the Sistine Chapel are rather confused, and admirable chiefly in their detail. Botticelli was fifty years old when he was profoundly aroused and disturbed by the violent preaching of Savonarola, despite his friendship for and gratitude to the Medici. Henceforth his work was to bear the trace of this conflict. In his last pictures – *The Communion of St. Jerome* in the Metropolitan Museum of Art, New York, the two versions of the *Pietà* at the Brera in Milan and the Old Pinakothek in Munich respectively, and *The Sacred Allegory* at the Fogg Art Museum, Cambridge, Mass. – the religious feeling is expressed with painful intensity.

One of the most important aspects of his work can be seen in his mythological scenes. They mark a big step forward. Before him, painters had confined themselves to Christian subjects. Thanks to Botticelli the gods of antiquity regained a foothold on earth, above all Venus, a Venus who seems faintly alarmed by her own reincarnation and by the attentions of Mars, Mercury, and others.

Botticelli, that "Pre-Raphaelite," who was somewhat neglected after the triumphs of Leonardo, Raphaël, and Michelangelo, came back into favor in the nineteenth century, and we shall have occasion to mention his posthumous influence.

Andrea Verrocchio (1435–1488) was goldsmith, sculptor, and painter. In the few pictures we have of his, *The Baptism of Christ,* for instance, we can see the attempt to depict volume by relief (as well as by outline) which was to be taken still further by his pupil Leonardo. Lastly, amongst these Florentine painters, we cannot fail to mention Piero di Cosimo (1462–1521), who painted mythological subjects with a remarkable taste for the fantastic.

The Sienese painters of the fifteenth century – such as Sassetta (c. 1400–1450),

BOTTICELLI · *Spring*
Uffizi, Florence

BOTTICELLI · *The Birth of Venus*
Uffizi, Florence

Sano di Pietro (1406–1481), Vecchietta (1412–1480), and Francesco di Giorgio (1439–1502) – carried on the artistic traditions of their predecessors while trying to assimilate the Florentine innovations. The results were often charming, as in Francesco di Giorgio's *Nativity* at San Domenico in Siena or Sassetta's *Madonna and Child with Six Angels*. But the persistence of these painters in capturing sweetness and elegance becomes exaggerated.

Similar characteristics are found in the works of the Umbrians Benedetto Bonfigli (1420–1496) and Fiorenzo di Lorenzo (1440–1522), but in the end the Florentine influence on Umbrian painting contributed to the production of artists of far more talent and personality.

It is only in the last twenty years that Piero della Francesca (1416–1492) has come to be regarded as one of the greatest of the Italian painters. Apart from a few small easel pictures, his painting is chiefly represented by the cycle of frescoes on the legend of the Holy Cross in San Francesco at Arezzo. Like the Florentines of his day, he was an able draftsman, but he sought above all to reduce the human body to broad simple volumes, bathing them in a clear light. In accordance with the subject, two of his frescoes are battle scenes; he achieved astonishing effects with charging horsemen and brilliant standards against a pale blue sky. In other frescoes he painted grave, impassive faces, singularly hieratical in style. Lastly, in the one of them in which an angel appears at night to the Emperor Constantine sleeping in his tent surrounded by his guards, we are struck by the skillful painting of the light shining straight

ANDREA VERROCCHIO
The Baptism of Christ (detail)
Uffizi, Florence

down from the angel onto the others. Amongst his small panels are *The Scourging of Christ* in the Palazzo Ducale at Urbino and *The Resurrection* in the Palazzo del Comune at Borgo San Sepolcro, in which we find the same pure light, the same passion for perspective, and the same dignified figures.

The painting of Melozzo da Forli (1438–1494) has neither the originality of Piero della Francesca's, its luminosity, nor the disdainful impassiveness of its figures.

It nonetheless deserves our attention for its remarkable qualities, its amplitude of form, and the wealth and intensity of its color. His heads of angels, fragments of a wall painting in the Vatican, and his fresco of *Sixtus IV Founding the Vatican Library* make us bitterly regret he has left us so few specimens of his work.

Luca Signorelli (1450–1523) painted a large number of works. In the Cappella Nuova in the Cathedral of Orvieto he depicted the overthrow of the Antichrist and the Last Judgment with great vigor and asperity. It is not effects of light or coloring that he emphasized here, but the rendering of the human body, whose anatomy he has obviously studied assiduously. Signorelli has also left us the frescoes in the Sagrestia della Cura in the Chiesa della Casa Santa at Loreto, with groups of apostles and innocent, graceful angels.

Compared with him, Pietro Vannucci, called Perugino (1450–1523), seems a less important figure despite his ability as a draftsman. In his pictures of the saints he has too often drawn the same types in the same attitudes with the same inexpressive faces. Imitators of Perugino began a long tradition of religious art which is not even today exhausted, although it has become more and more insipid with the centuries.

Though less original, Pinturicchio (1454–1513) is distinctly reminiscent of Benozzo Gozzoli. He, too, is an excellent storyteller, with a keen sense of the pic-

PIERO DI COSIMO · *The Wedding of Thetis and Peleus*
Louvre, Paris

turesque. Loquacious, so to speak, he is sometimes apt to lose his way in detail. He decorated the Borgia apartments in the Vatican and the Library of the Cathedral of Siena with brightly colored frescoes enhanced with gold. He was really a miniaturist, as the *Portrait of a Boy* in the Dresden State Picture Gallery proves.

In the fifteenth century, thanks to four princes of the house of Este, Niccolò III, Lionello, Borso, and Ercole, who were enthusiastic over art and display, the visual arts prospered at Ferrara. Mantegna and Piero della Francesca worked there. Lionello acquired a triptych from Rogier van der Weyden, when he visited Ferrara. Of the three chief painters produced by Ferrara in this century – Cosimo Tura, Cossa, and Ercole di Roberti – Cosimo Tura (c. 1430–1495) was the most remarkable. He depicted a world in

LUCA SIGNORELLI · *The Conversion of St. Paul*
Church, Loreto

which everything seemed made of metal, a world haunted by sad-looking people with tense expressions. There is a hint of German art in the complicated folds of the clothing.

Both Francesco Cossa (c. 1436–c. 1478) and Ercole di Roberti (c. 1450–1496) worked, as did Cosimo Tura, on the frescoes in the Palazzo Schifanoia ("Sanssouci") in Ferrara, in which contemporary scenes were mixed with astrological allegories. Less contorted and grimacing than Cosimo Tura's figures, Cossa's have small round heads with bulging foreheads. He infused his complicated themes with life. The same feeling for life runs through the series of scenes painted to illustrate the miracles of St. Vincent Ferrier, in which, small as they are, the characters are not lacking in grandeur.

Andrea Mantegna (1431–1506) worked at Padua and Mantua. A pupil of Squarcione, he was influenced in his early days by Uccello and Donatello. From Uccello he acquired his enthusiasm for perspective, from Donatello his love of classical antiquity and a bent for scru-

PERUGINO · *St. Mary Magdalen*
Palazzo Pitti, Florence

BERNARDINO PINTURICCHIO · *Portrait of a Boy*
State Picture Gallery, Dresden

PIERO DELLA FRANCESCA
Portraits of Federico Montefeltro and His Wife
Uffizi, Florence

pulously precise drawing. To him we owe many altar paintings, the frescoes in what is called the Cappella del Mantegna in the Eremitani in Padua, and in the Palace at Mantua (including many portraits of the Este family), and cartoons depicting *The Triumph of Caesar*. Side by side with his desire for strictly truthful representation was that for historical accuracy, and he zealously studied the ancients. He had something of the erudition of a humanist, but he never allowed his painting to be cluttered or dulled by it. Though many of his classical details are in fact arbitrary, the antiquity he portrays is unquestionably grand and imposing.

His knowledge of drawing, on the other hand, and still more his understanding of perspective, had a powerful influence on many Italian painters. One of his master drawings is the *Death of the Virgin* in the Prado. More moving than exact, it impresses by virtue of that feeling for grandeur which runs through all his work. He began his independent career as a painter by winning the competition held at Padua for the decoration of the church of the Eremitani. His career ended in Mantua, while he worked for the Gonzaga family, making occasional trips to work at Rome, Florence, or Verona. In 1474 he began the decoration of the Camera degli Sposi in the palace at Mantua. In 1490, when Isabella d'Este married Francesco Gonzaga, he became, thanks to the influence of the former, a leading figure in artistic circles. It was Isabella who gave him very precise instructions for the *Allegory of Vice and Virtue* now in the Louvre. The *Madonna della Vittoria*, also in the Louvre, was a

COSIMO TURA · *Madonna and Child*
National Gallery of Art, Washington

FRANCESCO DEL COSSA · *St. Lucy*
National Gallery of Art, Washington

votive offering by the reigning Gonzaga after the indecisive battle fought at Fornovo in 1495. No work shows better than Mantegna's that genius is not necessarily fettered by rules and instructions.

The Florentines who came to paint in Venice in the first half of the fifteenth century, Uccello and Fra Lippo Lippi,

did not fail to influence the Vivarini brothers, Antonio (c. 1415–1480) and Bartolommeo (1432–1490). The Byzantine tradition nevertheless persisted, and it can be distinctly seen in the panels painted with gold highlights by Carlo Crivelli (1430–1495). For him a picture was a decorative object, whose richness of color and wealth of gilt ornamentation

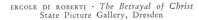

ERCOLE DI ROBERTI · *The Betrayal of Christ*
State Picture Gallery, Dresden

should make it rival an elaborate enamel in a jeweler's setting. As a matter of fact, both Mantegna and Giovanni Bellini occasionally used gold to underline the folds of a Madonna's veil or robes.

At this time, the Sicilian painter Antonello da Messina came to live in Venice. For a long time it was believed, on Vasari's authority, that he had previously been to Flanders, where he had picked up some of the technique of Van Eyck's painting. But it is not at all certain he ever went there, for he may equally well have seen Flemish painting at Naples, where, for example, King Alfonso possessed a Van Eyck. However that may be, his paintings show him to have been captivated by Flemish art, particularly in the matter of technique. For Flemish painters had by this time abandoned tempera for oil painting, and Antonello followed suit. He painted religious pictures and small portraits, which are remarkable for their great precision, particularly in the rendering of light. This quality may be seen in his *Portrait of a Man* and *Salvator Mundi* in the National Gallery, London; his Madonnas in the National Museum, Palermo, and in the Old Pinakothek in Munich; and his *Portrait of a Condottiere* in the Louvre. Both from an artistic and a technical point of view, Antonello had a decisive influence on Venetian painting.

GIOVANNI BELLINI · *Pietà*
Brera, Milan

ANDREA MANTEGNA · *The Death of the Virgin*
Prado, Madrid

VITTORE CARPACCIO · *The Sermon of St. Stephen*
Louvre, Paris

Venice gave him much, and he gave much in return. His religious pictures, such as the *Pala of San Cassiano* in the Kunsthistorisches Museum, Vienna, are certainly remarkable for their well-balanced composition as well as for their coloring, but what is most appreciated today are his portraits in oil, the heads always three-quarter-face and turned to the left. The modeling in the facial expressions is admirable. The face of the *Condottiere* expresses a ferocious, implacable will. The *Portrait of a Young Patrician* (Accademia, Venice) and another of a beardless man in the Palazzo Trivulzio in Milan bring their unknown sitters to life far more effectually than many a detailed

ANTONELLO DA MESSINA · *Portrait of a Condottiere*
Louvre, Paris

biography; indeed, Antonello da Messina's portraits must be regarded as among the masterpieces of his time. Jacopo Bellini (c. 1400–1470) was surpassed by his sons, Gentile (1429–1507), and still more by Giovanni (1430–1516), whose sister married Mantegna. Gentile liked to paint religious subjects in architectural settings, sometimes real, sometimes imaginary. His gift for color and his imagination were surpassed by Vittore Carpaccio, whose figure painting is shown at its best in the *Scenes from the Legend of St. Ursula* (Accademia, Venice), and the series of panels dealing with the lives of St. George, St. Stephen, and St. Tryphonius in the church of San Giorgio degli Schiavoni in Venice. With a close fidelity to nature, great precision, and a curious mixture of tenderness and naïve humor, he incorporated the details of everyday life in Venice into the oriental settings he imagined for the saint's life. Of these Venetians, Giovanni Bellini is the most remarkable, not merely for what he himself painted but for seeds he sowed which blossomed later in the works of Giorgione, Titian, Tintoretto, and Veronese, in their sense of light and feeling for color. In his early pictures we see the joint influence of Antonello da Messina and Mantegna, as in his *Presentation in the Temple* in the Accademia, Venice, and in his *Pietà* in the Brera, Milan. Later he gave more importance to the background landscapes of his religious paintings, getting more depth into his pictures as well as more light. He thus came to paint his finest works, *The Agony in the Garden*, in the National Gallery, London, *The Transfiguration*, in the National Gallery of Capodimonte, Naples, and, right at the end of his life, *The Feast of the Gods*, in the National Gallery of Art, Washington. He also painted many portraits and many Madonnas. Some of the latter are very vigorously painted; in others, such as the famous *Madonna of the Two Trees*, he used every resource to obtain an extremely smooth relief.

Giovanni Bellini exerted an excellent influence on several painters, including Cima da Conegliano (1459–1517), Marco Basaiti (1470–1528), and Bartolommeo Montagna (1450–1523).

Except for Leonardo da Vinci, Lombardy produced no painters in the fifteenth century to rival those of Tuscany, Umbria, and Venice. But Leonardo, though born in the middle of the century and a contemporary of Signorelli, Pinturicchio, and Carpaccio, was considerably in advance of his time in his conception of painting, and for that reason is rather to be regarded as a sixteenth-century painter.

Vincenzo Foppa (1427–1515) came from Brescia and worked in northern Italy. We can detect the influence of Jacopo Bellini and Mantegna in his painting, which is pleasant and picturesque, though somewhat devoid of character. The same can be said of Borgognone (1450–1523), who hesitated between the new tendencies of his day and the older traditions. Butinone (active between 1484 and 1507) and Zenale (1436–1526) were followers of Crivelli, as can be seen in their altar panels with gold highlights.

GOTHIC PAINTING IN FLANDERS

Italy was one of two great centers of painting in fifteenth-century Europe. The other was Flanders, which produced a large number of talented artists.

In those days the Flemish towns were commercial centers dealing not only with neighboring countries, but with Italy, Spain, and Portugal. They were also industrial centers famous for their cloth. They were very prosperous in the fourteenth century and still in the fifteenth, though their decline had already begun. Antwerp began to supplant its rival,

Bruges, whose navigable channels were silting up, and by the beginning of the sixteenth century it was the busiest port in the west.

In Italy painting was divided between murals done "al fresco" and panels done in tempera. Flemish painters rarely made wall paintings, and never used the fresco technique. Paintings for church decoration took the form of altarpieces, with or without wings, placed above the altar; they were painted in oil, as were portraits, which were smaller in size than altarpieces.

It has for a long time been recognized that Jan van Eyck was the inventor of oil painting, the technique that was to have so brilliant a history. There is no written record of the invention, however, and there was much argument before the matter was decided. According to the most plausible account, Jan van Eyck, by adding turpentine to oil, made it dry more quickly. This made work easier, and he obtained color of a brilliance and richness equal to stained glass.

Despite the differences that distinguish them, Flemish painters have much in common. Whereas the Italians aimed primarily at beautiful human forms, the Flemish artists sought to reproduce reality as faithfully as possible. They also strove to render depth, and to make air circulate among the objects represented. This they achieved by aerial perspective, the rendering of distance by color and light, rather than by linear perspective, for which they never shared the passionate interest of the Florentines. From the start, they liked to paint little landscapes, half real, half imaginary, as backgrounds for their paintings, whether religious pictures or portraits, and this fondness for landscape grew steadily through the century. Compared to the scenes found in Italian frescoes and panels, theirs may often seem to us rather stiff. For one thing, they may have felt somewhat cramped, painting their figures on small panels instead of having, like the Italians, a vast area of wall space to work on. They rarely tried to produce beautiful or clever combinations of lines and volumes, or to depict figures in movement, and in their Madonnas surrounded by saints and donors they were particularly given to symmetrical composition. But they were never behind the Italians in the deep seriousness of their art, a seriousness shown in their conscientious fidelity to nature, both in drawing and coloring, and in the dignified restraint of their works. No fifteenth-century Flemish painter can be accused of trying to show off his skill. We know little or nothing of their religious feelings, but, to judge from their painting, they were men of profound faith.

Jan van Eyck was probably born between 1390 and 1400. He died in 1441. He was the earliest of the Flemish painters, for his elder brother Hubert, supposed to have begun *The Adoration of the Lamb* in the Cathedral of Ghent, is so ill-defined a figure that some historians have denied his existence.

Jan van Eyck not only invented a new technique which vastly expanded the expressive potentialities of painting; he also was a great artist. Nor did he content himself, as did his fellow-painters, with amazingly faithful renderings of reality: he treated reality with such infinite devotion and humility as to transfigure it, yet without thereby making it seem less real. In the panels composing the altarpiece of *The Adoration of the Lamb*, as in the *Van der Paele Madonna* in the Royal Academy of Arts at Bruges, or *Giovanni Arnolfini and His Bride* at the National Gallery, London, time seems to be standing still. Familiar things that we as a rule take little notice of appear in an entirely new light; and Jan van Eyck teaches us to admire and to love them. That he should have succeeded in doing so is all the more remarkable for

JAN VAN EYCK
The Marriage of Giovanni Arnolfini and Giovanna Cenami
National Gallery, London

his making no effort, as the Italians did, to introduce figures of great beauty into his pictures. He took people as he found them, as worthy of being painted. This is also true of his landscapes. The broad, detailed landscape of his *Madonna and the Chancellor Rolin*, with the river, the bridges, the hills and towns, is justly famous.

As a rule, historians of Flemish art make little of Petrus Christus, who died about 1472. Admittedly he closely followed Jan van Eyck's style, but his *Lamentation over the Dead Christ* is beautifully composed and full of restrained feeling. Also by him are some remarkable portraits, such as the *Carthusian* in the Metropolitan Museum of Art, New York, and the *Young Woman* in the State Museum, Berlin-Dahlem.

The other great painter of this century is Rogier van der Weyden, also known as Rogier de la Pasture (c. 1399–1464). He seems to have learned his craft from a painter who was for a long time called the Master of Flémalle, but who is now identified by some authorities as a certain Robert Campin who was active during the first half of the fifteenth century and died in 1444. Diverse works have been attributed to him, such as the Mérode *Annunciation* recently acquired by the Metropolitan Museum of Art, New York, and *The Descent from the Cross* in the Walker Art Gallery in Liverpool, England. But whatever interest the Master of Flémalle's work may have, his forms often lack precision and his treatment of light is conventional.

Rogier van der Weyden, Van Eyck's great rival, lived in Brussels. He visited Italy, and spent some time in Rome and Ferrara. While Van Eyck's painting breathes serenity and acceptance of life as it is, Van der Weyden's expresses a deeply felt mysticism. His most moving paintings are *The Descent from the Cross* in the Prado, in which the Madonna is

swooning and the Magdalen writhes in agony, and *The Entombment* in the Uffizi, tragic in its simplicity. He also painted admirable winged altarpieces, particularly the one in the Old Pinakothek in Munich and the one in the Dahlem Museum, Berlin, *The Last Judgment* in the Hôtel-Dieu at Beaune, and *The Seven Sacraments* in the Royal Museum of Fine Arts, Antwerp. In the last

ROGIER VAN DER WEYDEN · *The Crucifixion* (center panel of *The Seven Sacraments*) Musée Royal des Beaux-Arts, Antwerp

named work he succeeds in combining figures of contemporaries with angels, without striking a discordant note. He also expresses what Bossuet called *l'inexprimable sérieux de la vie chrétienne* ("the extraordinary gravity of Christian life"). Not less remarkable are his portraits, such as the *Portrait of a Nobleman with an Arrow* in the Musées Royaux des Beaux-Arts, Brussels, and the *Woman with a Linen Cap* in the National Gallery of Art, Washington.

In the fifteenth century there was little difference between the northern part of the Low Countries (now Holland) and the southern part (now Belgium). The tendencies were the same; only the personalities differed. It would be difficult to point to any specifically Dutch features in the work of Dieric Bouts (d. 1475). His painting displays all the characteristics of the school as a whole: extreme precision in drawing, clear treatment, brilliant colors, distant landscapes, and skies painted in delicate blues and whites extending to the top. Dieric Bouts' originality asserts itself in his tall thin figures with impassive faces. This is most noticeable in his altarpiece in the Church of Saint-Pierre, Louvain, whose central panel with *The Last Supper* is surrounded by four smaller panels, depicting scenes from the Old Testament, which prefigure the Sacrament. Another example is found in the tall panels in the Musées Royaux des Beaux-Arts, Brussels, illustrating a legend about Emperor Otto III. Although the scenes include a beheading, an ordeal by fire, and the burning of a woman, the spectators are depicted as imperturbable.

Albert van Ouwater, active between 1430 and 1460, was another painter from the northern Low Countries. The only work that can be attributed to him with any certainty is *The Raising of Lazarus*, now in the State Museums, Berlin-Dahlem.

Hugo van der Goes, who lived in the second half of the fifteenth century, suf-

MASTER OF FLEMALLE
St. Barbara by the Fireplace
Prado, Madrid

DIERIC BOUTS · *Head of Christ*
Boymans-van Beuningen Museum, Rotterdam

fered from a mental disorder toward the end of his life, and retired to the Prieuré de Rouge-Cloître near Brussels, where he died in 1482. He painted one of the Flemish masterpieces of the period, the altarpiece of *The Adoration of the Shepherds* in the Uffizi at Florence, on whose side panels are shown the family of the donor, Tomasso Portinari, and their patron saints. In this picture, as in *The Madonna and Child with St. Anne and a Donor* in the Musées Royaux des Beaux-Arts, Brussels, the artist, though following the footsteps of his predecessors, has engaged in explorations of his own. He emphasized secondary figures and, in the foreground, added carefully drawn bunches of flowers or tufts of herbs, and irises and red lilies in a pot of Italian faience. His *Lamentation over the Dead Christ* and *Death of the Virgin,* which may have been inspired by his illness, display a vehemence and an intensity of expression that are quite new in Flemish art.

HUGO VAN DER GOES · *Madonna and Child with St. Anne and a Donor*
Musées Royaux des Beaux-Arts, Brussels

Hans Memling, or Memlinc (c. 1435–1494), was born at Mainz, and lived in Bruges. His paintings on the Shrine of St. Ursula in the Hôpital Saint-Jean belong in spirit more to illumination, but, perhaps because Bruges has many visitors, it is his most famous work. A reliquary in the form of a chapel, standing some three feet high, provided sufficient space on its wooden walls for a series of paintings representing the life of St. Ursula; and there are medallions on the roof showing the Coronation of the Virgin and more scenes of St. Ursula with her companions and angels. With an excellent sense of composition, Memling subordinated everything to the over-all decorative effect he intended: a shrine brilliantly ornamented with gold and precious stones.

He had more room in which to expand in his altarpieces of the Madonna and Child surrounded by angels and donors, and in the very fine panel depicting St. Maurus, St. Christopher, and St. Giles, dating from 1484. In the center St. Christopher is shown carrying the Infant Jesus on his shoulders across the water. On the left is St. Maurus, reading, and on the right St. Giles, holding a book and stroking a doe. In another picture William Moreel is accompanied by his patron saint and his five sons, while his wife Barbara Vlaenderberghe, with her patron saint, stands at the head of her eleven daughters. Here Memling is the painter of tender piety and hearts at peace, but these realistic yet serene figures are excellent examples of his art as a portraitist. He painted other fine portraits, including that of *Martin van Nieuwenhoven*, also in the Hôpital Saint-Jean at Bruges, that of the man reputed to be Jean de Candida in the Musée Royal des Beaux-Arts, Antwerp, and that of *Maria Portinari* in the Metropolitan Museum of Art in New York.

Born in Holland, Gheeraert (Gérard) David (c. 1460–1523) worked in Bruges. In his painting we find some of the solemnity of Dieric Bouts, but the style is less individual. His *Judgment of Cambyses and Punishment of Sisamnes* in the Royal Academy of Arts, Bruges, shows us an unjust judge being flayed alive, and in the whole work the only person whose face shows the slightest feeling is that of a small boy on the verge of tears. David's masterpiece is probably his *Madonna and Child in a Landscape* at the Boymans-van-Beuningen Museum, Rotterdam.

Art historians have long been puzzled over Joos van Wassenhoven, better known as Justus van Ghent, who went to Italy and worked at Urbino, where he came in touch with Piero della Francesca and Melozzo da Forli. His *Crucifixion*, a triptych with numerous figures, shows he was far from lacking in talent. To judge by his *Holy Communion* in the Palazzo Ducale at Urbino, he does not seem to have become Italianized.

Geertgen tot Sint Jans, who lived in the second half of the fifteenth century, worked in Leyden. Though he does not seem to have left Holland, he belongs to the Flemish school. His landscapes faithfully reproduce nature, and his figures are well integrated with their surroundings. These features which distinguish his art are found in his *Raising of Lazarus* in the Louvre and his *Lamentation over the Dead Christ* in the Kunsthistorisches Museum, Vienna. But to regard him as the forerunner of the seventeenth-century Dutch landscape painters is to go too far. In some of his pictures the invention is naïve to the point of puerility, as in the *Madonna* in the Boymans-van-Beuningen Museum, Rotterdam, in which the Virgin's face is as smooth as an egg and her eyes are like a bird's.

With Quentin Matsys (1466–1530), who is also called Metsys and Massys, we see the first signs of a change that was to gather momentum in the sixteenth century. His tendency to depict everyday reality is manifested in all his works, including *St. Mary Magdalen*, and *The*

HANS MEMLING · *Portrait of Maria Portinari*
Metropolitan Museum of Art, New York

GERARD DAVID · *Madonna and Child
in a Landscape*
Boymans-van Beuningen Museum, Rotterdam

Entombment, both of which are in the Musée Royal des Beaux-Arts, Antwerp. However, he is often grandiloquent, particularly in *Ecce Homo*, at the Prado. This is no longer the world of Van Eyck, Van der Weyden, or Dieric Bouts, realistic and at the same time fantastic, but a world that is thoroughly down to earth. Perhaps because of his humble submission to reality, his portraits are his greatest achievements. An excellent example is the *Man with a Carnation* in the Chicago Art Institute. Good as he is, however, most of us would prefer a portrait by Van Eyck or Van der Weyden.

At the end of the fifteenth century a strangely and powerfully original painter appeared in Flanders. His name was Hieronymus van Aken, but he went by the name of Bosch, after his birthplace Hertogenbosch, where he spent the whole of his life. He was probably born about 1450 and died in 1516. We know he belonged to a half-clerical, half-theatrical fraternity which performed mystery plays. We also know that Philip II of Spain acquired several of his works. For a long time Hieronymus Bosch was regarded as no more than a painter of amusing *diableries*, but during the last thirty years an attempt has been made to provide a philosophic or psychoanalytic explanation of his weird symbolism. A German authority, Wilhelm Fränger, seems to have really succeeded in deciphering Bosch's pictures. According to him, many of them are irreproachable in their orthodoxy, but others were painted for a heretical sect, the "Brothers and Sisters of the Free Spirit," whose members claimed to incarnate the Holy Ghost and thus to be absolutely pure, even though indulging in all the pleasures of the flesh. The innumerable episodes which fill Bosch's pictures are peculiar in that he drew, for the creation of his fantastic creatures, not only on the animal and vegetable kingdoms, but also on the kitchen and workshop. His monsters are all the more disconcerting for being modeled on familiar objects, such as spoons, bowls, hammers, etc. But Bosch's symbolism, however interesting, must not deflect us from his merits as a painter, which are great. His fantasy was based on close observation of reality. He was a wonderful landscape painter, and was the first to conceive such pictures on a large scale, placing his horizon very high so as to leave room for many figures and much activity in the foreground.

Nor should the ingenious fantasy of Hieronymus Bosch be allowed to make us overlook another of his merits, the skill and utmost refinement with which he handled color. Displaying the best qualities of the miniaturist, he at the same time anticipates, by his bold innovations, the great painting of the sixteenth century. His *Adoration of the Magi* in the Prado, Madrid, justly regarded as his masterpiece, shows his mastery both of landscape and of color in a scene of great tenderness. The *Christ Carrying the Cross* in the Museum of Fine Arts, Ghent, is the best evidence of his vigor. These pictures might be described as the two poles of his inspiration and craft.

Hieronymus Bosch is an important figure not only for the work he himself left, but also for the influence he exerted. Pieter Bruegel the Elder imitated his realism, though he stopped short at deliberate stress to ugliness. Similarly, Patinir certainly learned the art of composing vast landscapes from Bosch. (For Bruegel's work see *The Kermesse* at the National Gallery, London, *The Massacre*

QUENTIN MATSYS · *Madonna and Child*
Mauritshuis, The Hague

of the Innocents and *Christ Carrying the Cross* in the Kunsthistorisches Museum at Vienna; for Patinir, see *Paradise and Hell* and *The Flight into Egypt* at the Prado.)

SPAIN AND PORTUGAL

In the fifteenth century, Spanish art was beset by rival influences, Italian and Flemish, and it was the latter that gained the upper hand. Luis Borrassa, who died after 1424, mixed the Sienese style with that which we call "international Gothic," as in his altarpieces in Santa Maria at Tarassa, Santa Maria in Venice, and Santa Maria in Seva, the last two being in the Episcopal Museum at Vich. A Catalan, Bernardo Martorell, who died about 1445, is a curious painter who, though less gifted, reminds one of Pisanello. In the predella of his altarpiece *The Transfiguration*, he put a monkey, a dog with puppies, and some ducks.

In 1428 Jan van Eyck accompanied the ambassador sent by Philip the Good, Duke of Burgundy, to Spain. Three years later the Valencian painter Luis Dalmau (d. 1460) was ordered by the King of Aragon to go to Bruges. There is every reason to suppose he saw there the works of the great Flemish painter, and may well have painted in his workshop. Certainly his altarpiece in Barcelona, *The Madonna of the Concelleros*, is thoroughly Flemish.

There was one painter, however, who resisted this influence. This was the Catalan Jaime Huguet (d. 1492), whose works reflect local traditions. Discarding oils, he went back to working tempera with gold highlights, and painted figures that were not lacking in vigor, as may be seen in his *Prophet* in the Prado and in his altarpieces at Sarria and Tarassa.

The Flemish influence did not die, however. It dominated Bartolome de Car-

HIERONYMUS BOSCH · *The Hay Wagon*
(center panel)
Prado, Madrid

denas, called Bartolome Bermejo (d. after 1498), and Fernando Gallego (d. after 1507). The first of these was unquestionably the strongest personality in the Spanish art of the time. His most important work is the *Luis Desplà Pietà* in the Cathedral at Barcelona. By its strength, breadth, and its unrelieved pathos the composition can stand comparison with the most remarkable Italian works of the period. The broad landscape, with little storm clouds and a fantastic town in an orange sunset, reminds one of Hieronymus Bosch. One might also mention the *St. Dominic of Silos* in the Prado.

The expressionism and the angular folds of drapery in the work of Fernando Gallego bring to mind the German masters rather than the Flemish ones.

As a matter of fact, *The Beheading of St. Cucufa*, in the Barcelona Museum of Catalan Art, has finally, after long research, been attributed to a German, a certain Hans or Heinrich Brün or Brunn, whose name was converted by the Spaniards into Anye Bru. This picture, which came from the monastery of San Cugat des Valles, is chiefly remarkable for the figures of the two spectators, the expression of whose faces is unforgettable.

The personality, life, and works of an artist from Paredes de Nava, Pedro Berruguete, have long posed a historical problem, which is still unsolved. He was born in 1450 and may have worked with Gallego. He went to Italy and collaborated with Justus van Ghent at Urbino. In 1483 he was back in Spain, working on the church of St. Thomas at Avila. The scenes from the life of St. Thomas appear to be earlier than the work he did in Urbino, remarkable for its assurance and skill.

Jan van Eyck's stay in Portugal may well have influenced the painters there. But in contrast to Luis Dalmau, Nuno Gonsalvez (active between 1450 and 1480) was not content to be a docile imitator of the Flemish master. The example of Van Eyck may have encouraged him to depict nature more faithfully, but Gonsalvez never adopted the meticulous technique of the Flemish school. In his *St. Vincent Altarpieces* in the Lisbon Museum of Art, people of every sort – priests, noblemen, magistrates, sailors, and fishermen draped with their nets – are grouped round the figure of Henry the Navigator, kneeling before the saint, the treatment is as firm as it is broad and robust, the paint is thick and without transparent glazes. This work is

BERMEJO · *St. Dominic of Silos*
Prado, Madrid

sufficient by itself to place Gonsalvez among the great painters of his century.

No other Portuguese painter of the time attained his level. It is not known who painted the striking *Ecce Homo* in the Lisbon Museum of Art, in which Christ, with a rope around his neck, has his face half veiled. It is even thought the work may be a sixteenth-century copy. A painter who must be mentioned here, though he was active from 1515 to 1540, is Cristovao de Figueiredo. The two donors in his *Entombment,* painted between 1520 and 1530, are in the Gonsalvez tradition, but they have a breadth and technical assurance which reveal the new spirit of the Renaissance.

SECOND PERIOD OF GERMAN ART

In Germany, commercial and industrial prosperity during the fifteenth century furthered the growth of towns and the rise of a wealthy bourgeoisie interested in the arts. Three large cities, Cologne, Hamburg, and Nuremberg, where a lot

BERRUGUETE · *St. Peter's Grave*
Prado, Madrid

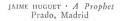

JAIME HUGUET · *A Prophet*
Prado, Madrid

of money was handled, became important art centers. Mural painting had gone out of fashion in church decoration, huge altarpieces being preferred, in which painting could be combined with sculpture, the latter being itself brightly colored and touched up with gold. As for foreign influences on German art, these came mostly from Flemish painting, occasionally from Burgundian, and only rarely from Italian.

In the Cologne school of painting, so much vaunted by later romantic writers, we do not find that tendency toward a strident expressionism which is one of the most constant attributes of German art. Instead, we find a great deal of refinement, even tenderness. The leading painter of the school was Stephan Lochner (d. 1451), whose *Madonna in a Rose Arbor* and the *Dombild* with *The Ado-*

ration of the Magi in the center are his masterpieces. In this last work as well as in *The Presentation in the Temple* in the Hessian Provincial Museum, Darmstadt, he combines gentle mysticism with a tendency to naturalism.

Two works of the Flemish school, Rogier van der Weyden's *Altar of the Magi* and an altarpiece by Dieric Bouts, were in Cologne at this period, and it is scarcely surprising that several local painters, whose names are unknown to us, were influenced by them. The most interesting is the Master of the Life of the Virgin whose *Nativity of the Virgin* in the Old Pinakothek, Munich, depicts the life of the time with a delicately intimate character.

Of all the Hanseatic cities, Hamburg was the one in which art flourished best. We know little of Master Franke, who was active in the first thirty or forty years of the fifteenth century. His style has been compared with that of Parisian miniatures, but his work could be quite dramatic, as his *Man of Sorrows* in the Hamburg Museum.

There was intense artistic activity in Nuremberg in the second half of the fifteenth century. The leading painters were Hans Pleydenwurff (second half of the century) and Michael Wohlgemut (1434–1519). Pleydenwurff's *Portrait of Count George of Löwenstein* in the National Museum, Nuremberg, and his *Crucifixion* in the Old Pinakothek entitle us to suppose that he visited Flanders, since we find in them many echoes of Van der Weyden and Dieric Bouts. It is the same with Wohlgemut's pictures. The hand of the latter's pupils is much in evidence, and they have in any case undergone repeated restorations. But with him the Flemish influence was soon ousted by his own tortured, angular style of drawing and unpleasantly hard color. The harshness and complication of his work will be met with again in Albrecht Dürer, transfigured by genius.

STEPHAN LOCHNER · *The Madonna of the Rose Arbor*
Wallraf-Richartz Museum, Cologne

In Westphalia, Konrad von Soest (early fifteenth century) suggests by the artless realism and restrained elegance of his painting that he may have been outside Germany and observed Burgundian painters.

The influence of the latter is visible in Swabia too, in an altarpiece by Lucas Moser at Tiefenbronn depicting scenes from the life of St. Mary Magdalen. In this work there is much that is awkward and the perspective is uncertain, but it is not lacking in naïve charm. Having signed and dated his picture, the painter added this bitter complaint: "Speak out, arts, speak out and complain, for today people have had enough of you." Many plausible explanations have been suggested for these bitter words.

Lucas Moser lived in the first half of the fifteenth century. One of the best things in his altarpiece is a little "seascape" on one panel, which may well have been inspired by Lake Constance. Another lake scene, more elaborately detailed, is included in Konrad Witz's most famous picture. Witz, the best painter of the Swabian school, was born about 1390 and died in 1447; he spent most of his life in Switzerland. Critics have detected

Flemish influences in his work, but what distinguishes it and gives it its value is his talent for simplifying form, and for hacking out his figures three-dimensionally, as though in wood. That is why for all the differences between a Swabian and a Florentine, he is comparable to Masaccio. In the panel in the Strasbourg Museum of Fine Arts, he did not merely give us a church interior with its aisles in perspective, but went on to make us aware of the empty space around the seated figures of St. Mary Magdalen and St. Catharine. In *The Miraculous Draught of Fishes* in the Museum of Art at Geneva he depicted the shores of the

KONRAD VON SOEST · *The Death of the Virgin*
Marienkirche, Dortmund

HANS MULTSCHER · *Christ before Pilate*
State Museums, Berlin-Dahlem

he has left us a work of prime importance in the Isenheim Altar, now in the Museum of Colmar, which alone would place him in the very first rank. It is composed of two large panels, six smaller ones, and a predella. They show scenes from the life of Christ, the Virgin, and the saints, particularly St. Anthony. Grünewald carried to the extreme that expressionism which, as we have seen, is one of the constant factors in German art. He seems determined to disturb the spectator's equanimity with gruesome or repulsive detail. The body of Christ on the cross covered with sores is unforgettable, as are the devils assaulting the hermit and the bristling, baleful vegetation. Lastly there are his colors, intense

MICHAEL PACHER · *Altar of the Church Fathers*
(detail) · Old Pinakothek, Munich

lake and the hills of Savoy with remarkable accuracy. On the other hand, the figures are quite out of proportion, while the distant view of the Alps with Mont Blanc has no relation to reality.

In Alsace, Caspar Isenmann (active 1436–1447) stands halfway between Konrad Witz and Martin Schongauer. He lacks the sense of volume and the crude power of Witz, but his *Entombment* in the Museum at Colmar is remarkable for the quiet resignation it breathes.

Born in Colmar, Martin Schongauer (c. 1445–1491) may have visited Flanders. He worked more as an engraver than as a painter. His *Madonna in an Arbor of Roses* in the Church of St. Stephen at Colmar is the only picture that can be ascribed to him with absolute certainty. It has the same character as his prints: a contorted gracefulness, with many angular folds of drapery.

The singular painter who is still known as Matthias Grünewald was in fact called Mathis Gothardt Nithardt. Born between 1450 and 1460 he died in 1528. Besides works such as *St. Erasmus and St. Maurice* at the Old Pinakothek in Munich,

and arbitrary, with which the painter, disdaining realism, seeks to act upon us directly.

The same vehement expressionism is found in Gabriel Maelskircher's *Crucifixion* in the National Museum at Nuremberg. In this picture Maelskircher, who lived in the second half of the fifteenth century, set out to paint figures so hide-

KONRAD WITZ · *The Miraculous Draught of Fishes*
Museum of Art, Geneva

ous as to border on caricature. This trait also appears in the work of Hans Multscher (c. 1400–1467), a painter and sculptor who worked at Ulm. His eight panels in the State Museums, Berlin-Dahlem, dealing with the life of the Virgin and the Passion, make an emotional appeal, seeking to arouse horror, pain, and anger, by portraying the Jews and executioners with the most hideous faces, twisted by hatred. And in the panel of *The Nativity,* the shepherds' faces, instead of being joyful, are sullen and even hostile.

In Austria, Flemish and Venetian influences may be seen in the pictures of Rueland Frueauf the Elder, active at Salzburg and Passau between 1478 and 1507. His son Rueland Frueauf the Younger (c. 1507–1545) painted small, pleasantly naïve panels in the style of the previous generation.

In the Tyrolean painter Michael Pacher (c. 1435–1498), Italian influence is obvious, especially Mantegna's, which makes his work stand out from that of other German painters. In the St. Wolfgang Altar, of which he sculpted the central part and painted the wings and the predella, we find no overwrought expres-

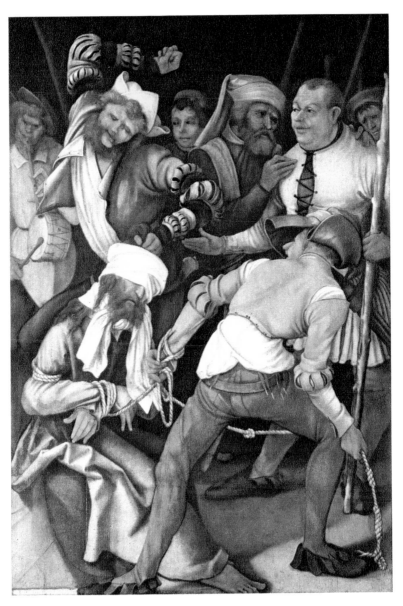

GRÜNEWALD · *The Mocking of Christ*
Old Pinakothek, Munich

sions, no stress on ugliness. In *The Raising of Lazarus* he used perspective with great skill to obtain a striking composition, and in *The Circumcision* there is a serenity lacking in his fellow painters. Avoiding both expressionism and prettiness, Michael Pacher learned from the Italians the value of simple, ample forms, radiance, nobility, and beauty.

At the cost of a bitter struggle the Confederation of Swiss Cantons won and maintained its independence and enlarged its territory in the course of the fifteenth century. By the end of the century it enjoyed considerable military prestige, though it still suffered from internal troubles. Not until the following century did Switzerland produce artists of note.
All the same, there were a few in the fifteenth century. First, there was a group of artists who signed their work with a

FRENCH SCHOOL · *Man with a Wine Glass*
Louvre, Paris

JEAN FOUQUET · *Juvénal des Ursins*
Louvre, Paris

carnation. Two among them gained some reputation: the Master of the Carnation, from Zurich (active late fifteenth century), and the Master of the Carnation, from Bern (active 1490–1501). Their paintings resemble German works and are of more documentary than artistic interest.

THE END OF THE MIDDLE AGES
IN FRANCE

The fifteenth century opened in France under unpromising circumstances. The mad king, Charles VI, was deposed by his uncles; a deadly feud raged between the Armagnacs and the Burgundians; revolts had broken out following the English invasion; and there was poverty, famine, and pestilence everywhere. Within thirty years, however, Joan of Arc had taken to the field. Little by little Charles VII drove the English from his kingdom. His successor, Louis XI, added new provinces to it. Then Charles VIII came to the throne. In 1495–1496 he led an invasion of Italy, which was to have a great influence on French art.

During the fifteenth century, little mural painting was done in France. One of the few examples was the angels painted on the vaults of the chapel at the Hôtel de Jacques Cœur at Bourges, built between 1443 and 1453. On the other hand, paintings on panels were numerous in various parts of the country.

Although we are dealing with painting here and have in general to ignore illuminations, we cannot fail to mention those done by an unknown artist in the middle of the fifteenth century for a romance of chivalry entitled *Le Cœur d'Amour Épris,* a work now in the National Library, Vienna. Whoever did them undoubtedly had some connection with Fouquet; he abandoned the meager twisted forms of his fellow illuminators and followed nature closely. Two of his illuminations – one of people in a room lit by artificial light, the other of a sunrise – are quite exceptional achievements for the art of that period.

Jean Fouquet (c. 1420–c. 1480) was both miniaturist and painter. He was undoubtedly conversant with Flemish art and saw the work of the Florentines and the Umbrians during a visit to Italy. With his delicate, harmonious coloring, he proved himself a remarkable miniaturist in the *Heures d'Etienne Chevalier* and the *Antiquités Judaïques,* and then, abandoning vellum for the wooden panel, proved himself no less remarkable a painter. In his *Madonna and Child* at the Musée Royal, Antwerp, and in the portraits of *Charles VII, King of France* and *Juvénal des Ursins,* he shows an ability to reduce the human body to broad simple volumes such as we find much later in Georges de la Tour, Ingres, and Corot. Could he have been the painter of the Nouans *Pietà,* distinguished especially for its restrained feeling? All we can say is that we can point to no

FRENCH SCHOOL · *Margaret of York*
Louvre, Paris

other painter of the period who could have done it.

It must be added that we are only beginning to learn about Fouquet's life and work. Famous as he was in his day, he fell into neglect in later centuries. Thanks to scholars he has been restored to a place of honor, following George Brentano's discovery at the beginning of the nineteenth century of forty miniatures from the *Heures d'Etienne Chevalier,* now in the Musée Condé, Chantilly, thanks to the Duc d'Aumale. The next works to be identified as his were *Etienne Chevalier présenté par St. Etienne,* and (with somewhat less certainty) the *Antiquités Judaïques,* now at

JEAN FOUQUET · *Portrait of Charles VII, King of France*
Louvre, Paris

by the authorities to date from 1460. The painter is unknown. As in the Nouans *Pietà*, there is no violent gesticulation, but the feeling is all the more concentrated and intense. In this admirable work one already sees that mistrust of grandiloquence which has been one of the constant features of French art, differentiating it sharply from German art. In a less accentuated form, the same spirit prevails in another anonymous Provençal work, the *Rétable de Boulbon* (Boulbon altarpiece) now in the Louvre. In the presence of the angular-faced donor and St. Agricola in bishop's vestments, Christ is emerging from the tomb. Behind, the head of God the Father appears, while the third member of the Trinity, in the form of a Dove, soars between. One member of the school whose name we know is Enguerrand Quarton, or Charonton of Laon, active at Aix, Arles, and Avignon between 1444 and 1466. His *Coronation of the Virgin* in the Hospice of Villeneuve-les-Avignon is a work of great quality, generously decorative, and delicate in its treatment of light. At the bottom of the picture is a broad landscape, half-real, half-imaginary, which reminds one of Corot. Enguerrand Quarton was also the painter of the *Madonna of Mercy*, a picture of great tenderness which is in the Musée Condé, Chantilly. Almost prosaic in its naturalism is the *Triptyque du Buisson Ardent* (The Burning Bush) in the cathedral of Saint-Sauveur at Aix-en-Provence, a triptych showing the episode told in Genesis which is interpreted as a prefiguration of the Annunciation: the Madonna appears at the top of the picture inside a circular hedge. The saints and donors shown on the wings are by an artist who enjoyed painting truthfully and vigorously what he has seen with his own eyes. And there is the same feeling for reality, the same sense of space and volume, in *The Annunciation* at Aix, painted by an unknown hand c. 1443. The central panel

the Bibliothèque Nationale. Since then, learned discussions of his life and works have gone on apace. The probable facts are that he was born at Tours, learned his trade in a Paris workshop, spent three or four years in Italy, and then on his return to France was appointed Painter to the King. In that capacity he had not only to paint miniatures and pictures, but also to be responsible for monuments and ceremonies. He seems to have died before 1481.
There existed in this period, in Provence, a group of artists of similar character and accomplishment. The finest work produced by this school – one of the masterpieces of French painting – is the Avignon *Pietà* in the Louvre, estimated

is in the church of Sainte-Marie-Madeleine at Aix-en-Provence. The wing showing Jeremiah is in the Musées Royaux des Beaux-Arts, Brussels. The other, showing Isaiah, is in the Boymans-van Beuningen Museum, Rotterdam, except for the top part, a still life showing books, which is in the Rijksmuseum at Amsterdam.

Another anonymous painter has been called the Master of St. Sebastian because of some panels depicting St. Sebastian's life which have been attributed to him (now in the Johnson Collection in the Philadelphia Museum of Art). He may have been Josse Lieferinxe, from the Hainault, who lived at Avignon and Marseilles. In the latter place he was employed in 1497 on an altarpiece, also of St. Sebastian. But if the painter of these panels was of Flemish origin, he had completely acclimatized to the spirit of French art, for his works have a discreet charm and naturalness which place him definitely in the Provençal school.

Louis Bréa of Nice is also regarded as a member of that school. His beautiful and touching *Madonna between St. Martin*

SCHOOL OF AVIGNON · *Pietà*
Louvre, Paris

1480 and 1500 an anonymous painter was working there who has been given the name of the Master of Moulins. His triptych in the cathedral of Moulins suggests that he was familiar with Flemish painting, in particular Hugo van der Goes. The central panel shows the Virgin in glory surrounded by angels, and the wings the Duke and Duchess of Bourbon presented by their patron saints, St. Peter and St. Anne. In this triptych, as in *The Nativity* in the Autun Municipal Museum (with Chancellor Rolin as donor), there is a passion for truth which makes him a remarkable portrait painter (see also his *Mary Magdalen with a Donor* in the Louvre), as well as an obvious affection for children. The light from the Virgin's multicolored halo glows differently in the

MASTER OF MOULINS · *Portrait of a Child*
Louvre, Paris

MASTER OF MOULINS · *Mary Magdalen with a Donor*
Louvre, Paris

and St. Catherine, done in 1475, is in the church of Cimiez, near Nice. The influence of nearby Italy is not very noticeable, but it became dominant in his later work.

Thanks to the Dukes of Bourbon and to a Valois princess, Anne de Beaujeu, the daughter of Louis XI, who was regent during the minority of her younger brother Charles VIII, the town of Moulins became an artistic center towards the end of the fifteenth century. Between

SCHOOL OF AMIENS · *The Madonna as High Priestess*
Louvre, Paris

various faces of the angels, according to their position. These angels are painted most realistically as little girls, yet at the same time made to look like angels. Whereas Fouquet in his Antwerp *Madonna* stylized the Infant Jesus, the Master of Moulins in his *Madonna* in the Musées Royaux des Beaux-Arts, Brussels, represents the Infant as a real newborn child. It has been suggested that this painter's name was Jean Perréal, a Parisian born about 1452 who worked for the Bourbons and went with Charles VIII and Louis XII to Italy, where he would have met Leonardo da Vinci, but this matter has yet to be proved beyond all doubt.

The Dukes of Burgundy employed French artists, but they also commissioned works from Flemish painters and invited a number of them to Dijon. The latter gradually adopted the French style. This can be seen in several fine portraits by anonymous hands, such as the one of the man with the brutal face in the Worcester (Massachusetts) Art Museum thought to be of Claude de Toulongeon, and the one of Jeanne de Montaigu in the Rockefeller Collection, New York.

III

THE RENAISSANCE

The art of the sixteenth century, that supreme expression of the Renaissance, which has had such a vast influence on succeeding centuries, was centered in Lombardy, Venice, and Rome. Its artists—Leonardo, Raphael, Michelangelo, and later Titian, Veronese, Tintoretto, and the Carracci family—were its principal masters in Italy. They not only stimulated but often served as models for the painters of Germany, Flanders, Holland, Spain, and France. We shall discuss them all, but we must give first place to the Italians, for their inventiveness, the quality of their achievement, and the quantity of great works they produced.

When we go to the Sistine Chapel and look at the frescoes on the walls done by the *quattrocentisti*—Botticelli, Ghirlandaio, Signorelli, Perugino, etc.—and then turn to the ceiling and the east wall painted by Michelangelo, we grasp at once the immense difference between the painting of the fifteenth and the sixteenth century. In the passage from one to the other a revolution had taken place under the guidance of three painters of genius: Leonardo da Vinci, Michelangelo, and Raphael.

From the beginning of the sixteenth century, the extensive commissions from the popes and from other local patrons had led to Rome's supplanting Florence as the artistic center of Italy, and the work that was done there now began to influence the rest of the country.

What were the characteristics of this new school?

The principal preoccupation was with relief, which was carried so far as to give volumes an almost sculptural quality. Color took a secondary place. Form acquired amplitude, monumentality. Picturesque and variegated costume gave way to draperies with elaborately arranged folds. The custom of introducing contemporary personalities into a fresco or a picture was discontinued along with that of including supernumerary figures added only because the painter had been struck by their appearance or posture. These new artists sought to give an idealized image of man, to confer nobility and dignity upon him, and at the same time to express all the subtlety of his feelings. They also aimed at an effect of balance by the harmonious arrangement of lines.

All these new features reflect the in-

LEONARDO DA VINCI · *Mona Lisa*
Louvre, Paris

LEONARDO DA VINCI · *St. John the Baptist*
Louvre, Paris

fluence of classical sculpture, which painters studied far more thoroughly in the sixteenth than in the fifteenth century. The *quattrocentisti* had been prompt to exploit a decorative motive or an architectural detail borrowed from classical antiquity, but they never allowed classical sculpture to come between them and nature. The *cinquecentisti*, on the other hand, were so deeply in love with classical work that they wanted their own to come as close to it as possible. They did not see the danger: the classical art they took as their model was sculpture, with the result that they often neglected color, which was not restored to its rightful place until the advent of the Venetians.

It is not surprising that Rome should have been the center of an enthusiastic cult of classical sculpture, for here fresh classical remains were being uncovered constantly, and the city was a favorite with archaeologists and collectors alike. Artists had by this time acquired a

slightly more elevated social rank and were in a position to associate with the humanists and other men of learning for whose approval they were anxious and whose advice they were ready to take.

LEONARDO DA VINCI

What strikes one first about Leonardo (1452–1519) is that he was in advance of his times. He was only three years younger than Ghirlandaio and two years younger than Signorelli, while Pinturicchio was two years younger than he. Yet the works of these three painters seem to antedate his by half a century. His style changed little in the course of his life. Almost as soon as he began to work, he was what he was to be for the next forty years. He has left few works, and some of them are unfinished. A man of prodigious intellectual gifts, he studied the problems of representing form by line and modeling in just the same way as he studied anatomy or the formation of mountains. Whatever he took up, his approach was always in terms of problems to be solved – problems of composition, of form, of expression. In his famous *Last Supper* in the refectory of the convent at the Church of Santa Maria delle Grazie at Milan, he tried by an elaborate arrangement of curves to bring the different groups of apostles on either side of Christ into formal relation, and also to give their faces the expression which would best convey their individual feelings. In his *Madonna and Child with St. Anne* in the Louvre he tried to mold into a harmonious group the bodies of two women and a child. All his life he was haunted by one facial type, which reappears again and again in his work, and the most celebrated instance of which is the *Mona Lisa.* If this is the portrait of a real person, she was the personification of his ideal type.

Leonardo was unquestionably a genius,

MICHELANGELO · *The Last Judgment*
Sistine Chapel, Rome

MICHELANGELO · *The Creation of Adam*
Sistine Chapel, Rome

but it is legitimate to ask whether he was a painter of genius, because neither color nor texture plays an important part in his paintings. Accordingly, his paintings give us little more than his drawings do. That he was a very great draftsman is indisputable. He drew the human body with as much nobility and beauty as truth, and his knowledge of surface relief was a great inspiration to his contemporaries. However, painting was only one of his many occupations. His enigmatic figure strides across the Renaissance like a sort of Faust, whose Mephistopheles was the Demon of Knowledge and whose Gretchen, the poor little girl whom he occasionally deigned to caress, was painting.

MICHELANGELO

Sculptor, painter, and architect, Michelangelo Buonarroti (1475–1564) was a man utterly different from Leonardo. Art to him was not a mode of knowledge, but a means of expression. In the Sistine Chapel he set out to create a whole world of forms which would embody all the torments of his restless spirit. His painting was in fact the outward sign of his tortured sensibility. The man who on the ceiling of the Sistine Chapel painted a *Creation of the World* that no one else has ever equaled, himself created a superhuman humanity, beings that are the plastic realization of the psychological concept of the hero. Nourished on classical art, the Old Testament, and Dante, he rose to such heights, that beside the tremendous creations of his imagination those of other artists seem pale indeed.

He had already produced two or three paintings of unusual power when, in 1508, having received a formal order from Julius II, he painted single-handed the ceiling of the Sistine Chapel – a surface of 130×40 feet – finishing it in October, 1512. He undertook the work unwillingly, complaining that he was not a painter but a sculptor, but in fact he made full use of all his talents – as sculptor, architect, and painter – for he introduced architecture and statues into these paintings of prophets and sibyls, and did not shrink from including figures of nude young men, though their role was purely decorative. The colors are subdued: pale grays dominate, touched up with pale blues and faded greens, but in this case relegation of color to a secondary place was artistically justified.

The work is so charged with genius as to be quite overwhelming, and it is only too easy to understand how discouraging it can have been to painters of lesser fiber who attempted to employ the same plastic language, but without Michelangelo's genius.

In this work Michelangelo made a titanic effort to achieve a synthesis between the Renaissance, with its cult of classical sculpture, and his own fervent Christian ideals. Therein lay the conflict that was to torment him all his life, and increasingly with advancing years. Within him were two beings, one passionately in love with the beauty of the human body, the other devout, austere, focused upon God rather than man, yet fearing His severity. From this conflict sprang the dramatic quality of his work, its restlessness. His figures seem to be haunted by some terrible, painful secret. Michelangelo has been reproached for his emphasis upon musculature, and it has been said

that in the Sistine Chapel he has proved himself more of a sculptor than a painter. Actually, to stress bone and muscle both at rest and in movement was his way of expressing the tumult of an exacerbated sensibility. He thought in terms of bodily rhythm, the way Beethoven thought in terms of musical rhythm.

Between 1536 and 1541 Michelangelo went back to work on the decoration of the Sistine Chapel at the behest of Pope Paul III, and painted *The Last Judgment* (17×13 meters) on the east wall. This terrible scene – a well-worn subject of Christian iconography – Michelangelo succeeded in investing with incomparable movement and grandeur. He has been criticized for having made the Christ too stern a God, but this is simply to ignore the subject of the fresco: the judgment of sinful mankind. Michelangelo could hardly have shown Him punishing the wicked and blessing the chosen at the same time, and the somber, uneasy nature of his own faith accounts for his choice of the first rather than the second of these attitudes.

A more serious criticism which may be raised is his tendency to overemphasis, to the multiplication of figures to a degree verging on confusion. These faults are most marked in his frescoes in the Pauline Chapel, also in the Vatican, *The Conversion of St. Paul* and *The Crucifixion of St. Peter;* here unrelieved vehemence becomes a little monotonous.

With his preference for the tall figure with small head, hands, and feet, with his passion for postures involving frequent changes of axis, and lastly with his sometimes frenzied dramatization of feeling, Michelangelo moved away from the classical serenity and harmony which had formed the Renaissance ideal. Here we may sense the coming of the Baroque. In fact we might say that the greatest masterpiece of the Baroque was Michelangelo's *Last Judgment*, a work very different from the ceiling of the Sistine

Chapel and one in which the nudes of classical antiquity are used to express the epic Christian vision of the end of the world, much as St. John the Divine used the Greek of Sophocles and Plato to write the Book of Revelation.

RAPHAEL

Raphael Sanzio (1483–1520) is yet another personality, quite different from either of the two we have been discussing. Son of a mediocre painter of Urbino, he studied successively under Timoteo Viti, Perugino, and Pinturicchio. In the course of these apprenticeships, he proved he had the gift of assimilation, one of the important elements in his make-up. But this was not his only gift, and his genius was much more than the sum of what he had learned from others.

He spent four years in Florence, and his painting, which had so far been delicate

RAPHAEL · *Pope Julius II*
Uffizi, Florence

and feminine, acquired breadth and depth. He painted at that time some fifteen Madonnas, each of which represented for him a fresh problem in equilibrating volumes and lines, and also gave him an outlet for his conception of physical beauty.

In 1508 his uncle, Donato Bramante, then architect of St. Peter's and the Vatican, persuaded Pope Julius II to entrust the decoration of a suite of rooms to this young painter of twenty-five. From the start, he showed himself a master, capable of undertaking the most difficult tasks, and accomplishing them in a way that opened up new vistas in painting.

In his work three essential elements may be distinguished. First, he was not a powerful, clear-cut personality, nor was he a visionary; but, as we have already suggested, he had in high degree the gift of turning to advantage everything that came his way. Second, he had an innate sense for beauty, harmony, and nobility. What he found in nature he examined in the light of the ideal, and, if it passed the test, he used it. Third, he had a great gift for drawing, and a genius for composition, which meant that he could always create beauty by a happy arrangement of lines and volumes. Like a ballet master, he maneuvered his figures on a three-dimensional stage. And he did not merely try to satisfy the eye. His aim was to expound as plainly as possible, in the language of forms, the action of the story he was depicting. He was also an excellent storyteller, and in this respect heir to Giotto and Masaccio.

In his early works, such as *The Vision of a Knight* in the National Gallery, London, we see a rather shy, boyish gracefulness. But already his work in Florence shows the development of his powers. His Madonnas are mothers now, though scarcely matrons, for they still have the modesty of girls. From his arrival in Rome onward, we begin to recognize the Raphaelite type of woman-

RAPHAEL · *Portraits of Angelo and Maddalena Doni*
Palazzo Pitti, Florence

hood. We see it in *The Parnassus* and even more impressively in the *Sibyl* painted for Santa Maria della Pace, and the robust women in *The Myth of Psyche* at the Villa Farnesina.

It has been said that Raphael lacked a sense of color, and there is no doubt that he failed to take full advantage of the opportunities offered by oil paint. Nevertheless, there were exceptions such as his *Mass of Bolsena* and *Deliverance of St. Peter*, in which his frescoes achieve a richness of color not even surpassed by Titian much later in oil. Lastly, he was a remarkable portrait painter, and, in this field too, he made color come into its own on occasion, as in *Balthazar Castiglione* in the Louvre and the *Portraits of Angelo and Maddalena Doni* (Palazzo Pitti, Florence). But his talent for idealizing and ennobling the figures he painted, for endowing them with natural elegance

and dignity is peculiarly his. Like Michelangelo, he was much misunderstood, and his successive imitators have often produced academic – that is to say artificial – art. For this much of the blame lies with his later Madonnas and the famous *Transfiguration*.

Raphael had many pupils, wl ɔ had a hand in his major works, such as the decoration of the *Camere* of the Vatican. The only one of any interest to us is Giulio Pippi (1499–1546), known as Giulio Romano. His wall paintings are inventive, but tend to bore us with detail.

Leonardo da Vinci exerted a palpable influence on several artists from Lombardy. Bernardino Luini (c. 1475–1532) was one, whose frescoes are mildly pleasant and graceful. Another was Giovanni Antonio Bazzi, known as Sodoma (1477–1544), who did much of his work in

PONTORMO · *The Adoration of the Magi*
Palazzo Pitti, Florence

Siena, and then went to Rome. He too had a great sense of feminine grace, as is shown by his *Marriage of Alexander and Roxana* in the Villa Farnesina at Rome. Few painters have been so unequal, however. More interesting pupils of Leonardo are Ambrogio da Predis (1472–1517) and Giovanni Boltraffio. All of them excellent draftsmen, they were less distinguished for their use of color.

THE MANNERISTS

The style tendencies current in Florence in the early sixteenth century are represented by three painters who were regarded as great masters until about sixty years ago, but are now neglected. Mariotto Albertinelli (1474–1515) was assistant to Fra Bartolommeo della Porta (1475–1517), who was for a time a Dominican. Both painted in a cold, hard way. Andrea del Sarto (1486–1531) is a more attractive painter, though he failed to make the most of his gifts. An excellent draftsman but a poor colorist, he aimed at little more than charm and elegance.

During the first half of this century, certain painters appeared who have subsequently been dubbed "Mannerists." For a long time they were despised on account of their affectation, but it has finally been recognized that they did some remarkable work. Their position was not an easy one, for they followed masters of exceptional genius. To escape the domination of the latter, they exploited idiosyncrasies and sought for refinements, and they feminized the human type created by Michelangelo. Hence the disturbing sensuality of the Madonnas by Parmigianino (Francesco Mazzolo, 1503–1540), and the complicated compositions of Pontormo (Jacopo Carucci, 1494–1557). However, the former also produced the charming frescoes in the Rocca di Fontanellato near Parma, and the latter the two frescoes in the Medici villa at Poggio a Caiano near Florence, perfect in their simplicity and naturalness. Pontormo also painted the *Entombment* in the Church of Santa Felicità in Florence, the delicate colors of which are worthy of a less painful subject. These two painters also have admirable portraits to their credit.

More interesting is Angelo di Cosimo, called Bronzino (1507–1572). In his frescoes in Florence dealing with scenes from Genesis, his one concern was to group human figures in attitudes that would best show off their physical beauty. In his rare mythological pictures he succeeded in making the female body seem of marmoreal purity, and yet sensuous, in a way that must have delighted Ingres. He was also a remarkable portrait painter, whose heads are especially impressive. Apart from the Venetians, Bronzino was the only painter of this epoch who had real originality in his handling of oils.

Included among the Mannerists is the Sienese painter Domenico di Pace, called Beccafumi (1484–1551), who employed fantastic lighting in his intricate compositions.

Il Rosso and Primaticcio, who were also Mannerists, will be dealt with in the section on the sixteenth century in France, for the bulk of their work was done in that country.

THE VENETIAN MASTERS

Owing to their long and busy trade with the East, the Venetians clung to the Byzantine tradition for a long time, and with it kept a warm feeling for color.

Until the end of the fifteenth century painters in the rest of Italy had used two mediums: pigment diluted in water for wall paintings and tempera for panels. Neither medium afforded the possibility of achieving strong contrasts between transparent shadows and opaque impastos, needed to render depth more effectively.

The Venetians soon discovered that in their damp, salty climate fresco painting quickly deteriorated. Being great shipbuilders they knew all about canvas, and before long they realized that, instead of decorating their public buildings with frescoes, they would obtain better results by decorating them with large paintings on canvas.

Giovanni Bellini's last works show a growing awareness of the potentialities of oil painting. But it was left to two younger painters to grasp fully the advantages of the new medium. They were Giorgio Barbarelli, called Giorgione (1477–1510), and Tiziano Vecelli, called Titian (c. 1477–1576). So alike were they in their early efforts that major works, such as the *Concert Champêtre* in the Louvre and the *Concert* in the Palazzo Pitti, are attributed to Giorgione by some historians and to Titian by others. An added complication arises from the fact that Titian completed some of Giorgione's works after the latter's premature death; and we are not even sure what exact meaning to give the term "completed."

These two young artists were at one in wanting to break away from the precise drawing of their predecessors, in wanting to deal more massively with form, to soften contours rather than to emphasize them, and in wanting to paint with layers of translucent oil colors.

Few works can be attributed with certainty to Giorgione. The most remarkable are the *Madonna with St. Francis and St. George* at Castelfranco, the painting at the Kunsthistorisches Museum, Vienna, entitled *The Three Philosophers*, who in fact represent the Three Magi, *The Tempest* in the Accademia, Venice, and *A Knight of Malta* in the Uffizi. Giorgione continued the researches of Leonardo, endeavoring like him to express forms in relief, but he enveloped them more richly and was more of a colorist than Leonardo. All that his successors were to exploit both technically and aesthetically

GIORGIONE · *The Tempest*
Accademia, Venice

is already implicit in his work: flesh bathed in light, ample volumes, transparent glazes, the love of country life. Titian lived the best part of a century. He began to paint in his early youth and only laid down his brush at the very end. He accordingly left a vast quantity of work behind him, which had a great influence on painting. Thanks to his application and skill he soon acquired great facility. He was anxious to please and to succeed. It is not surprising that he was a favorite with the art patrons of his day – the Council of Venice, the Dukes of Ferrara, the Dukes of Mantua, Charles V, Philip II, and several popes. At the same time he was on friendly terms with many artists and writers of his time.

He was a pupil of the Bellini brothers, but fell out with them, and then worked for a long time with Giorgione, whose style was so close to his own. His typical work in this period is *Sacred and Profane Love*. Later, he moved toward a style of greater amplitude, one of the best examples of which is *The Assumption* in the Accademia at Venice.

It was Titian who bequeathed to Venetian painting the majority of its characteristic features. The styles of Veronese and Tintoretto, to name only two, are highly individual, but the principles Ti-

tian laid down are still alive in them, as well as his rules of composition, manner of drawing, and even ways of mixing paint.

Titian was one of the greatest colorists the world has ever known. He knew how to get the most varied effects from relatively limited means. He was above all the painter of all that the visible world has to offer in the way of beauty – beautiful human types, sumptuous fabrics, harmonious landscapes. A religious subject was for him simply another opportunity for a seductive arrangement of forms and combination of colors. He is best of all with the nude (*Sacred and Profane Love* in the Palazzo Borghese, Rome, the *Venus of Urbino* in the Uffizi, the *Danaë* in the Prado) and the portrait (*Flora* and the so-called *La Bella di Tiziano* in the Palazzo Pitti, *Pope*

TITIAN · *The Venus of Urbino*
Uffizi, Florence

VERONESE · *The Marriage at Cana*
Louvre, Paris

Paul III and His Two Grandsons in the National Gallery of Capodimonte at Naples, *Charles V at the Battle of Mühlberg* in the Prado), in which he recaptured the essentially human in moments of splendor and plenitude.

In his last years he painted in a freer way, using more varied brushstrokes and obtaining a more shimmering effect. At the same time he discarded his carmines and ultramarines, restricting his palette to browns, reds, and gold, as in *The Nymph and the Shepherd* in the Kunsthistorisches Museum, Vienna. His last religious pictures, such as the *Pietà* in

the Accademia in Venice, are stamped with a depth of feeling hitherto absent from his work. It is as though the pagan serenity of this great voluptuary has been shaken by the approach of death. There is already in these works a prefiguration of Baroque tendencies.

No similar last period can be found in the career of Paolo Caliari, called Veronese (1528–1588). He was born in Verona. His father, a sculptor, wanted him to follow in his footsteps, but the young Paolo was set on being a painter. He was put to study under his uncle, the painter Antonio Badile, but his most formative influence seems to have derived from another painter, Giovanni Caroto, who was particularly assiduous in the study of perspective. Veronese soon made a name for himself in decoration, and was soon employed on ambitious undertakings, first in Mantua, then in Venice. Apparently it was the sight of the work of Michelangelo and Raphael during a visit to Rome that put the final touch to his development as a painter. Back in Venice, he turned out work after work – mythological and historical scenes, religious pictures and portraits. What his contemporary Vasari wrote about his *Marriage Feast at Cana* shows well what Veronese's admirers saw in him and expected of him: "This picture, by its size, by the number of figures it contains, by the variety of the costumes and the wealth of invention, is marvelous. . . . There are more than a hundred and fifty heads, all different and painted with infinite care."

Variety, invention, magnificence. Add his gifts for color and composition, and you have Veronese complete, the painter of luxury, joyousness, and sensuality. He was above all a decorator; his talent was to serve up feasts for the eyes. He painted huge canvases for the Doges' Palace, for churches and monasteries, and frescoes for the Villa Giacomelli (Villa Masèr) near Treviso. It would not be fair to expect him to show religious feeling as well in his pictures. A biblical subject was for him an opportunity to stage a magnificent spectacle with shimmering silks and sumptuous colors backed by towers and pinnacles rising against a turquoise sky -- witness *The Martyrdom of St. George* in the church of San Giorgio in Braida at Verona, *The Banquet of Gregory the Great* in the refectory of the convent at the Basilica de Monte Bèrico near Vicenza, and *The Supper in the House of Levi* at the Accademia, Venice. His *Marriage Feast at Cana* in

the Louvre is surely the most wonderful banquet of its kind, but we cannot easily pick out the figure of Christ among the many wedding guests. For all of that, accepting his limitations, we must recognize Veronese as a prodigious painter, as good a colorist as Titian – in fact, a more varied one – and a more original explorer of his craft. When his coloring is examined closely, it often is found to consist of a small number of carefully chosen tones, grouped together over the entire picture surface, as in the *Finding of Moses* in the Prado.

Jacopo Robusti, called Tintoretto (1518–1594), is quite different from his two great rivals, and also from all the other Venetian painters of his day.
The saying goes that he wrote upon the wall of his studio: "Michelangelo drawing and Titian color." Whether true or not, there is no doubt that he knew very well what he wanted to achieve – a highly personal style – and he lost no time going after it, thereby completing the Venetian trinity of Titian, Veronese, and Tintoretto. He was gifted with prodigious facility, based upon a perfect knowledge of his craft, and he was another who never tired of painting. Vasari tells us he worked without letup, regardless of whether he was properly paid. He would even work for nothing. The heads of the confraternity of San Rocco, wanting a Crucifixion, asked him to submit a preliminary sketch before they would give him the commission. Tintoretto set to work at once, but on an enormous canvas, and he then and there painted the picture itself. The monks were annoyed. He had promised them a sketch before they made their decision, and had no right to go ahead. Tintoretto answered that that was his way of doing a sketch, and that it had to be full size, "so that no one should be taken in." In any case, if they didn't want the picture, they needn't pay for it; he would give

VERONESE · *The Finding of Moses*
Prado, Madrid

TINTORETTO · *Susanna and the Elders*
Kunsthistorisches Museum, Vienna

it to them, all the same, as an offering to San Rocco. With that he put down his picture next to the preliminary studies of the other competitors—and it was he who was commissioned to provide the decoration still to be done. Here, too, the kind of man he was explains the kind of painter he was. His early works, such as *The Miracle of St. Mark* in the Accademia, Venice, show that he could handle color as ably as Titian, happily combining the richest pigments. But he very soon toned down his palette, re-

stricting himself to more somber harmonies, streaked with silver and gold. With Fra Angelico and Rembrandt one of the greatest of Christian artists, when painting a religious subject he confined himself strictly to its meaning. He succeeded because he was both a visionary and a realist, able to make use of all the life around him. His *Last Supper* is not a brilliant joyous feast, as Veronese's, but a portrayal of Christ passing the bread and the wine He has blessed to the humble fishermen of Galilee.

Tintoretto was an expert and forcible draftsman, who could take difficulties in his stride and juggle with the most risky extremes of foreshortening. But he never used his gifts merely to show off his virtuosity. He used them to express the message within him. His genius for composition was as great as Raphael's; in fact, it was bolder and more inventive. In composing a picture, he placed his lines and volumes asymmetrically, to create lines of force which would draw the spectator's eye to key points in the armature of the whole. Besides admirable works like *The Last Supper* in the church of San Trovaso, the picture on the same subject in San Polo, and *The Descent from the Cross* in the Accademia – these three in Venice – there are some nudes which are astonishing in their breadth and power, such the *Danaë* in the Palace of Art, Lyons, the *Susanna and the Elders* in the Kunsthistorisches Museum, Vienna, and *The Milky Way* in the National Gallery, London. His portraits, such as the *Jacopo Soranzo* in the Castello, Milan, and the *Antonio Capello* in the

Accademia, Venice, are among the most remarkable of the period. His crowning achievement, however, consists of the canvases that decorate the Scuola di San Rocco in Venice. In this series of very well thought out scenes from the Old and New Testaments he reveals to the full his visionary genius. His *Crucifixion* stands beside Rembrandt's *Three Crosses* as the sublimest portrayal of the Passion.

The remaining Venetian painters of this period were inspired more by Titian than by either Veronese or Tintoretto. Paris Bordone (1500–1570) painted groups of lovely well-fleshed bodies with a great wealth of color, but added little to what had already been said by the Master. The same may be said of Palma Vecchio (1480–1528), whose sensuous nudes are rather massive. Sebastiano Luciani, called Sebastiano del Piombo (1485–1547), is difficult to classify, for, having adopted the style of Giorgione, he then went to Rome, where he set out to imitate both Michelangelo and Raphael. His *Scourging of Christ* in the church of San Pietro in

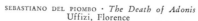

SEBASTIANO DEL PIOMBO · *The Death of Adonis*
Uffizi, Florence

Montorio in Rome is a capable but impersonal work. His *Death of Adonis* in the Uffizi is not lacking in grandeur.

Another painter who stands apart is Lorenzo Lotto (1480–1556). He is unequal but engaging. A restless, changeable figure, he worked in many places and came under many influences, including those of Titian and Correggio. In addition to excellent portraits, often curiously embellished with symbolic accessories (the *Old Man* in the Brera, Milan, and the *Young Gentleman* in the Accademia, Venice), he painted some commonplace pictures, but also some that are subtle in their lighting as the *Nativity* in the National Gallery of Art in Washington. His two masterpieces are the frescoes in the chapel of the Villa Suardo at Trescore near Bergamo, and the scenes from the legend of St. Lucy in the library at Iesi, in which he shows great inventive power and an astonishing degree of observation.

Jacopo da Ponte, called Bassano (1510

LORENZO LOTTO · *The Birth of Christ*
National Gallery of Art, Washington

or 1518–1592), had four painter sons. Accordingly, it is not easy to be certain what work is entirely by his hand. He treated religious subjects in a rustic style, scarcely varying the types he painted or the attitudes he placed them in. Often he has put a squatting peasant woman with tawny shoulders in the foregrounds of his pictures.

Venetian influence spread across Lombardy. We find it in the massive forms of Alessandro Bonvicino, called Moretto da Brescia (1498–1554). At Verona there was Giovanni Battista Moroni (1523–1578), who did nothing but portraits. These are excellent. Disdaining brilliance of texture and wealth of color, and confining himself more often than not to harmonies of grays, blacks, and whites,

GIOVANNI BATTISTA MORONI
A Master of Titian's School
National Gallery of Art, Washington

CORREGGIO · *The Holy Night*
State Picture Gallery, Dresden

ANNIBALE CARRACCI · *Fishing Scene*
Louvre, Paris

he appears to have had no other ambition than to depict his sitter faithfully; but the expression of the face and the lighting are rendered with sureness, restraint, humility, and contempt for ostentation. These qualities can be seen in *The Master of the School of Titian* in the National Gallery of Art, Washington, and in *The Prioress Lucrezia Cattaneo* in the Metropolitan Museum of Art, New York.

At Ferrara, Giovanni dei Luteri, called Dosso Dossi (1479–1542), was curiously romantic in his pictures, mostly mythological subjects set in landscapes, e.g., his two Circes, one in Washington, the other in the Palazzo Borghese, Rome. But his work would be more pleasing if he had more feeling for color.

Antonio Allegri da Correggio (1494–1534) does not enjoy quite the same reputation as he once did, when he was regarded as the equal of Titian. His delight in gracefulness and in a smoothly graded chiaroscuro gives much charm to his *Leda* in the State Museums, Berlin-Dahlem, his *Io* in the Kunsthistorisches Museum, Vienna, and his *Danaë* in the Palazzo Borghese, Rome. But he is less felicitous in his religious pictures, with the exception of his *Holy Night* in the State Picture Gallery in Dresden. His Virgins, angels, and saints eye the onlooker and smile at him in altogether too seductive a manner. All the same, there are some really exquisite frescoes done by him in grisaille in a small room in the Convento di San Paolo, Parma. In the dome of the cathedral in that town he painted an immense *Assumption*, pale and harmonious, which served as model for a great many painters, both Italian and foreign, of the seventeenth and eighteenth centuries.

Federico Baroccio, called Barocci (1526–1612), was another who carried gracefulness to a morbid degree. He is chiefly interesting for his pearly coloring and his effects with pinks, sky-blues, and pale yellows, which recall the harmonies so dear to the French painters and tapestry-makers of the eighteenth century.

THE CARRACCI

We come now to the three artists who bore the name of Carracci and who exerted a considerable influence, most of all by their imposing work in decorating the Palazzo Farnese in Rome. Reacting against Mannerism, they sought to revive a more weighty, eclectic kind of painting which would carry on the tradition of the great masters. Ludovico Carracci (1555–1619) was the eldest and the cousin of the other two. The churches and palaces of Bologna have many of his altarpieces and frescoes treating religious or mythological subjects. They are certainly serious works and unexceptionable as such, but they are conventional. Of the two brothers, Agostino (1537–1602) was a thinker, an organizer, and a good teacher. He was less of a painter than an engraver. The third, Annibale (1560–1609), was a much more picturesque character. Their carefully executed religious pictures

may well be thought lacking in fervor. No great depth of feeling seems to animate their figures. But what Annibale, assisted by Agostino and his pupils, Domenichino and Albani, achieved in the Palazzo Farnese justifies their reputation. For this princely palace they were commissioned to decorate the oblong Galleria or hall on the second floor and they rose to the occasion wonderfully. Above the cornices, within a painted architectural framework, the lovers of the classical gods and goddesses are depicted in panels held up by caryatids and beautiful naked boys. It is obvious that Annibale was inspired by Michelangelo's ceiling in the Sistine Chapel. But he translated that sublime Biblical poem into a sensual pagan language. There is no attempt here to endow the human body with superhuman qualities, but rather to portray the gods as all-too-human. Where the Sistine Chapel is both heroic and pure, the Palazzo Farnese is

ALBRECHT DÜRER · *Self-Portrait*
Louvre, Paris

ALBRECHT DÜRER · *Self-Portrait*
Prado, Madrid

the sumptuous exaltation of eroticism. The Carracci and their school exerted a great influence both in Italy and France. The interior decoration of Versailles was inspired by that of the Palazzo Farnese. But the reaction they launched was destined to die, for it was based on eclecticism, which offers no solution when it is not backed by genius. Genius seeks greener pastures. A real artistic revolution involves a radical revaluation. When such a genuine renewal finally occurred, causing profound repercussions, both in Italy and elsewhere, it emanated from the strong personality of Caravaggio.

THE GREAT CENTURY
OF GERMAN PAINTING

The sixteenth century is the great century of painting in the Germanic countries. Both in Germany and in Switzerland artists abounded. It is interesting to see how they reacted to the painting of the Italian Renaissance, the spirit of which

ALBRECHT DÜRER · *Self-Portrait*
Old Pinakothek, Munich

was so profoundly different from their own. How did German art, always fond of forceful and sometimes vehement expression – and rarely concerned with rendering physical beauty – react to Italian art, which, inspired by classical sculpture, liked nothing better than to depict beautiful types of humanity, to idealize nature, and to produce works notable for their order and harmony? In fact only Albrecht Dürer, among the German artists – because he was a genius – succeeded in assimilating the basic qualities of the Italian Renaissance, without repudiating his own Germanism. The others did little more than borrow from their colleagues on the other side of the Alps a number of new decorative motives. As for Holbein, whom we shall discuss presently, he remains much of an enigma. Though this work is primarily concerned with painting, we cannot refrain from pointing out that all the German painters of this period also produced engravings and woodcuts of truly great originality. Some of them put the best of themselves into their prints, rather than their paintings.

Pupil of Wohlgemut and the brothers of Martin Schongauer, Albrecht Dürer (1471–1528) was a child prodigy. His astonishing skill is shown in the drawing he did of himself at thirteen (in the Albertina, Vienna) and in the portrait he painted of his father when he was only nineteen (in the Uffizi, Florence). His early self-portrait in the Prado, his portrait of *Oswolt Krell* in the Old Pinakothek, Munich, and of *Elsbeth Tucher* in the State Picture Gallery at Cassel are stunning in the meticulousness of their drawing and in their easy mastery. His first religious pictures, on the other hand, in spite of their obvious excellence lack confidence, and are so crowded as to be confusing. But the serene, picturesque *Adoration of the Magi*, in the Uffizi, and the powerful *Hercules*

ALBRECHT DÜRER
Portrait of Hieronymus Holzschuher
State Museums, Berlin-Dahlem

LUCAS CRANACH THE ELDER · *Venus*
Louvre, Paris

and the Stymphalian Birds, in the Bavarian National Museum, Munich, show
how rapid was his progress. There is
some doubt about an earlier visit he is
supposed to have paid to Italy, but he
certainly went to Venice in 1505 and
stayed a year. We know moreover from
his letters to his friend Willibald Pirck-
heimer how intensely interested he was
in all he saw there. The influence of the
Italian masters is visible in the work he
did at that time–in *the Feast of the
Rosary* (Strahow Monastery, near
Prague), for instance, and the *Madonna
with the Goldfinch* (Berlin), and most of
all in the *Portrait of a Young Woman*
(Berlin) which shows how thoroughly he
had assimilated Giovanni Bellini's lighting and modeling. His interest in the
proportions of the human body and its
harmonious representation is shown in

HANS BALDUNG GRIEN · *The Three Graces*
Prado, Madrid

his *Adam* and his *Eve* (both in the
Prado), while Italian influence is again
obvious in *The Four Apostles* in the Old

Pinakothek, Munich, in which the simple, flowing drapery is so different from the complicated, angular folds common in his other paintings and prints. We cannot fail to mention a few of his later portraits, which are even finer than the early ones—*Michael Wohlgemut* (Munich), *An Unknown Man* who might have been Johann Imhoff (Prado), and *Hieronymus Holzschuher* (Berlin).

The work of Albrecht Dürer is so rich and varied, his versatile personality so fascinating, that we regret having to pass over him so briefly. We should have liked to deal with the theorist, the painter of delightful watercolor landscapes, animals, and plants. We should have liked to speak of the engraver and to discuss that extraordinary combination in him of realistic observation and visionary imagination. That imagination, his gift of depicting something never seen with perfect credibility, is shown to the full in his prints, which have so often inspired less imaginative artists.

If Hans Süss von Kulmbach (c. 1480–1522) and Hans Schäufelein (c. 1480–c. 1540) merely reflected Dürer, the same cannot be said of Hans Baldung Grien, more often called Hans Baldung (c. 1484–1545), who had a genuine personality of his own and deserves our attention for a moment. His use of color is rather hard, but he has plenty of imagination, with a leaning to the weird and the macabre. His *Coronation of the Virgin*, part of the altarpiece in the cathedral at Freiburg, and his *Adoration of the Magi with St. George and St. Maurice* in the State Museums, Berlin-Dahlem, count among his best works. In his *Pyramus and Thisbe*, also in Berlin, he puts his figures into contemporary costume, which gives the classical scene an unexpectedly romantic character.

Italian influence is so obvious in the work of Hans Burgkmair (1473–1531) that he is presumed to have been in Italy. He had great facility and produced a great deal of work. His painting deserved respect, though it is difficult to see much personality in it.

Lucas Cranach (1472–1553) was an ardent Protestant, a wholehearted admirer of Luther. For a long time he was in the service of the Electors of Saxony, Frederick III and John. In spite of the undeniable qualities of his *Crucifixion* (Munich) and *Rest during the Flight to Egypt* (Berlin), his religious pictures are not the most engaging part of his work. His portraits are generally preferred. They are full of emphasis and quite unforgettable. Among them are the *Portrait of a Young Lady* in the Louvre, who seems to be the same person shown in *Portrait of a Young Lady* (Art Gallery, Zurich). *Dr. Johannes Cuspinian* in the Oskar Reinhart Collection at Winterthur, is intensely expressive, and there is also

HANS BURGKMAIR · *St. John on Patmos*
Old Pinakothek, Munich

the magnificent *Johannes Schöner,* geographer and astronomer, one of the masterpieces in the Musées Royaux des Beaux-Arts, Brussels. Of this last it may be said that a single human being has rarely been represented with such penetration and power.

Lucas Cranach and his numerous assistants turned out innumerable pictures of women taken from mythology, history, or the Scriptures. Whatever the characters depicted, they were always of the same type: a long sinuous body with small round breasts, an affected pose, and an ambiguous smile. A rather surprising type coming from a fervent Lutheran; but perhaps the need to please his clients made him tolerant on this score.

Albrecht Altdorfer (c. 1480–1538) had a highly individual imagination. He painted small religious pictures which never lapsed into dullness. He had a feeling for landscape, particularly as seen at night. In his *Susanna and the Elders* and his *Wooded Landscape with St. George and the Dragon,* which are both in Munich, in his *Flight into Egypt* and *The Nativity,* both in Berlin, one might suppose the works had been conceived to explain their subjects to children. The last of these is especially delightful, spontaneous and poetic, showing the Holy Family sheltering in a half-demolished barn building while cherubs fly through the night sky. There is here the same desire to recapture the artlessness of childhood that will appear in the nineteenth century in Ludwig Richter and Moritz von Schwind.

Probably of Dutch origin, as is suggested by his name, Bartholomäus Bruyn (1493– c. 1555) painted some remarkable portraits which have something in common with those of Jan van Scorel. Outstanding pictures by Bruyn include the grave *Johannes von Ryht, Burgomaster of Cologne* (State Museums, Berlin-Dahlem), *Arnold Brauweiler* (Wallraf-Richartz

Museum, Cologne), and *Dr. Fuchsius* (National Gallery, London). On the other hand, his religious pictures are overcrowded and exaggerated, presenting all the faults of the Flemish Romanists. Italian influence, and particularly that of Bronzino, is visible in the austere portraits of Georg Pencz (c. 1500–1550). His decorations in the Hirschvogel House in Nuremberg, however, are ostentatious imitations of Michelangelo and Raphael. It is also as a portrait painter that Christoph Amberger (c. 1500–1561) is most memorable; see his portrait of the geographer Sebastian Münster in the State Museums, Berlin-Dahlem. He was the favorite painter of the Fuggers, the great banking family.

When one compares the work of the German-language painters of the fifteenth and sixteenth centuries with that of Holbein, his unlikeness to them is immediately apparent. First of all with subjects drawn from the Bible or from classical antiquity he shows none of the personal imagination evinced by Dürer, or even by Baldung or Altdorfer. When he paints what he has not seen with his own eyes, the result is pure rhetoric. As for his famous *Dead Christ* in the Museum of Art at Basel, it is moving as a study of a corpse, but what has it to do with Jesus?

In his portraits on the other hand, where invention is not demanded, he is incomparable. Oscar Wilde once complained to Bernard Berenson that a portrait painter for whom he had sat had merely made a map or landscape of his face. And that is exactly how Holbein worked. We would swear he did nothing but copy what was in front of him, patiently and conscientiously, omitting nothing and giving every detail the same importance, as much to the pattern and texture of a dress or tablecloth, as to his sitter's eyes and mouth. Actually he left out what he didn't think necessary, but we feel this without being able to say just what it

HANS HOLBEIN · *Portrait of a Nobleman with a Falcon*
Mauritshuis, The Hague

may have been. He shows so little un-evenness of execution that it is difficult to select any one portrait as superior to the others. Since we must cite some, let it be the portraits of a *Nobleman with a Falcon* in the Mauritshuis, The Hague, that of *Georg Gisze* in the State Museums, Berlin-Dahlem, which includes a wonderful still life, *Richard Southwell* in the Uffizi, and the virginal *Christina of Denmark, Duchess of Milan* in the National Gallery, London. But there are plenty of others just as good. There are also his drawings.

His personality is as puzzling as his painting. How did it come about that, amid his German and Swiss contemporaries, all of whom were given to passionate, vehement statement, and haunted by themes of religious faith and mortality, this one calm, well-balanced, objective painter appeared? He might almost have belonged to another race.

The most plausible explanation is to be found in the circumstances of his life. He was born at Augsburg in 1477 and died in London in 1543. A considerable number of those years were spent in England – from 1526 to 1528 and from 1532 till his death – thirteen years during which he was the painter of kings, lords, and great ladies. He created a type of portrait which is equally pleasing to artists and to sitters and their families, a type of picture in which likeness can only enhance the work of art. For a long time he set the standard for portrait painting in England. Before going there he had worked in Basel, a city of humanists which maintained close contacts with Italy and France. Holbein traveled in northern Italy and the south of France, becoming interested in French medieval sculpture no less than in Leonardo. A wanderer in other lands, long absent from his own, a court painter, how could he have kept an exclusively German character? He had to be what he was, what his life had made him. We must

NIKOLAUS MANUEL DEUTSCH · *The Judgment of Paris*
Museum of Art, Basel

regard him as a school in himself. He had many admirers and quite a few imitators, but no outstanding pupils. Next to him figures like John Bettes in England, Bruyn and Amberger in Germany fade into insignificance.

This period was remarkable not only for painting in Germany, but also in Switzerland.

Hans Fries of Fribourg (1460–c. 1523) is very uneven. The work he did at the end of his life is full of trivial detail and is disagreeable in color, while in his early work, such as his *St. Barbara* and *St. Christopher* in the Fribourg Municipal Museum, he is morbidly pathetic.

Nicolas Manuel Deutsch (c. 1484–1530), who was from Bern, was not only a painter but a soldier, a politician, and a satirical poet active on behalf of the Reformation. His best works, *The Beheading of St. John the Baptist, The Judgment of Paris,* and *Pyramus and Thisbe,* all in the Basel Museum of Art, show a highly individual, very attractive imagination and a bold and subtle use of color.

Urs Graf (1485–c. 1528), who was from Zurich, deserves to be mentioned for the remarkable drawings depicting his adventurous life as a mercenary, rubbing shoulders with Death itself. Tobias Stimmer (1539–1584) came from Schaffhausen. He spent some time at Como and had copied Mantegna, Titian, and Bronzino, and his own work is stamped with Italian influence. His paintings on the façade of the Haus zum Ritter in Schaffhausen are vivacious, if a little overexuberant. In his portraits of *Conrad Gessner* and *Martin Peyer* in the Schaffhausen Museum, and *Jacob Schwytzer and His Wife* at the Basel Museum of Art, he shows himself almost the equal of Holbein.

JOACHIM PATINIR · *Landscape with St. Jerome*
Prado, Madrid

THE RENAISSANCE
IN THE LOW COUNTRIES

In Flanders as in Holland the sixteenth century is a somewhat equivocal period. Most of the painters were making desperate efforts to keep abreast of Italy; at the same time they clung to their patrimony, the qualities that had brought such glory to their forebears in the preceding century. We must cite a few, though their paintings are no more than half convincing. Two artists, however, stand out: Joachim Patinir and, more unmistakably, Pieter Bruegel the Elder. Joachim Patinir (c. 1480–1524) has not yet enjoyed the reputation he deserves, either with the general public or with the experts. As we have already pointed out, he borrowed from Hieronymus Bosch the idea of taking a religious subject as a pretext for an enormous landscape with the horizon placed very high, to make room for all sorts of incidental episodes –laborers at work, knights on horseback, hermits praying, etc.–while a broad river flows away toward the sea, just visible in the distance. His work, like that of Bosch or Bruegel, shows how in those days the public liked to go over a picture detail by detail as we might run through the illustrations of a book. Patinir incidentally was the first to abandon the untroubled skies that invariably promised fine weather in the works of his predecessors, and to introduce clouds of every shape and color. Looking at his *St. Christopher*, in the Escorial, his *Landscape with St. Jerome*, in the Prado, or his *Baptism of Christ*, in the Kunsthistorisches Museum, Vienna, we are led to suspect that he was less interested in his religious subjects than in the wide country vistas within which he could put so many things. The delight with which he did so is at the root of the indefinable lyricism and serenity which radiate from his work. As for the painters called "Romanists" –Barend van Orley (c. 1488–1541), Joost

van Cleef (d. 1548), Jan Gossaert, called Mabuse (born c. 1475), and Frans de Vriendt, called Floris (1516–1570)–there is no gainsaying the fact that both their religious and mythological pictures are totally lacking in homogeneity. It is useless to put the blame, as is so often done, on their having gone to Italy and studied there. Rubens and many others did the same without ill effect. The real failing of the Romanists was an inability to learn what the Italians had to teach them. Mabuse's *Neptune and Amphitrite* (Berlin) and his *Metamorphosis of Hermaphrodite and Salmacis* (Boymans-van Beuningen Museum, Rotterdam), Barend van Orley's *Christ on the Cross with the Madonna and St. John* (Boymans-van Beuningen Museum, Rotterdam), Joost van Cleef's *Death of the Virgin* (Old Pinakothek, Munich) and *Holy Family* (Kunsthistorisches Museum, Vienna), and Floris's *Fall of the Angels* (Musée Royal des Beaux-Arts, Antwerp) are all rather tedious. But, as is so often the case with painters lacking imagination, when they came to paint portraits, dealing with what was before their eyes, their hands at once recovered an inherent skill handed down to them by their forefathers. Then they managed to forget Michelangelo, Raphael, and Leonardo, and the garlands and architecture of classical antiquity, and to concentrate simply on how to achieve the best possible likeness of their sitters. It is thus a pleasure to look at Orley's *Dr. Zelle* (Musées Royaux des Beaux-Arts, Brussels), Joost van Cleef's *Woman with a Rosary* (Uffizi), and *Queen Eléonore of France* (Kunsthistorisches Museum, Vienna), Mabuse's *Donor and His Wife* (Brussels) and Jan Gossaert's *Unknown Man* in the Boymans-van Beuningen Museum, Rotterdam, and Floris's *Man with a Falcon* (National Museum, Brunswick). In none of these was the painter content to give us a mere likeness; each of them tells us something of the sitter's personality as well.

This same desire to reproduce a human face honestly and accurately is found in the *Portrait of a Young Woman* (Museum of Fine Arts, Ghent) by Frans Pourbus the Elder (1545–1581), and in the *Portrait of the Anselme Family* by Maerten de Vos (c. 1531–1603) at the Musées des Beaux-Arts, Brussels.

With Pieter Aertsen (c. 1507–1575) and his nephew Joachim Beuckelaer (c. 1533–1573), painting became more secular, with scenes of family life a common subject. From both of them we have vigorous market scenes and kitchen interiors full of things to eat and things to cook them in.

In the second half of the century we find three landscape painters – Paulus Bril (1545–1626), Josse de Momper (1564–1635), and Roelandt Savery (c. 1575–1639) – who did not follow the panoramic

<small>MABUSE · *The Metamorphosis of Hermaphrodite and Salmacis*
Boymans-van Beuningen Museum, Rotterdam</small>

traditions of Bosch and Patinir, as Bruegel was to do a little later. Arriving at Rome in 1582, Paulus Bril stayed there for the rest of his life, painting landscape frescoes in churches and palaces. In these there is a harmonious simplicity which persuades us that he was one of the founders of the classical landscape and a precursor of Claude Lorrain. Presumably Josse de Momper went to Italy too, acquiring on his way, no doubt, that taste for mountain scenery which was to be a feature of his work. In his landscapes we find a free and unexpected use of color, a happy blend of realism with a romantic feeling for nature, and a sense of grandeur. His *Mountain Landscape*, in the Kunsthistorisches Museum in Vienna, and his *Winter Scene*, in the State Picture Gallery, Dresden, are only surpassed by Pieter Bruegel. Roelandt Savery also made use of the Alps, painting the jagged slopes of the Tyrol with a strange hardness and a coldness of color. A typical example is his *Wall of Rock* in Baron Hatvany's Collection in Budapest.

Like so many of his fellow painters, Pieter Bruegel the Elder (c. 1525–1569) went to Italy. He brought back some excellent drawings of the Italian countryside, but they are the only trace of Italian influence in his work. He went there a Fleming and a Fleming he returned, and ever remained. Starting off, as we have seen, from the type of picture invented by Hieronymus Bosch, one with a high horizon, leaving plenty of foreground to fill with people and things, he set to work to illustrate popular tales, proverbs, etc. (see *The Battle between Carnival and Lent* in Vienna), With immense gusto and humor, he shows both a remarkable gift for observation and a keenly inventive fantasy. All the same, he was a painter first and last, and his humorous comment is never allowed to spoil the picture. He went on to paint religious pictures, such as *The Massacre of the Innocents* (Vienna)

PIETER BRUEGEL · *The Massacre of the Innocents*
Kunsthistorisches Museum, Vienna

and *The Numbering at Bethlehem* (Musées Royaux des Beaux-Arts, Brussels), placing the scenes in his native Flanders, and introducing all that was familiar to him in Flemish life. As with Degas and Toulouse-Lautrec, each person, even the most minor figure, is given an individual physiognomy and personality. His backgrounds of heavy storm clouds, pallid suns in wintry skies, and exquisitely colored brick houses are all perfect in their rendering. Occasionally he painted a straight landscape, like *Hunters in the Snow* (Kunsthistorisches Museum, Vienna), *Harvest* (Metropolitan Museum of Art, New York), and *The Dance beneath the Gallows Tree* (Museum, Darmstadt), which show a feeling for the country such as will not be found again until the nineteenth-century landscape painters. Certain art historians have credited Bruegel with profound philosophic inten-

113

LUCAS VAN LEYDEN · *The Sermon*
Rijksmuseum, Amsterdam

been set up in the farmyard and not a detail of costume or furnishings has been omitted. *Hunters in the Snow* is set in a familiar landscape with houses, trees, and skaters. *The Pilgrimage of Molenbeck*, in the Albertina, Vienna, is a "snapshot" of a village scene, like *The Peasant and the Birdnester* (Vienna), the *Kermesse* (National Gallery, London), or *The Honey Harvest* (London). The caricatures, the comic incidents, have been painted on the spot. Even the religious scenes are almost always given the same local Flemish flavor.

Sixteenth-century Holland had no Bruegel, nor even an equal of Dieric Bouts or Ouwater. Hard and needlessly complicated, the religious pictures of Cornelis Engelbrechtsen (1468–1533), such as his *St. Constantine and St. Helen* at Munich and his *Calvary* at the Municipal Museum in Leyden, or those of Maerten van Heemskerck (1498–1574), are of no more than documentary interest. It is true that Heemskerck did some very interesting portraits, such as *Pieter Bicker and His Wife* in the Rijksmuseum, Amsterdam. Another able portrait painter was Jan van Scorel (1495–1562), as may be seen in his *Portrait of a Boy* in the Boymans-van Beuningen Museum, Rotterdam, his charming *Agatha van Schoonhoven* in the Palazzo Doria, Rome (which might be regarded as a forerunner of Vermeer's *Girl in a Turban*), and his grave *Pilgrim to Jerusalem* at the Cranbrook Academy of Art, Bloomfield Hills (Michigan). Lucas van Leyden (1494–1533) should be regarded less as a painter than as an engraver, in which capacity he did outstanding work. In his *Moses Striking the Rock* (Museum of Fine Arts, Boston), *The Sermon* (Rijksmuseum, Amsterdam), and his *Adoration of the Magi* (Art Institute of Chicago), we can certainly see something of that imagination and gift for observation that make his prints so excellent, but his color is crude and his lighting conventional.

tions. They exaggerate; in any case it is enough for us that he was a great painter who could enter into and depict the pleasures and the toil of simple people.

The setting of *The Massacre of the Innocents* is a village in winter. The sky is gray and the roofs are covered with snow. Against the white, the browns and yellows of the houses stand out, as the soldiers carry on their ruthless search and the victims look on. The scene of *The Numbering at Bethlehem* is much the same. In *Village Wedding* a table has

PAINTING IN SPAIN - EL GRECO

Spanish painting of the sixteenth century has few strong personalities, and only one man, a foreigner, stands out above all the rest – El Greco. The influence of the Italian Renaissance completely overpowered Juan de Juanes, sometimes called Macip (1523–1579), who merely copied Raphael. Juan Fernandez Navarete (1526–1579), called El Mudo (The Mute), carried eclecticism to the extent of following Titian, Correggio, and Hieronymus Bosch in turn. Francisco de Ribalta (c. 1552–1628) is more interesting, for in his religious pictures there is a soft realism which anticipated Murillo. Luis Morales (d. 1586) was a Mannerist who came to grief when he painted enormous pictures showing long-faced Madonnas with bulging foreheads. Yet his sentimentality went down so well with his age that he was called El Divino.

There was an extremely interesting portrait painter in Spain at this time, however, Antonio Moro (1512–1575), who came from Utrecht, his real name being Antonis Mor, but better known in England as Sir Anthony More. Philip II of Spain made him his court painter. His severe portraits are painted on a dark ground with relentless veracity and firm technical control. His *Duke of Alba* in Brussels (Musées Royaux des Beaux-Arts) and his *Mary Queen of Scots* in the Prado bear evidence to his undeniable skill. Born in Spain, though of Portuguese origin, Alonzo Sanchez-Coello (1531–1590) was a pupil of Moro and succeeded to his place in royal favor. Of less technical proficiency than his master, he painted some portraits that are gripping in their honesty, like the one of Philip II in the Prado.

Domenico Theotocopoulos, called El Greco (1541?–1614), was born in Crete, where he had been taught rudiments of painting in the monasteries. He went to Venice early in life, and learned to admire Tinto-

retto. A little later he spent some time in Rome, where his original talents were noticed. At a date unknown he moved on to Spain, no doubt hoping to be employed by Philip II at the Escorial. He settled in Toledo. He was commissioned to paint *The History of St. Maurice and His Companions*, but the King was dissatisfied with it. For the remainder of his life he stayed in Toledo, where, despite the strangeness of his painting and his idiosyncracies, he did a great deal of work for churches and monasteries.

There is a curious mixture of elements in El Greco's painting – some relics of Byzantinism due to his Greek origin and early training, a craftsmanship and a sense of color gained during his apprenticeship in Venice, a feeling for form derived from the Mannerists of Florence and Rome. In the first works he did in Spain, *The Trinity* in the Prado and the *Pietà* in the Béraudière Collection in Paris, his treatment, particularly the care to endow his figures with physical beauty, is still very Italian. Soon, however, his own personality asserted itself, and his painting acquired an extraordinary originality, as may be seen in his *St. Maurice and His Companions* at the Escorial, his *Espolio* (the disrobing of Christ) in the Toledo Cathedral, his *Burial of Count Orgaz* in the Church of Santo Tomé at Toledo. He took greater and greater liberties with the visible world in order to create a world of his own. He elongated his figures and clothed them in heavy draperies, which he painted with transparent glazes of intense color; behind them he painted dark, ragged clouds which both provide a background for them and divest the picture of depth. His handling became freer too, more elliptic.

In the pictures of his last years we can see an odd but quite definite reversion toward the Byzantine style – the enthusiasm of his childhood – though he kept this passion for movement and expres-

EL GRECO · *Christ Driving the Money-Changers from the Temple*
National Gallery, London

sion. His figures gesticulate and their attitudes are contorted, so much so that we can see in this Cretan turned Spaniard the coming of the Baroque. Looking at *The Pentecost* in the Prado, *The Baptism of Christ* in the hospital of San Juan Bautista in Toledo, and the *Christ Driving the Money-Changers from the Temple* (National Gallery, London), we scarcely wonder that his contemporaries found his art disconcerting. How could they have taken without a murmur a style so different from the current one? As for the idea which has been put forward that El Greco's distortions were due to a defect of eyesight, it does not hold water for a moment. Had he seen all bodies as more elongated than is normal, he would have had to paint them in normal size for them to appear elongated to him.

Because El Greco lived in a century that

produced great mystics – he was a contemporary of St. Theresa and St. John of the Cross – he has been regarded as the artist who expressed the mysticism of Spain. It must be observed, however, that his style of painting is utterly unlike that of the great Spanish religious painters, Ribera, Zurbarán, and Murillo. He was a visionary, who borrowed from reality no more than he needed to express in painted forms the images that haunted him, while the other Spanish religious painters were strictly realistic in their treatment, even when dealing with the most mystical subjects. His visionary qualities did not prevent El Greco being a remarkable portrait painter, as is proved by his *Man with a Sword* in the Prado or his *Cardinal Niño de Guevara* in the Metropolitan Museum of Art, New York.

ITALIAN INFLUENCE IN FRANCE

Are we right, when we deal with the history of French art, to go on speaking of the so-called School of Fontainebleau? To be sure, in the sixteenth century, the kings of France no longer spent most of their time in the region of the Loire; they preferred the Ile-de-France and busily decorated their châteaux in and around Paris. But how can we speak of a French school of Fontainebleau considering that we find there as few French pupils as masters? Louis Réau rightly stresses the international character of this pseudo-school and regards it as "the meeting point between Holland and Italy."
With Italy and Italian influences predominating from the first, the patronage of Francis I made Fontainebleau, and thereby the Paris region, the successor of Rome. Two Italian painters, Il Rosso and Primaticcio, supplied the teaching staff. Was this Italian influence on the French artists of the period a good one or a bad one? The question has been much debated,

SCHOOL OF FONTAINEBLEAU · *The Huntress*
Louvre, Paris

not always factually or without national bias. In any case, it is not the sort of question to which a final answer can ever be given.
Historians of French art rightly maintain that in architecture and sculpture the creative forces of the nation were not exhausted, and in support of this statement they cite such remarkable architects as Philibert Delorme, Androuet du Cerceau, and Pierre Lescot, and sculptors

117

such as Jean Goujon and Germain Pilon. But it has to be admitted that, when it comes to painting, this century was the poorest in French history, and it is a mistake to put the blame on the fondness of kings and courtiers for Italian work, for there were many French painters who, like their Flemish colleagues, were only too ready to imitate the Italians. One of them was Jean Cousin the Elder, who died about 1560, and who seems to have been the painter of *Eva Prima Pandora*, a work saturated with Italianism. And there is still more in *The Last Judgment* (Louvre) by Jean Cousin the Younger, who died in 1593, the picture being merely a Mannerist imitation of Michelangelo. Many pictures of women naked to the waist were painted at this time, such as *Gabrielle d'Estrées and Her Sister*, a portrait of them together in their bath, which is also in the Louvre, and

the *Poppaea* in the Geneva Museum of Art, an imaginary historical portrait. These works have little more than a documentary interest. They clearly show the characteristics of the Italian painters who were invited to France by Francis I, and who became what is called the School of Fontainebleau.

Italian painters had been crossing the Alps to work in France since the time of Louis XII. A pupil of Leonardo's, Andrea Solario, worked from 1507–1509 on a fresco in the chapel of the Château de Gaillon. Leonardo himself came to France in January, 1516, at the invitation of Francis I, and died at Cloux near Amboise on May 2, 1519. In 1518 or 1519 Andrea del Sarto spent a few months at Fontainebleau. To decorate the château there, Francis I procured two Italian Mannerists, Giambattista de' Rossi, called Il Rosso (1494–1540), who came to France in 1530, and Francesco Primaticcio (c. 1504–1570), who joined him the following year. With the help of numerous collaborators, they covered the walls of the Château de Fontainebleau with frescoes framed with stucco figures and ornaments in high relief. In them we find the typical caracteristics of the Mannerists who took over Michelangelo's style of treatment – emphasis on musculature, contorted postures, elongation of the figures – but to serve the purposes of sensual elegance rather than to celebrate the heroic. Although the work of both these painters is affected, and despite the self-conciousness with which they displayed their skill, their pictures are redeemed by a coquettish sensuality.

Side by side with the Italian influence on French painting was a Flemish one, expressed in small portraits, both in color and in line drawing, which were then very fashionable. Jean Clouet, who died in 1540, was the King's valet, and his son François (b. before 1522; d. 1572) followed in his footsteps. Attributed to

FRANÇOIS CLOUET · *Elizabeth of Austria, Queen of France*
Louvre, Paris

CORNEILLE DE LYON · *Portrait of Clément Marot*
Louvre, Paris

Jean Clouet is the *Francis I* in the Louvre, which has some of the qualities of illumination, and the very carefully worked *Claude d'Urfé, Seigneur de Château Neuf*

at Hampton Court. François Clouet painted the botanist, *Pierre Cutte*, in the Louvre, a tight-knit portrait, and the *Diane de Poitiers in Her Bath* in the Cook Collection at Richmond. Also attributed to him are the *Charles IX* in the Kunsthistorisches Museum, Vienna, and the *Elizabeth of Austria* in the Louvre. One is sometimes tempted to think, however, that the Clouets were at their best in their drawings. The more keenly observed sovereigns, royal families, and the great lords and ladies of the period come to life before our eyes.

Drawings were the fashion then, and others besides the Clouets practiced the art. The Dumoustier brothers, for instance, obtained many commissions from the Court. Corneille de Lyon – so called from his long residence in that town – came originally from the Low Countries. He died in 1574. He painted small portraits, hardly bigger than miniatures, in which, however, he avoided the stiffness and meticulousness of miniatures. A typical example is his *Clément Marot* in the Louvre.

IV

THE CENTURY OF BAROQUE

The French seventeenth century has been called the *Grand Siècle* because, under the personal rule of Louis XIV, it produced such writers as Corneille, Racine, Molière, Bossuet, and La Fontaine. But was it not also the "Great Century" of European painting? A man who went around Europe in the middle of the century would have met great artists everywhere: Rubens in Antwerp, Rembrandt in Amsterdam, Louis le Nain in Paris, Poussin in Rome, and Velazquez in Madrid. What a pity we do not possess the record of such a journey – even though a contemporary would have been more likely than we are to miss Georges de la Tour, who was painting in Lorraine, and Caravaggio, who died in 1610.

A generation ago no one would have thought of calling this period, as we often do today, the century of Baroque, for that word had acquired, with the classical revival at the end of the eighteenth century, a derogatory sense which long persisted. Whatever its origin, the term "Baroque" designated to the contemporaries of Winckelmann and Quatremère de Quincy a style that was grotesque, overelaborate, peculiar, in short, not worthy of serious admiration.

Today the word has lost its derogatory meaning. It is used in two senses. First, it serves as a generic term for European art in the phase when it stopped imitating classical antiquity – particularly classical sculpture, which, as we have seen, was the only statuary known to the Renaissance – a phase extending from Michelangelo or the sack of Rome in 1527, down to a date which varies with the country concerned, somewhere between 1650 and 1750. Second, the term "Baroque" unquestionably indicates a state of mind (Eugenio d'Ors). Can a state of mind be defined in so many words?

Moreover, can something characterized by constant change be described with any precision – something that is now progressive, now reactionary? Just where does the Renaissance end and the Baroque begin – or, as the Germans put it, how are we to distinguish between the *Spätrenaissance* and the *Frühbarock*?

An attempt has been made (by Louis Réau) to contrast Renaissance and Baroque art in terms of their particular inspiration, and especially according to the relative importance given to drawing on the one hand and to color on the other. The art of the Renaissance, it is suggested, is essentially static, aiming at equilibrium, that of the Baroque essentially dynamic, aiming at movement, for which purpose it employed in painting an oblique or diagonal composition. The art of the Renaissance is essentially linear, in love with line as such; the art of the Baroque is given to molding its forms by contrasts of light and shadow; it is in love with picturesque and powerful effects of mass. All this is true to a great extent, but the formulas do not fit all periods or all countries.

We might also regard the Baroque as one of those inevitable swings of the pendulum – like the late Gothic reaction against earlier austerity, like the reaction of Romanticism against Classicism, or like the present-day reaction of Abstract art against what preceded it. But that brings us back to the definitions of Baroque as a state of mind.

Perhaps the best solution is to use the term to designate the long interval between the Renaissance and Neoclassicism, and then, in each school or country, to distinguish between what was handed down from the past and revolts against it or innovations.

There is no gainsaying the fact that, at certain times and places, artists have deliberately set out to make something new. Other innovations in art are derived from influences outside art.

Eminent art historians such as Werner Weisbach, Emile Mâle, and Louis Réau see Baroque art as a consequence of the Counter-Reformation inaugurated by the Council of Trent, a Counter-Reformation which took the form of a Counter-Renaissance, with the Society of Jesus as the chief agent of reform (hence the term *style jésuite* often given to the Baroque in France). A regenerated Catholic Church took back control over art, and did not merely confine itself to banning nudes and mythological subjects. It eliminated from the lives of the saints – and thus from iconography – anything that might be seized on as a pretext for derision. It forbade artists to add anything of their own invention to pictures of sacred subjects, or anything which might lead simple minds astray. Lastly, a new iconography gave prominence to the cult of the Virgin and to the ecstasies, miracles, and martyrdoms of saints. At the same time – to continue this line of argument – Baroque artists were attached to the courts of kings and princes and their painting was pompous, luxury-loving, and ostentatious in the period of growing absolutism and nationalism. There were thus two opposing currents in the Baroque, the one restraining art, the other giving free rein to the imagination and the senses.

Some recent art historians, however – V. L. Tapié, for instance – have undermined this theory. The identification of Baroque art with Jesuit art has been shown to be an exaggeration. The theologians of the Council of Trent, we are told, were much too humanistic to banish literature and the fine arts from the spiritual education

DOMENICHINO · *Girl with a Unicorn*
Palazzo Farnese, Rome

of Catholics. No doubt at their instigation a reaction, often violent in its expression, was set in motion against the sensual and pagan outlook of the Renaissance, but the new style that was formed under their guidance reconciled a portion of the Renaissance heritage with the religious ideal laid down by the Council. So richly diverse an art, these historians argue, could not have come about at the instigation of a single religious order. To take one example: the Gesù, the mother church of the Jesuits in Rome, far from expressing an original conception, confined itself to subordinating Renaissance elements to the ideals of the Counter-Reformation and the special rules of the Society of Jesus.

Born in Rome, Baroque art remained Roman. Indeed, in seventeenth-century Europe it became an accepted principle that every artist must go to Rome. And almost all the important artists went to Rome, were sent there by their government, through such agencies as the Académie in France. And what a lesson Rome was! Besides the Carracci and Domenichino, there were Raphael and Michelangelo to look at as well. The most diverse artists were to be found there – Rubens and Vouet, Claude Lorrain, Poussin and Velazquez. Every sort of artistic talent could find some nourishment. We have only to take a glance at the various schools there during the Baroque period.

In Italy Guido Reni and Lanfranco continued the tradition of the Carracci. Then came Caravaggio, a highly original artist, and he was followed by Guercino, Cavallino, Luca Giordano, Feti, Procaccini, Monsu Desiderio, and all the other Italian painters of the seventeenth and eighteenth centuries.

As for France, Vouet, Poussin, Le Sueur, Claude Lorrain, and Le Brun followed the tradition of Raphael and the Carracci, but the brothers Le Nain and Georges de la Tour modeled themselves on Caravaggio. Philippe de Champaigne, on the other hand, and those who were henceforward to be called the *peintres de la réalité* turned to the Low Countries.

In this northern province of European art, Rubens and his school – Jordaens, Van Dyck – provided the Catholic world with a rich, sensuous, and even voluptuous art, while a more sober spirit prevailed in the Protestant north (most of present-day Holland), as may be seen from Frans Hals's portraits, Vermeer's interiors, Ruisdael's landscapes, etc.

In Spain there were Herrera, Ribera, Zurbarán, Murillo, Velazquez, Valdes Leal. The above list is enough to show what an infinite range of painting is included in the art we call Baroque.

THE BAROQUE IN ITALY

In Italy the eclecticism of the Carracci exerted a strong influence, the more so because their style of painting had a grandiloquent quality which made it equally suitable for altarpieces and the domes of churches and mythological or historical scenes in palaces. Domenicho Zampieri, called Domenichino (1581–1614), displays great skill, though he tends to academism, in his frescoes in the church of the monastery at Grottaferrata and in various churches at Rome and Naples. His two best works are the panel of the *Girl with a Unicorn* in the Palazzo Farnese and *Diana Hunting* in the Palazzo Borghese, in which he gives expression to his love of landscape and of youthful gracefulness. Guido Reni (1575–1642) painted some fine mythological scenes in Rome, inspired by classical sculpture as well as somewhat sentimental religious pictures. Pietro Berettini, called Pietro da Cortona (1590–1669), was both architect and painter. He produced a great many frescoes and easel paintings. Sensual, graceful, vividly colored, they

CARAVAGGIO · *The Supper at Emmaus*
National Gallery, London

are not without charm in their somewhat operatic style. Much the same may be said of Giovanni da San Giovanni's frescoes in the jewel rooms of the Palazzo Pitti in Florence, some of which are unquestionably attractive.

It was this type of painting, whose qualities were chiefly borrowed from the great masters or from classical sculpture, that Michelangelo Amerighi da Caravaggio (1565–1610) rebelled against. He attacked the eclecticism of the Carracci, and his influence was felt throughout Europe.

Born in Lombardy, Caravaggio came at an early age to Rome. He found a few patrons there, but was sharply attacked for his realistic treatment of religious subjects, and his violent character got him into trouble with the police. He had to seek refuge in Naples, then in Malta, and then in Sicily; on his way back to Rome, he caught a fever, and died alone at Port'Ercole.

The two principal traits of Caravaggio's work are what might be called his plebeianization of religious subjects, and his strong contrasts between light and shadow. Caravaggio turned his back on the Mannerists and on the Carracci, regarding their work as affected and conventional. He wanted to renovate and re-invigorate the painting of his day, not merely by painting life as it was, without embellishment, but by choosing his models from the humbler levels of society. He portrayed the Virgin as a peasantwoman, and the apostles as men hardened by toil. In the foreground of his *Entombment,* he shows Nicodemus as an old man with varicose veins.

From the point of view of historical accuracy Caravaggio was of course right: the characters of the Gospels were humble people. He was right, too, from an artistic point of view. Stripping these figures of a nobility that had become artificial, he restored them to a simplicity that brought out their authentic grandeur.

From what we know of his wild, disordered life, we can hardly suppose Caravaggio to have been a man of deep faith, but his pictures are nonetheless painted with all the seriousness of a believer. He did not aim at new picturesque effects, he sought the truth. Stripped of all decorative accessories, all pretentiousness, all artificial idealizing, perennial subjects recovered their natural dignity, and glowed with deep conviction. These are the qualities of his *Death of the Virgin* in the Louvre, so poignant in its restraint, his *Calling of St. Matthew* in San Luigi dei Francesi, Rome, and *The Entombment* in the Vatican.

Reacting against the use of pale colors, Caravaggio liked his forms to be silhouetted against opaque shadows, which bring to mind the black backgrounds of certain paintings from Pompeii. Significantly, he is one of the few Italian painters who never went in for the fresco

technique; it would not have suited what he was trying to do. He was also a master of composition, which his contemporaries tended to neglect. The curves of the angel who is leading the Evangelist by the hand in his *St. Matthew* in the State Museums, Berlin-Dahlem, are calculated with extraordinary subtlety; the same is true of Christ's hand as it emerges from the shadow in the *Supper at Emmaus* in the National Gallery, London, and the arrangement of the figures in *The Entombment,* or in *The Conversion of St. Paul* in Santa Maria del Popolo, in Rome.

Caravaggio's innovations were revolutionary, and they profoundly influenced many Italian painters. To portray people and things in a manner hitherto unknown is the privilege of genius.

Orazio Gentileschi (1545–1638) painted religious scenes with the veracity of Caravaggio but without his violent contrasts and in cooler colors. His *Flight into Egypt* (Corporation Art Gallery, Birmingham) and his *Finding of Moses*

DANIELE CRESPI · *Pietà*
Prado, Madrid

(Prado, Madrid) give a good idea of his style, which is studied but fearlessly truthful.

Another of these *tenebrosi*, as Caravaggio's disciples were called, was Giovanni Francesco Barbieri, also known as Guercino (1591–1666). At first a disciple of the Carracci, he shifted his allegiance to Caravaggio. But if he bathed his figures in shadow, he saw to it that the shadows were translucent, not opaque. His *St. William of Aquitaine* in the Accademia, Bologna, his *Deliverance of St. Peter* in the Prado, and his fresco of *Aurora* in the Casino dell'Aurora, Rome, are among his best works. Giovanni Serodine of Ticino (1594–1631)was a colorist of great sensibility who worked golden tones into the Caravaggesque shadows, and in this respect sometimes reminds one of Rembrandt. His most accomplished work is the *St. Lawrence* in the convent of Valvisciolo near Sermoneta, to which must be added *The Sons of Zebedee* in the Church of St. Peter and St. Paul at Ascona, and his *St. Jerome* in the Grecchi-Luvini Collection at Lugano. There is every reason to believe that, if Serodine had not died at the age of thirty-seven, he would have been an outstanding representative of the Caravaggio school.

Bernardo Cavallino (1622–1654) was also a disciple of Caravaggio, but he had a taste for elegance and gracefulness as well; witness his *Martyred Saint* in the collection of the Proto d'Albaneta at Naples and his *St. Cecilia* in the National Gallery of Capodimonte in Naples. Unfortunately, owing to poor preparation of the canvas, his pictures have greatly deteriorated. Bartolomeo Manfredi (c. 1580–1620) and Carlo Saraceni (1585–1625) obediently followed the master, as we can see from *The Denial of Peter* by the former (National Museum, Brunswick) and the beautiful and serious *St. Cecilia* by the latter (in Rome). Mattia Preti, called Il Calabrese (1613–1705), and

DOMENICO FETI · *Melancholy*
Louvre, Paris

Luca Giordano (1632–1705) combined admiration for Caravaggio with a taste for grandiose scenes filled with innumerable figures. Giovanni Battista Crespi, called Il Cerano (1576–1632), and Piero Francesco Mazzuchelli, called Il Morazzone (1571–1626), treated emotional subjects with passionate emphasis. Crespi painted the scenes from the life of St. Charles Borromeo in the Milan Cathedral and a *Madonna with Saints* in the Reale Pinacoteca, Turin; Mazzuchelli painted *St. Joseph's Dream* in the State Museums, Berlin-Dahlem. Giulio Cesare Procaccini (1548–1626) seasoned his Caravaggism with Mannerism and an obtrusive sensuality (the *Magdalen* and *The Mystic Wedding of St. Catherine*, both in the Brera, Milan). The three last-named painters collaborated in *The Martyrdom of St. Rufina and St. Secunda*, also in the Brera, which is one of the most representative pictures of the Italian Baroque. Giovanni Battista Crespi's son, Daniele

Crespi, lived from 1592 to 1630. His paintings, unlike the works of the artists just mentioned, are distinguished by their realism and restraint, witness his *Pietà* in the Prado and his *Feast of St. Charles Borromeo* in Santa Maria della Passione, Milan. Domenico Feti (1589–1624) was an eclectic whose style varied a great deal. His *Melancholy* (Louvre) and *Elias in the Desert* (Berlin) owe much to Caravaggio, while his series in the State Picture Gallery, Dresden, illustrates the parables of Christ in a contemporary setting. The theatrical romanticism of Francesco Maffei (c. 1620–1660) is not devoid of interest, while Giovanni Antonio Fumiani (1643–1710), who displays his love of color and movement in his large frescoes in San Pantaleone, Venice, almost anticipates Delacroix. Finally, there is the priest from Bergamo, Eva-risto Baschenis (1617–1677), who specialized in still lifes. The Surrealists have rescued from oblivion a painter whom the Italians called Monsu Desiderio, but who was a native of Lorraine, Didier Barra. We know he worked at Naples from 1617 to 1647, painting scenes of a wild and fantastic romanticism with strange lighting effects.

Fifty years ago the Italian painters of this period were held in little regard. They were looked upon as the decadent successors to the great masters of the Renaissance. Today their merits have been recognized. The revolution effected by Caravaggio is now thought to have been necessary, and even though, apart from him, Italy had no outstanding masters in the seventeenth century, we know that it produced a number of artists of unquestionable value.

NICOLAS POUSSIN · *Bacchanalian Revel before a Term of Pan*
National Gallery, London

THE GRAND SIÈCLE IN FRANCE – POUSSIN

Three tendencies may be discerned in seventeenth-century French painting. First, there were the painters who, whether they had been to Italy or not, derived their inspiration from classical sculpture and the eclecticism of the Carracci, and occasionally, with respect to color, from the Venetians. In this group we have Simon Vouet, Nicolas Poussin, Gaspard Dughet, Claude Lorrain, Eustache le Sueur, and Charles le Brun. Second, there were the painters influenced directly or indirectly by Caravaggio: Georges de la Tour, Robert Tournier, and Valentin. Third, there were the painters who in their search for realism turned to the Low Countries rather than Italy: the three Le Nain brothers, Philippe de Champaigne, Jacques Blanchard, Jean Jouvenet, and Charles de la Fosse. In addition, there was also a small group of still-life painters who set themselves modest tasks and performed them well: Baugin, Louise Moillon, Jacques Linard, and Sebastian Stosskopf. Finally we must mention two isolated figures: Claude Vignon and Sébastien Bourdon, whose manner was extremely varied and who imitated all other painters.

Simon Vouet (1590–1649) went to Italy at the age of twenty-two and stayed there for sixteen years. His style was of course influenced by so long a stay. He first was influenced by Caravaggio, but later he acquired a preference for the light and color of the Venetians. Nothing much has survived of his decorative paintings, but we can appreciate both his color and his composition in *Wealth* in the Louvre and in *Lot's Daughters* (privately owned). After long neglect, his work is now increasingly appreciated. Simon Vouet's return to France is an important date in the history of that country's art.

Nicolas Poussin (1594–1665) spent an even greater part of his life in Italy,

CLAUDE LORRAIN · *St. Paula of Rome Embarking at Ostia*
Prado, Madrid

where he went at the age of thirty. He settled in Rome, and died there at the age of seventy-one. Nevertheless, Poussin remained profoundly French. As a young man, he had admired Titian's color and had nothing but contempt for the slick facility of his Italian contemporaries, and he looked upon Caravaggio as the Antichrist of painting. He was attracted to Rome, because he worshiped classical antiquity, which he never stopped studying. For him it was a sort of Paradise

127

Lost, and his painting is a constant evocation of it. He was a man of reason, clarity, and logic, very scrupulous in matters of craftsmanship and contemptuous of boastful virtuosity. Yet he was not in the least pedantic. If he admired, even worshiped, classical antiquity, he also loved all that was beautiful in nature –the human body, trees, mountains, and rivers. His genius was a mixture of strict discipline with fervor, vigor, and charm. He appeals to both the senses and the mind. So well did he assimilate classical models, they never obstructed expression of the emotions aroused in him by nature. His work, far from being cold, throbs with life.

Working on canvases of relatively small size, Poussin treated religious and mythological subjects. He left no portraits, apart from one of himself, and, despite his long stay in Italy, he never painted frescoes. He loved beauty, but subordinated it to order; he loved color, but it was not allowed to have first place; he loved truth, but cleared of all accidental and commonplace features. It is difficult in Poussin's case to select works of outstanding importance, but the following may be taken as representative of his genius, which, despite his devotion to classical antiquity, was truly original: *The Young Jupiter Nursed by Amalthaea* (State Museums, Berlin-Dahlem), *Venus Sleeping* (State Picture Gallery, Dresden), *Summer (Ruth and Boaz,* in the Louvre), *Bacchanalian Revel before a Term of Pan* (National Gallery, London). It would be idle to look in his pictures for richness of color or texture; incidentally many of them have darkened because their priming coat of red-brown has discolored the surface layers of paint. But Poussin enchants us by his composition, his sense of order. Nothing has been left to chance; the artist created a personal style which expresses the spirit of Western humanism in the language of form and color.

Poussin's brother-in-law Gaspard Dughet (1613–1675) also lived and worked in Rome, painting landscapes of the Roman countryside. Though related to Poussin's work, they are distinguished by their greater faithfulness to nature.

Claude Gellée, also known as Claude Lorrain (1600–1682), left his native Lorraine at an early age, and spent the rest of his life in Rome. He became a master of what was later to be called "the historical landscape," that is to say, a composition which does not merely depict a given site, but in which the natural elements such as streams, trees, and hills are harmoniously blended with temples, houses, palaces, or ruins, so that the result is an imaginary landscape. If he treats a subject derived from classical mythology or history, it is the landscape that is often stressed. A Claude Lorrain does not give us truth in the raw, as the Impressionists do. In his art, nature is transfigured, purified; it expresses the emotions it arouses in the artist contemplating it; his landscapes are almost musical evocations of nature, rather than naturalistic representations. *Morning* (Duke of Westminster's Collection, Eaton Hall), *Acis and Galathea* (State Picture Gallery, Dresden), and *Seaport: St. Paula of Rome Embarking at Ostia* (Prado, Madrid) are excellent examples of his peaceful, serene style. Claude Lorrain's deep love of nature can be seen in his admirable wash drawings, which often recall Chinese landscapes.

Eustache le Sueur (1617–1655) never lived in Italy, but looking at his works, we might suppose he had. He owes nothing to the Carracci, but a great deal to an earlier master with whom he had affinities: Raphael, the Raphael of the Florence period, who painted the Madonnas. Whether treating religious or mythological subjects (*The Family of Tobias Giving Thanks to God* at the Museum of Grenoble, *The Three Muses* and *Cupid Receiving the Homage of the Gods* in

EUSTACHE LE SUEUR · *Cupid Receiving the Homage of the Gods*
State Picture Gallery, Dresden

the Louvre) Le Sueur is always incomparably polished, yet never insipid. He might be described as a Fra Angelico who had appeared after the Renaissance and studied both Raphael and classical sculpture.

Charles le Brun (1619–1690) was indeed a painter, but to have a proper idea of his personality, we must recall that he was the "supervisor" of the team of painters, sculptors, and decorators who were hired to embellish the château and park of Versailles and to glorify Louis XIV, the *Roi-Soleil*. In his religious pictures for churches, such as *Christ Served by Angels* (Louvre), in his gigantic decorative works for Versailles, such as *The Entry of Alexander into Babylon* (Louvre), and in his cartoons for tapestries, he shows his skill in the art of composition, but only rarely did he make use of all resources, as he did in his magnificent *The Entry of Chancellor Séguier* (also in the Louvre).

As for the French painters influenced in varying degrees by Caravaggio, the greatest of them was Georges de la Tour (1593–1652). Born in Lorraine, he was content to stay there, and never went to Paris, let alone to Italy. He was so little known in the centuries that followed, that his works were attributed to others. He was rescued from obscurity by the German art historian Hermann Voss in 1914. Georges de la Tour's painting is original and enigmatic. Because the light in his paintings is often provided by a candle or a lamp, his work has been compared to that of his Dutch contemporary, Gerard van Honthorst. But Georges de la Tour was not concerned with lighting effects for their own sake. He employed a reduced light and deep shadow, primarily for greater intimacy. He had simplicity and great restraint, with respect to both form and color; his ochers and golden whites are punctuated by orange vermilion. He liked to arrange his figures in unusual groupings (*The Prisoner*, which actually portrays Job and his wife, at Épinal and *St. Joseph the Carpenter* in the Louvre), to modulate his colors so that the volumes are bathed in light, and to render his figures as large simple masses. His vision is intensely individual, but unlike Caravaggio, he never tries to impose it brutally, or to baffle and surprise us. His paintings, e.g., *The Discovery* of *St. Alexis' Body* (Museum, Nancy), *The Education of the Virgin* (private collection, Paris), *St. Sebastian with St. Irene* (State Museums, Berlin-Dahlem), and *The Newborn* (Museum, Rennes), are imbued with intense poetry. He treats his subjects with humility and truth, and their atmosphere is one of peace and mysterious silence.

Valentin de Boullongne (1591–1634) went to Rome, where he died young. He treated religious subjects, such as *The Tribute Money* (Louvre), but more often groups of musicians, guardsmen, or gambling scenes *(The Fortune-Teller* in the Louvre, *Cheaters* in the State Picture Gallery, Dresden). Some of his works have been attributed to Caravaggio, so great is the resemblance. Robert Tournier (1604–c. 1670) studied under Valentin in Rome, but was less influenced by Caravaggio. In such paintings as *The Entombment* at the Museum of Fine Arts, Toulouse, and *The Pilgrims at Emmaus* at the Museum of Fine Arts, Nantes, the subjects are treated with great seriousness and veracity.

Other French painters of this period turned for enlightenment, not to Italy, but to the Low Countries, to the Dutch and Flemish masters. Foremost among them were the Le Nain brothers, Antoine (c. 1588–1648), Louis (c. 1593–1648), and Mathieu (c. 1607–1677). The eldest, Antoine, painted interiors with groups of figures; his composition is awkward and his craftsmanship weak. Mathieu, the youngest, painted over-meticulous small group portraits, similar to those that were done in Holland. Louis Le Nain, however, is one of the finest French painters and a profoundly original artist despite his similarity to Dutch painters. He treated scenes of peasant life, and even when he attacked religious or mythological subjects he placed them in a rustic setting, as in *The Nativity of the Virgin* in the church of Saint-Etienne-du-Mont in Paris or *Venus in Vulcan's Forge* (Museum, Reims), in which the goddess is a buxom countrywoman. What is so enchanting in the work of Louis Le Nain –in *The Forge*, for instance, *The Cart, The Peasant Repast,* or *The Peasant Family,* all of which are in the Louvre–is the veracity and seriousness with which he treats his subject, the complete absence of rhetoric or embellishment: he paints his peasants as he sees them, as they really are. There is also the quality of his light, the beauty of his colors, which, though limited in range–browns, ochers,

GEORGES DE LA TOUR
St. Joseph the Carpenter
Louvre, Paris

LOUIS LE NAIN · *The Peasants' Meal*
Louvre, Paris

grays, and whites – are never dead, never monotonous. In his treatment of light and his color, Louis Le Nain anticipates Corot. His peaceful family scenes anticipate Chardin. Finally, the restrained expressiveness of his faces brings to mind certain fifteenth-century painters, Fouquet and the Masters who painted *Man with Wineglass* and the Avignon *Pietà*. Louis Le Nain's art is a typical example of the tempered realism which is one of the constant features of French painting.

Of Flemish origin, Philippe de Champaigne (1602–1674) painted religious pictures that were conscientious and dull. On the other hand, he has left us several portraits of great veracity and deep feeling. Such works as the *Portrait of Cardinal Richelieu* and the *Portrait of Louis XIII* (both in the Louvre) show that he assimilated the fine technique of seventeenth-century Flemish painting, while treating his subjects with typically French dignity and restraint.

Jacques Blanchard (1600–1638) has not yet acquired the fame he deserves. He spent a considerable time in Rome and Venice and was nicknamed "the French Titian." As a matter of fact his taste for shimmering pink flesh tones brings him nearer to Rubens than to Titian. His love of opulent nudity is shown in *Charity* (Lee of Fareham Collection), *Angélique and Médor* (Metropolitan Museum of

Art, New York), and *Cimon and Ephigène* (Louvre). His painting, which is imbued with a healthy sensuality, is unfortunately represented by very few works; he died at the age of thirty-eight.

The painter most deeply influenced by Flemish art was Jean Jouvenet (1644–1717), whose large religious works recall Rubens by their colors (*The Descent from the Cross*, in the Louvre) and the fine portrait, also in the Louvre, thought to be that of Dr. Raymond Finot. As for Charles de la Fosse (1636–1716), his nacreous tones and smiling graceful figures (*Moses Saved from the Water*, in the Louvre) seem to belong rather to the eighteenth century.

Claude Vignon (1593–1670), who lived for a while in Rome, treated all religious subjects and other subjects in a theatrical,

PHILIPPE DE CHAMPAIGNE · *Cardinal Richelieu*
Louvre, Paris

picturesque style, made up of elements taken from classical antiquity and everyday life with oriental admixtures. Examples of his work are: *The Farewell* in the Musée Magnin, Dijon, *The Washing of the Feet* in the Museum of Fine Arts at Nantes, and the *Death of a Hermit* in the Louvre.

Sébastien Bourdon (1616–1671) tried his hand at many genres; he was a kind of Proteus of seventeenth-century painting. He imitated the masters so skillfully that his products were often sold as theirs. His *Solomon Sacrificing to False Gods* in the Louvre seems to have come straight from the Carracci. His *Camp with Gypsies and Soldiers*, also in the Louvre, is one of the genre paintings that were called *bambochades* at the time. Too versatile to have any character of his own, Bourdon nevertheless painted one fine picture, *The Lime Kiln*, in the State Picture Gallery at Dresden, in which light and shadow are admirably contrasted. There is also a remarkable self-portrait with an unknown musician, in the Benson Collection, Lichfield (England).

There were artists in France at that time who, in still lifes, portrayed humble everyday objects. Nothing is known of the life of Baugin, who painted the *Still Life with Chessboard* in the Louvre and the *Still Life with Candle* in the Palazzo Spada, Rome. Louise Moillon (1616–c. 1674) and Jacques Linard (of whom we know only that he was living in Paris in 1629) specialized in vases of flowers and baskets of fruit. Sebastian Stosskopf (1599–1657) was the most attractive of this group, and he is relatively free from archaisms, as may be seen from his *Strawberries* and his *Basket with Glasses*, both of which are in the Museum of Fine Arts at Strasbourg.

The seventeenth century in France was not merely a period of great activity; it also laid the foundations of the splendid edifice that French painting was to become.

CLAUDE VIGNON · *The Death of a Hermit*
Louvre, Paris

distinguished themselves in this tradition in every period of French painting are too numerous to be mentioned here. We may say that the great masters of this century laid the foundations of French painting. Whenever French artists have rebelled against academism and looked for new sources of inspiration, it has been to these great ancestors that they turned.

THE GOLDEN AGE OF DUTCH PAINTING

In the seventeenth century, in what then went by the name of the United Provinces and is now called Holland, painting was the major art and took on characteristically Dutch features. For one century Dutch painting enjoyed a prodigious burst of talent. It was characterized by a conception of pictorial art which differed totally from any that had been known in other countries.

Suffering from religious persecution and

Poussin and Le Sueur created what used to be called "historical painting," a genre that was later taken up by David, Géricault, Ingres, Delacroix, and Puvis de Chavannes. But Poussin was also a great landscape painter; so was Claude Lorrain. And in that field, French painting stepped into the front rank in the nineteenth century with Corot, Millet, Courbet, Manet, Monet, Renoir, and Cézanne.

Louis Le Nain and Georges de la Tour are highly original artists; their realism is typically French, with neither the harshness of Caravaggio and the Spaniards nor the ponderousness of the Dutch; it is a quiet, restrained realism imbued with humanity, such as will be found again in Chardin, Corot, Millet, Daumier, and Degas.

As for Philippe de Champaigne, he continued the tradition of French portrait painting begun by Fouquet and the Clouets, and added a new note of grandeur and dignity. The painters who

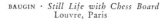

BAUGIN · *Still Life with Chess Board*
Louvre, Paris

heavily taxed, the Dutch rose against their oppressors near the end of the sixteenth century. With great courage and tenacity they threw off foreign rule in a struggle that lasted thirty years. An armistice was concluded in 1609, but the war continued. The independence of the United Provinces was not recognized by

GERARD VAN HONTHORST · *The Doubting Thomas*
Prado, Madrid

other European powers until 1648, with the Treaty of Münster. But though Holland was at war with Spain during the first half of the century and with England and France during the second half, and though throughout the century is was torn by internal political and religious struggles, this was nonetheless a golden age of Dutch painting. We have another example here of what we have already seen: that the flourishing of the arts is not in the least dependent on a country's wealth.

In his book, *Les Maîtres d'Autrefois,* Eugène Fromentin has shown very clearly what Dutch painting (apart from Rembrandt and his pupils) was in the seventeenth century. For this "practical, bourgeois people, seldom contemplative, never mystical, fiercely anti-Latin, devoted to a religion without images," an art was needed which would "appeal to it, represent it, and be comprehended by it." In short, "an art which painted its own portrait," that is to say portraits of people, their manners and customs, their cities, and their villages. The curious thing is that, in painting this portrait of their country, the Dutch painters completely left out all allusion to the struggles in which the Dutch were then engaged. Looking at their work, we might well come to the conclusion that they were at peace. Admittedly, there are pictures of naval battles, but the ships are seen in the distance and there are no

ABRAHAM VAN BEYEREN · *Still Life with Fish*
Frans Hals Museum, Haarlem

more than a few wisps of smoke to hint at the carnage.

What sort of an idea would one form of the lives of these seventeenth-century Dutch from their pictures? That the peasants spent most of their time in the inns, drinking, smoking, and quarreling, and that the burghers spent their time playing musical instruments, making love, drinking Spanish wine, and having banquets. One thing is totally missing: work. Holland was at that time one of the leading nations of Europe in agriculture, commerce, and industry. The painters did not record work in the fields, the conduct of business, weaving, printing, the making of pottery, shipbuilding, or distilling. Settling down to paint the portrait of their own people, the painters chose to represent them in their leisure hours.

Another thing lacking in these paintings is lyricism. Except for Rembrandt and a few of his pupils, the Dutch completely ignored two fields of lyrical inspiration, religion on the one hand and classical mythology and history on the other. And although Dutch navigators explored the coasts of Asia, Africa, and the two Americas, the painters were untouched by the glamour of far-off places.

But considering the narrow field to which the painters restricted themselves – always making exception of Rembrandt and his pupils – it is a miracle they achieved so much, and the explanation is, no doubt, that these painters really were painters. They were all the more faithful to the intrinsic values of painting for being indifferent to the more extrinsic ones. They were good craftsmen, but not especially interested in the study of form. Hardly any of them were remarkable for their drawings. It was much the same with composition. The subjects they undertook – landscapes, portraits, still lifes, three or four people in a room – did not pose them any great problems. None of them, except Vermeer, stands out as a really original colorist. For them, color was at the service of inherent values, no more. But when it came to portraying the deployment of volumes in depth or to determining the exact quality of a color in a given light they were incomparable. It must be added that they were thorough in all matters of craftsmanship. Their oil paintings are in excellent condition today.

Three painters stand apart from the others, for the fact of having spent time in Italy and there having fallen under the spell of Caravaggio. They are Hendrick Terbruggen (1585–1629), Gerard van Honthorst (1590–1656), and Dierck van Baburen (born c. 1590). They turned to everyday life for their subjects, and painted with frank realism, using the same settings as for Biblical themes. From Terbruggen we have *The Calling of St. Matthew* (Le Havre Museum) and *The Singer* (Museum of Art, Basel). From Honthorst, who was called Gherardo della Notte because, like Georges de la Tour, he had a preference for night scenes, we have *The Fortune-Teller* (Uffizi, Florence) and the *Dentist* (State Picture Gallery, Dresden). From Baburen we have *Lot and His Daughters* (Landry Collection, Paris) and *The Descent from the Cross* (San Pietro in Montorio, Rome).

Since the object of Dutch painting was to depict man in his everyday life, it is not surprising it should begin with a school of portrait painters, who received commissions, not only from the aristocracy, but also from merchants. Many of the latter belonged to the civil guards in the towns, and they enjoyed being portrayed with their sashes and standards at banquets. Thus, two sorts of portraits came into existence, portraits of individuals and portraits of groups. The syndics of the various corporations, too, liked to have group portraits. Bartolomeus van der Helst (1613–1670), Michiel van

BARTHOLOMEUS VAN DER HELST
The Banquet of the Civic Guard
Rijksmuseum, Amsterdam

Mierevelt (1567–1641), and Jan van Ravensteyn (1572–1657) were alike in being conscientious craftsmen without either genius or originality. They painted people just as they saw them.

In contrast to these stands a very different figure, the great painter Frans Hals (1580–1666). He never did anything but portraits. His subjects, men or women, were almost always dressed in black, according to the prevailing fashion, with broad ruffs of starched white linen. Their faces were those of respectable burghers whose minds were upon the daily routine of their lives and the prosperity of their businesses. The material Hals had to work on was not too exciting; the marvel is that he nonetheless was able to develop his great gifts. His technical skill was prodigious. His vision was always down to earth: he did not embellish what he saw. His technique was everything: in a few bold nervous strokes he could delineate a human face and bring its owner to life. His palette was limited in the extreme: white, black, brown, ocher, and Venetian red. It is as though he had restricted it on purpose, to show how much he could do with it. But when, occasionally, he painted a banquet of

civil guards, with their colorful flags and sashes, he was able to make something brilliant. His earlier portraits are careful and accurate, but stiff. As the years went by, his manner became freer and more elliptical and he reduced the number of brush strokes necessary to paint a face, a hand, or a lace collar. He was a virtuoso who never became trivial or slap-dash. The brilliance of his execution is always based on a solid feeling for reality. He has been reproached for painting only the exterior of his subjects, for neglecting their psychology, their inner life. As a matter of fact, most of his subjects had little personality and still less inner life. The astonishing thing is the amount he has to tell us about such commonplace creatures. For he succeeds in really interesting us in the *Old Woman* in the Boymans-van Beuningen Museum, Rotterdam, in the rakishly smiling *Jolly Toper* in the Rijksmuseum, Amsterdam, and even in the dull, sour-faced *Woman with a Prayer Book* in the Museum of Fine Arts, Boston. Hals is indeed far from being merely a clever technician. His pictures of the craft guilds are always skillfully composed: while making every face that of a real human being,

FRANS HALS · *The Jolly Toper*
Rijksmuseum, Amsterdam

he maintained the unity of the picture. This can best be seen in his paintings in the Frans Hals Museum at Haarlem, such as *The Banquet of the Officers of the Arquebusiers of St. George*, *The Assembly of the Officers of the Arquebusiers of St. Andrew*, and *The Governors of the Elizabeth Hospital*.

Two years before his death, when he was already over eighty, Hals undertook two large group portraits, of the governors and governesses, respectively, of the hospitals for old men and old women. His sight was failing and his hand was shaky, but these two paintings are masterpieces extraordinarily free in treatment. We might almost imagine he had thrown the paint on haphazardly. Nevertheless, his figures are intensely alive.

Besides such portraits, the Dutch painters did many genre scenes, both of burghers and of peasants, in their leisure moments. For the scenes of peasant life, we have Adriaen van Ostade (1610–1685), who painted the *Two Peasants Smoking* in the State Picture Gallery, Dresden, *The Open-Air Tavern* in the Rijksmuseum, Amsterdam, and *The Schoolmaster* in the Louvre. It is interesting that the picture he did of himself and his family (also in the Louvre) shows this painter of the poor to have been a prosperous burgher who lived in a comfortable house. His feeling for rustic poverty went in all probability no further than the realization of its picturesqueness, which he exploited because there was a good market for it. Cornelis Bega (1620–1664) painted similar subjects with greater simplicity.

The painters interested in a higher social class depicted ladies doing their own housework, cavaliers watching elegant women playing the spinet or lute, and gentlemen taking a glass of wine together. Such were Gabriel Metsu (1629 or 1630–1667), who painted *The Music Lovers* (Mauritshuis, The Hague), *Breakfast*, and *The Huntsman's Gift* (both in the Rijksmuseum, Amsterdam), and Jan

Steen (1626–1679), who painted the *Festival in a Tavern* (Louvre), *The Feast of the Kings* (State Picture Gallery, Cassel), the *Scene in an Interior* in the Rijksmuseum. Gerard Terborch (1617–1681) occupies with Pieter de Hooch a special place. He had a rare feeling for values and knew how to use black with great subtlety. Examples of his work are the *Child and His Dog* (Old Pinakothek, Munich), *The Concert* (State Museums, Berlin-Dahlem), and *Chamber Music* (Cassel). Pieter de Hooch (1629–1683) gave as much importance to the setting as to his figures. Whether treating an interior or a small garden, his real interest was in subtle changes of light and shadow. Thus, in *The Still Room* (Rijksmuseum), *The Card Players* (Buckingham Palace), and the *Dutch Interior* (Berlin), Pieter de Hooch obtains strong contrasts between his walls, which are dark, and the windows or doors, which give into brightly lit courtyards. In the *Courtyard of a Dutch House* (National Gallery,

PIETER DE HOOCH · *Dutch Interior*
National Gallery, London

JACOB VAN RUISDAEL
The Mill at Wijk bij Duurstede
Rijksmuseum, Amsterdam

London), and the *Courtyard* (Rijksmuseum), he exploits the soft light typical of Holland's maritime climate. His color is always exquisite, for he did not aim at strong but at accurate effects. His principal subjects are not the cooks and card players who figure in his works, it is light – light in so far as it serves to create three-dimensional space.

Two other artists must be mentioned: Jacobus Vrel, of whom all we know is that he lived in the middle of the seventeenth century, and Esajas Boursse (1631–1672). Both painted the interiors of humble people – people not at the extreme of poverty, but to whom every penny counted. There is no show of picturesqueness here, as with Van Ostade or Jan Steen, no note of patronizing, but in these simple rooms, generally occupied by one woman alone, there is an effect of quiet intimacy. From the hand of Vrel we have *The Street* (Hamburg), *Interior* (Musées Royaux des Beaux-Arts, Brussels), *The Washerwoman* (private collection, Rotterdam), while Boursse painted *The Sleeping Servant* (Heilgendorff Collection, Berlin), *Woman Cooking* (Wallace Collection, London), and *The Good Housekeeper* (Museum, Bonn).

Emanuel de Witte (1617–1692) and Gerard Houckgeest (1600–c. 1653) specialized in church interiors. These Protestant churches had been stripped of their statues, their pictures, and their stained-glass windows, and the bare white naves contrast sharply with the dark wooden pews. These two painters rendered many-faceted qualities of light very faithfully, and it is for this reason that their work delights us, despite their otherwise rather impersonal manner.

There were few Dutch painters of the seventeenth century who did not specialize to some extent. Among the landscapists, some specialized in the sea and the coastline, others in the countryside, and still others in the buildings and monuments of the cities. Many rendered the peculiarly flat Dutch landscape with its piled-up skies over a low, distant horizon line. Among such painters were Philip de Koninck (1619–1688), Jacob van Ruisdael (1628 or 1629–1682), Hercules Seghers (c. 1590–1643?), Jan van Goyen (1596–1656). For examples of their work we have Koninck's *Landscape in Gelderland* (National Gallery, London), Ruisdael's *View of Haarlem* (Mauritshuis), and Seghers' *View of Rhenen,* which has a romantic feeling recalling Rembrandt's landscapes. Jan van Goyen uses only grays and pale yellows in his *Meuse near Dordrecht* (Rijksmuseum), *Canal in Holland* and *View of Dordrecht* (both in the Louvre). Limited as the color is, the light is represented with great subtlety. Aert van der Neer (1603–1677), on the other hand, was fond of moonlit scenes, as in his *Moonlit Scene* (Rijksmuseum)

WILLEM VAN DE VELDE THE YOUNGER
The Harbor of Amsterdam
Rijksmuseum, Amsterdam

141

MEINDERT HOBBEMA · *The Watermill*
Rijksmuseum, Amsterdam

and *Landscape by Moonlight* (Louvre), with dove-gray clouds contrasting delicately with a pale bronze light faintly touched with pink. Willem van de Velde the Elder (1611–1693) and his son Willem van de Velde the Younger (1633–1707) were both marine painters. They painted the fleet in action and riding out a storm. *The Cannon Shot* by the younger is in the Rijksmuseum, and his *Harbor of Amsterdam* in the same museum. To these names must be added Jan van de Cappelle (1624/25–1679), whose *River Scene* is in the National Gallery, London, and

Ludolf Bakhuizen (1631–1708), whose *Rough Sea* is in the Rijksmuseum. Another painter, Meindert Hobbema (1638–1709), is famous for his *Avenue of Middelharnis* in the National Gallery. His other works are less inspired – *The Mill,* for instance, in the Rijksmuseum. Albert Cuyp (1620–1691), a conscientious painter, included animals as a feature of his landscapes, as in his *Cows in the Country* (Louvre) and *Two Dappled Gray Horses* (Boymans-van Beuningen Museum, Rotterdam). A similar painter is Paulus Potter (1625–1654) with his *Landscape with*

JAN VERMEER · *Lady Weighing Pearls*
National Gallery of Art, Washington

PAULUS POTTER · *The Young Steer*
Mauritshuis, The Hague

Cattle (Rijksmuseum) and his famous picture *The Bull* (Mauritshuis).

Some Dutch painters went to Italy and tried to find a compromise between its climate and their own. They painted country scenes which they thought to make more beautiful and distinguished by giving them a southern light. These golden landscapes, though quite artificial, are not destitute of idyllic charm. That group included Jan Both (c. 1610–1652), Nicolaes Berghem (1620–1683), and Karel du Jardin (1622–1678), who enjoyed a far greater reputation in their lifetimes than they do today.

The cities had their painters too, such as Jan van der Heyden (1637–1712) and Gerrit Berckheyde (1638–1698). From the first we have *The Westerkerk at Amsterdam* (Wallace Collection), from the second the *Flower Market at Amsterdam*

(Rijksmuseum). But the cities do not seem to have attracted artists of great originality, save for Vermeer.

Among all these landscape painters, Jacob van Ruisdael is by far the greatest personality. He, too, confined himself to a sober palette of browns, grays, and ochers. He differs from his contemporaries by his fondness for scenes of untamed nature, without figures, as *Underwood* (Louvre) and *Mountain Scene with Waterfall* (State Picture Gallery, Cassel), or the stormy seascape, as *The Sea near Haarlem* (Musées Royaux des Beaux-Arts, Brussels). Ruisdael gives the impression of being a restless, unsociable man, who chose scenes in nature to reflect his own anxiety.

The distinctive features of the best Dutch painting of this epoch – correct rendering of light and values, emphasis on depth, a rare quality of pigment–we find fully developed in the works of Jan Vermeer (1632–1675). He began with religious and mythological subjects, such as *Christ at the House of Martha and Mary* (National Galleries of Scotland, Edinburgh), *Diana and the Nymphs* (Mauritshuis, The Hague), and allegories in a contemporary setting, such as *The Allegory of the Faith* (Metropolitan Museum of Art, New York) and *The Allegory of Painting* (Kunsthistorisches Museum, Vienna). He soon settled down, however, to genre paintings of interiors which were frequently treated by his Dutch contemporaries. He surpassed them all. He was exceptionally skillful in his rendering of light. Like Flaubert, who could not bear to think there was a single misplaced word in his writings, Vermeer was determined there should not be a single touch in a picture which missed the mark. Everything in his paintings is bathed in a crystalline light of the utmost purity, as in *A Woman Weighing Gold* in the National Gallery of Art, Washington. Thanks to his scrupulous veracity he suggests better than anyone else the actual space of a room and the depths at which the various objects are situated. For this purpose, he often puts objects in the foreground as a foil, making the objects in the background seem more distant: this is the function, for instance, of the Persian rug and the basket of fruit in the *Lady Reading a Letter at an Open Window* (State Picture Gallery, Dresden), of the drapery in the shadow of the *Young Lady Adorning Herself with a Pearl Necklace* (State Museums, Berlin-Dahlem), and of the dark framework in *The Love Letter* (Rijksmuseum, Amsterdam). In addition to his faithful rendering of light, Vermeer is distinguished for his exquisite colors, his subtle harmonies of blues and lemon-yellows, and his glassy, enamel-like texture, which he often obtained, as in *A Maidservant Pouring Milk* (Rijksmuseum), by the use of tiny drops of color in the modeling of his forms. His tones are delicately graded, without ever being blurred.

Vermeer might appear to have seen in nature nothing but paintable objects, and among them to have made no distinction between a face, a carpet, or a jug. Yet his painting is never cold, never inhuman. On the contrary, it gives off an intense and radiant poetry. Vermeer is in every respect the complete opposite of Rembrandt, and yet these two artists equally differ from all their Dutch contemporaries in their ability, each in his own way, to go beyond visual appearance.

Vermeer's two landscapes, *A Street in Delft* in the Rijksmuseum (Amsterdam) and the *View of Delft* in the Mauritshuis (The Hague), were his last works. The color is so absolutely true and so delicate that all other Dutch landscapes seem superficial in comparison. They have also a marvelous texture, smooth as lacquer.

To Vermeer, familiar objects–pottery, glass, silver, fruit–were merely elements of a greater whole. Other Dutch painters of this century specialized in those objects. Unconcerned with the human face or the countryside, these painters reproduced, with extreme accuracy, glasses, goblets, Delft pottery, and oriental china, together with lemons, grapes, silver-scaled fish, delicate pink ham, and crusty brown loaves. In the three still lifes by Willem Claesz Heda (c. 1594–c. 1682), Pieter Claesz (1596–1661), and Hendrick van Streek (1659–1713), which are in the Dresden State Picture Gallery, the Budapest Museum of Fine Arts, and the Louvre respectively, or in *Fruit and Flowers* by David de Heem (1570–1632) in the Hamburg Museum, the glint of metal, the glitter of glass, the softness of the pile of a rug, etc., are rendered with unerring skill. Perhaps the best of this group was Willem Kalf (1622–1693), whose *Still Life* is in the Louvre and whose *Venetian Glass in a Niche* is in the Hamburg Museum.

REMBRANDT · *The Jewish Bride*
Rijksmuseum, Amsterdam

REMBRANDT

We now come to the great genius who is not only the dominant figure among seventeenth-century Dutch painters but stands head and shoulders above all the others. We must begin with a brief biographical outline of Rembrandt's life, for his work was closely linked with the events that marked it.

Rembrandt Harmensz van Rijn was born in Leyden in 1606, son of a miller. He began to paint at an early age. At twenty-eight he married a girl of good family, Saskia van Uylenborch, who died in 1642 leaving him a son, Titus. Rembrandt was then thirty-six. So far he had met with great success: his work, much of which was done for the wealthy merchants, was much appreciated, and he earned a handsome living.

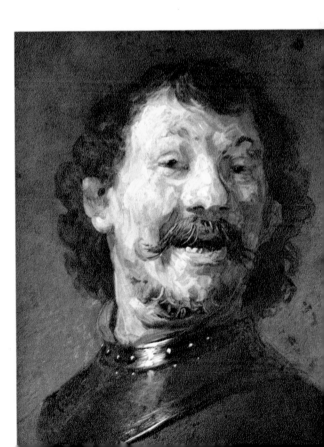

REMBRANDT · *Self-Portrait*
Mauritshuis, The Hague

Three years after his wife's death his style began to change: he painted with increasing freedom and originality, to the dismay of his admirers. At the same time, his financial situation deteriorated. He had spent a great deal of money on paintings, prints, and curiosities, and had also engaged in unfortunate speculations, as a result of which he went bankrupt. In 1654 the Consistory of the Reform Church of Amsterdam censured him publicly for living in sin with his servant Hendrickje Stoffels, who had given him a daughter. About 1664 she died; in 1669 his son Titus died, too, leaving a young wife and a daughter. Rembrandt died a few months later at the age of sixty-three, a lonely and virtually forgotten man.

Rembrandt was one of the greatest masters, but his genius was slow in asserting itself. Until he was nearly forty his work fell into two categories. First, there were his portraits, painted with skill and assurance but no particular originality. In fact, in his handling of light, he failed to achieve the high quality that seemed bred into the works of his fellow-painters. Among these works are *The Anatomy Lesson* (Mauritshuis, The Hague) and the *Shipbuilder* (Buckingham Palace). Second, there were his mythological and religious pictures treated in a grandiloquent, sometimes almost vulgar style, such as in *The Rape of Proserpine* (State Museums, Berlin-Dahlem) and *The Blinding of Samson* (Staedelsches Kunstinstitut, Frankfurt). If Rembrandt had died in 1644, he would certainly be regarded as a talented painter, but there would not be very much to his credit beyond the celebrated *Night Watch* in the Rijksmuseum, Amsterdam. (Incidentally, despite this traditional title, the scene is a daylight one.) But at about 1644, his style changed. The talented painter turned out to be a genius, the conscientious craftsman an artist of incredible freedom and boldness, the rhetorician a visionary who, as the years went on, became increasingly simple.

Just what happened to him will never be known. We can only guess. The lack of understanding which greeted *The Night Watch*, the intrusion of Hendrickje Stoffels into his life, and his bankruptcy and ruin may well have spurred on an artistic development which might otherwise have been slower. However that may be, there is no gainsaying the fact that this second and altogether different Rembrandt was a far more complex personality. He was at once sensual and mystical, a realist and a visionary. Relentlessly he aimed at expressing something which had seemed beyond the reach of painting, the life of the heart and the mind. At the same time he was very much interested in technical problems. Like all great artistic personalities he was torn by inner conflicts, and it was only gradually that he found his path. In this second period of his life, his painting became increasingly homogeneous. In the earlier period, there had been little or no relation between his realistic works—portraits and genre painting—and his religious or mythological compositions. Later, the differences between these two types of painting tended to disappear. One of his last works, the admirable *Jewish Bride* (Rijksmuseum, Amsterdam), has actually been interpreted as a Biblical scene, a genre painting, and as a portrait of Titus with his wife.

Complex as Rembrandt's painting is, two major features stand out. First, unlike the other Dutch painters of his day, who painted only what they saw, he stepped out of his age and country to re-create mythological scenes or Biblical episodes in an imaginary oriental setting. Second, while all other seventeenth-century Dutch painters, except Hals, sought primarily to reproduce nature, and especially light, with scrupulous fidelity, Rembrandt, as he grew older, confined himself to an ever increasing extent to the essential elements of form, and treated light with the utmost freedom, concentrating, dispersing, or dimming it according to his fancy.

When he wanted, he could render nature masterfully, witness his nudes – *Danaë* (Hermitage), *Bathsheba after Her Bath* (Louvre) – or his portraits: *Nicolaes Bruyningh* (State Picture Gallery, Cassel), *The Syndics (The Staalmeesters)* (Rijksmuseum, Amsterdam), and his numerous self-portraits. He was also an extraordinary visionary: *The Conspiracy of Claudius Civilis* in the National Museum in Stockholm brings to mind Shakespeare, by its imaginative power. While the other Dutch landscape painters prided themselves on the accuracy of their rendering of nature, he painted only romantic landscapes, like those in the National Museum of Brunswick and the Wallace Collection in London. Above all, he was a religious painter of unique originality, witness his *Pilgrims at Emmaus* (Louvre), *David Playing the Harp before Saul* (Mauritshuis, The Hague), *The Return of the Prodigal Son* (Hermitage, Leningrad). He was sensitive to the mysterious grandeur of the Old Testament as much as to the humanity of the New, to those simple texts which make us feel the presence of God made Man.

Rembrandt had many pupils. The portraits and Biblical scenes by Govert Flink (1615–1660) and Ferdinand Bol (1616–1680) are honest, careful works, somewhat banalized Rembrandts. Carel Fabritius (c. 1620–1654), who died at the age of thirty-four when the powderworks at Delft blew up, arrived at a deeper understanding of his master. He has left us a number of paintings of exquisite craftsmanship and refined color, such as *The Old Woman, The Goldfinch* (Mauritshuis, The Hague), and *Portrait of a Man* (Boymans-van Beuningen Museum, Rotterdam). Nicolaes Maes (1632–1693) spe-

CAREL FABRITIUS · *Self-Portrait*
Boymans-van Beuningen Museum, Rotterdam

cialized in genre paintings. The colors in his *Benedicité* (Louvre) and his *Girl at the Window* (Rijksmuseum, Amsterdam) are of great delicacy. Aert van Gelder (1645–1727), like Rembrandt, treated Biblical subjects in oriental settings. His *Christ among the Doctors* (Rijksmuseum), *The Three Angels* (Boymans-van Beuningen Museum, Rotterdam), and *The Holy Family* (State Museums, Berlin-Dahlem) are imaginative and display his gifts as a colorist, but for all their attractiveness they strike us as somewhat theatrical.

RUBENS AND FLEMISH PAINTING

Flanders had been through terrible ordeals in the sixteenth century. Its people, always independent by nature, revolted

149

PETER PAUL RUBENS · *Angelica and the Monk*
Kunsthistorisches Museum, Vienna

against the Habsburgs and embraced the
Protestant faith, less from religious conviction than from hatred of their oppressors. But Spain was too strong for
them. After a long struggle, she re-
established her authority; the Flemings
became Catholics again, and even ardent
Catholics.

In the seventeenth century Flanders recovered its peace and prosperity, and
with it came a magnificent revival of
painting. This revival was brought about
by Rubens, an artist whose powerful
personality gained him such prestige that
he influenced almost all the Flemish painters of his time.

Peter Paul Rubens (1577–1640) had a
happy life. He produced a large number
of paintings, was showered with honors
and fame, and distinguished himself as
a diplomat as well as an artist. He was
a polished man, courteous, well educated,
sincerely religious. At the age of twenty-
three, having studied under two mediocre
painters, he went to Italy, where he spent
eight years in the service of the Duke
of Mantua, visiting Venice, Rome, and
Genoa. Later he traveled in Spain, England, and France. In Italy he sketched
from classical models and copied works
by illustrious predecessors. Many Flemish
artists had gone to Italy before him, only
to have their native gifts smothered by
the foreign influence. Rubens had a
vigorous personality, and his own genius
was strengthened by what he assimilated.
Although he was a cultivated man, even
a humanist, there is none of the dust of
erudition on his work; no paintings have
ever been more sensual, more alive than
his. Yet his art, so realistic, so eager to
catch the softness of flesh, the shimmer
of satin, the play of light on quivering
leaves, is transfigured by a great lyrical
impulse. To see in Rubens simply a
realist is to misunderstand him completely. Before all else, he was a poet, in
love with the whole of creation, men,
animals, scenery, fruit, and flowers. It

was because he was a poet that he could often – and felicitously – mix allegory with reality, as when he painted sirens emerging from the water to salute Maria de' Medici, and the gods of Olympus surrounding her throne.

Rubens treated subjects of all kinds – Biblical scenes, episodes from the lives of the saints, mythological and historical themes, the life of the countryside, landscapes, and portraits. Admittedly, his portraits were not his greatest achievement. *Dr. Van Thulden* (Old Pinakothek, Munich), *Jacqueline van Caestre* (Musées Royaux des Beaux-Arts, Brussels), *Maria de' Medici* (Prado), and the delightful *Child of the Artist* (State Museums, Berlin-Dahlem) are excellent paintings in their way, but one must not expect Rubens to enter deeply into the soul of his sitter. He was too excited by the spectacle of all there was in the world to concentrate on a single individual. His work is overpowering by its inexhaustible wealth, its unceasing inventiveness, and its seeming effortlessness. In addition to rare natural gifts, he had great technical proficiency, which accounts for his immense production (however, it must be noted that he had many collaborators whom he had trained admirably). He acquired his skill by dint of great perseverance, as we can see by examining his early works, which are heavy, overemphatic, crude in color, and coarsely shaded. The technique he finally developed was not a complicated one. He did not go in for subtleties or refinements; but he knew how to obtain a great variety of effects with great economy of means. A great colorist, he was also a great draftsman, and rendered forms with truth and lyrical feeling. What he gives us is more than life, it is life transfigured.

He had studied classical antiquity, and he made full use of what he had learned. Delacroix was right in saying that there is no painter more Homeric than Rubens.

Yet, in dealing with classical subjects, it never occurred to him to divest his figures of flesh and blood, to renounce the autumn-tinted leaves and clouded skies he knew so well. From the whole Graeco-Roman store of accessories he borrowed no more than a few details, and even these he modified as suited his fancy. The rest he invented, unhesitatingly mixing contemporary details with classical ones. In *Decius Committed to the Gods of the Underworld,* in the Liechtenstein Collection, the Chief Priest wears a magnificent piece of Genoese damask over his white robe. His mythological pictures, such as the *Diana Returning from the Chase* (Royal Museum of Fine Arts, Dresden), the *Drunken Silenus* (Old Pinakothek, Munich), the *Bacchanalia* (State Museums, Berlin-Dahlem), the *Angelica and the Monk* (Kunsthistorisches Museum, Vienna), and that profusion of nudes like a basket overflowing with fruit entitled *Diana and Callisto* (Prado) are a confession of his abundant love of life and his healthy sensuality. It is easy to imagine that when he read one of those ancient classical stories, his mind was peopled by intensely vivid creatures disporting themselves in some stupendous landscape. So keen was his imaginative power that his allegorical figures are every bit as alive as those painted from life, as we can see in *The Joys of the Regency* in the admirable series of paintings in honor of Maria de' Medici in the Louvre and also in the equally admirable *Horrors of War* in the Uffizi at Florence. He put the same vitality into his theological allegories, such as *The Triumph of the Eucharist* and *Divine Love,* both of which are in the Prado.

Many people today are left unmoved by Rubens' religious pictures or even frown upon them. They admit the qualities of such works as *The Descent from the Cross* (Antwerp Cathedral) or *The Adoration of the Magi,* and *The Last Com-*

munion of St. Francis of Assisi (Musée Royal des Beaux-Arts, Antwerp), but they complain of overstatement, superficiality, lack of sincerity. It must be granted that Rubens' way of treating religious subjects, though it satisfied his contemporaries, does not quite come up to our ideas of how such work should be done. But to accuse him of insincerity would be unjust, showing a lack of historical understanding.

This cultured diplomat, who rubbed shoulders with the highest in the land, was able to paint the country and depict peasant life with the authenticity of a Bruegel, as we see in *Winter Scene* (Windsor Castle) and the *Farm at Laeken* in Buckingham Palace. He even tried his hand at the romantic landscape, e. g., his *Shipwreck of Aeneas* in the State Museums, Berlin-Dahlem.

Rubens exerted a considerable influence,

JACOB JORDAENS · *The Satyr*
Rijksmuseum, Amsterdam

153

SIR ANTHONY VAN DYCK · *Charles I, King of England*
Louvre, Paris

not merely on his immediate followers, but on later generations. Van Dyck and Jordaens are deeply indebted to him, and out of Van Dyck came the English school of portrait painting from Hogarth to Lawrence. The series of large canvases extolling the life of Maria de' Medici unquestionably exerted a profound influence on the whole of eighteenth-century French painting, from Watteau to Fragonard. Pictures like *The Garden of Love* in the Prado and *The Garden of the Château de Steen* in the Kunsthistorisches Museum in Vienna have already the atmosphere of a *scène galante* by Watteau. In the nineteenth century, Gros, Géricault, and Delacroix frequently turned to Rubens for inspiration, and who else could have prompted the pearly, opulent complexion of Renoir's women?

As for Jacob Jordaens and Anthony van Dyck, there is a tendency to regard the first as a heavier Rubens, the second as a more delicate one. This view, without being completely false, makes the mistake of considering these two artists as mere imitators of their master.

Admittedly Jacob Jordaens (1593–1678) was a disciple who learned an immense amount from Rubens, but he was by no means a mere reflection. Like Rubens, he painted religious and mythological pictures, genre paintings, and portraits. Good examples of his work are *The Marriage of St. Catherine* (Prado), *The Miracle of the Tribute Money* (Rijksmuseum, Amsterdam), *The Allegory of Fecundity* (Musées Royaux des Beaux-Arts, Brussels), *The Education of Bacchus* (State Picture Gallery, Cassel), and the *Satyr* (Rijksmuseum). To these must be added the series of twelve pictures illustrating the signs of the Zodiac, which Jordaens painted to hang in his own home. Bought by the French government in 1801, they are now in the Luxembourg Museum, and have recently been restored. These impressive paintings, full of the cleverest and most daring simplifications, constitute a mas-terpiece of Baroque decoration and deserve to be much better known. With Jordaens the paint is thicker and more opaque, lacking the pearly translucence of that of Rubens. The color is more emphatic and the light and shade more contrasted. And though he is capable of lyricism, Jordaens is closer to nature and more intent on realism. He was an excellent workman with solid, assured craftsmanship and his pictures impress us with their well-balanced composition, the weight and amplitude of their volumes, and the quiet strength they give off.

Sir Anthony van Dyck (1599–1641) worked under Rubens, then spent five years in Italy, mostly at Genoa. He did not stay long in Antwerp, on his return, for in 1632 he went to London, where he was appointed painter in ordinary to Charles I. He painted religious pictures as well as portraits. *The Crown of Thorns* in the Prado and *The Lamentation over the Body of Christ* in the Old Pinakothek in Munich are beautifully painted, but with scant religious feeling. In subjects such as these he saw an opportunity to use his great knowledge and skill in the painting of flesh, hair, draperies, etc.; and he frequently gave elegance and distinction to subjects in which these qualities were not needed. His feeling for elegance and distinction found a worthier outlet in his portraits of the aristocracy of the time. *King Charles I* in the Louvre, *Béatrice de Cusance, Princesse de Cantecroix* in Windsor Castle, *Maria Louise von Thurn and Taxis* in the Liechtenstein Gallery, Vienna, are all highly flattering portraits, but Van Dyck was none the less a shrewd observer of the society he was dealing with.

Some of the portraits painted towards the end of his life, when he was basking in success, unquestionably show too much of the handiwork of his pupils. But his portraits of *The Organist Liberti of Antwerp* (Old Pinakothek, Munich), of *James Stuart, Duke of Lennox* (Metropolitan

DAVID TENIERS · *The Deliverance of St. Peter*
State Picture Gallery, Dresden

Museum of Art, New York), or of *The Painter Frans Snyder and His Wife* (State Picture Gallery, Cassel) give us an intimate view of the personalities of his sitters. As for the *Portrait of an Old Woman* in the Liechtenstein Gallery, Vienna, painted by Van Dyck at the age of nineteen, it has all the dash and directness of a Hals.

Other portrait painters of this school who must be mentioned are the vigorous and serious Cornelis de Vos (c. 1585–1651) and Justus Sustermans (c. 1597–1681) who worked in Florence as court painter to the Medici family. Sustermans' *Maria Magdalene of Austria* in the Villa di Poggio a Caiano near Florence is a really splendid portrait, and the same can be said of his *Pandolfo Ricasoli* (in the Palazzo Pitti). If Sustermans often re-

minds us of Van Dyck, there are some pictures of his with white faces standing out against a dark background which give us a foretaste of Manet's early work.

Frans Snyders (1579–1657) assimilated the Rubens style so well that he painted most of the animals, fruit, and flowers in the pictures of both Rubens and Jordaens. He also painted on his own some still lifes of game, fish, and vegetables that are excellently done.

David Teniers the Younger (1610–1690) had a very distinguished career. He married Bruegel's granddaughter, whose godfather was Rubens. He became official painter to the Governor of the country, the Archduke Leopold William, and the curator of his superb collection of pictures. During his long life he never ceased turning out scenes of peasants smoking, drinking, and quarreling at the village taverns, a body of work that won him three centuries of fame. In the end, however, it has come to be realized that he was a mediocre painter, with little sense of either form or color, who had won success by his superficial competence. Not so Adriaan Brouwer (1605–1638), who also painted peasant scenes, and who had a fine sense of color and an opulent technique. His *Peasants Quarreling over Dice* in the State Picture Gallery, Dresden, and his *Landscape at Dusk* (Louvre) are painted with quite modern freedom and accent. Jan Siberechts (1627–c. 1696) is the only Flemish landscape painter of this period entirely uninfluenced by Rubens. His views of the countryside, such as *Ford near a Château* (Musée Royal des Beaux-Arts, Antwerp) and *Landscape with a Meadow* (Old Pinakothek, Munich), are painted in grays and cold greens with the rigorous precision of a primitive.

THE GOLDEN AGE IN SPAIN

The Spaniards rightly use the expression "golden age" to denote the great period from 1560 to 1700, which produced such writers as Cervantes, Lope de Vega, and Calderon; such mystics as St. Theresa, St. John of the Cross, and Louis Ponce de Léon; such sculptors as Juan de Juni, Gregorio Fernandez, and Montanes; such painters as Velazquez, Zurbarán, and Ribera.

At the beginning of the seventeenth century Francisco de Herrera the Elder (1576–1656) painted scenes from the Bible and the lives of the saints with almost brutal vehemence, as in his *Pentecost* at the Hospital, Seville, or his *Peter's Repentance* in the Prado. Jusepe de Ribera (1588–1656) settled in Naples, where he came under the influence of Caravaggio and also of the Neapolitan school. He

painted religious pictures of relentless naturalism and fine color, among them *The Trinity*, *The Martyrdom of St. Bartholomew*, and *Jacob's Dream* (all in the Prado). He painted many saints and ascetics as wrinkled and weatherbeaten old men. His picture of an aged toothless peasant woman holding a hen (in the Old Pinakothek, Munich) is typical of his realism.

Francisco Zurbarán (1598–1664) did a great deal of his work for churches and monasteries. He may have been indirectly influenced by Caravaggio, through Ribera, but it is quite possible that he had an innate tendency to realism. Even when painting visions, he remains a thoroughgoing realist: his angels and apostles seem to have been taken from ordinary life. This may be seen in three of his pictures in the Prado: *St. Peter Nolasco Visited by an Angel*, *The Crucified St. Peter Appearing to St. Peter Nolasco*, and *St. Bonaventura Visited by an Angel*. The same feeling for everyday reality may

JUSEPE DE RIBERA · *The Old Usurer*
Prado, Madrid

JUSEPE DE RIBERA · *The Martyrdom of St. Bartholomew*
Prado, Madrid

also be seen in his admirable *St. Bonaventura Visited by St. Thomas* in the
State Museums, Berlin-Dahlem, in which
the saint's books and the furniture of
his cell are painted with the accuracy of
the Dutch. And the *St. Casilda* in the
Prado is a contemporary Spaniard.

The chief events in the life of Diego
Rodriguez de Silva Velazquez (1599–
1660) were Rubens' visit to Madrid in

1628 and the two journeys he made to
Italy, in 1629 and 1649. Leaving his
native town of Seville, he went to Madrid, where he soon attracted the attention of Philip IV, who recruited him to
his service. From the start his real master
was nature. No doubt he profited by the
painting he saw in Italy, as well as by
Rubens' advice, but he needed no one as
an intermediary between himself and

nature. He communed with her directly, and what she told him he put down without embellishment or disguise. At court he painted innumerable portraits and never flattered anyone.

He painted what he saw and he painted it as he saw it. That was his great virtue: it was also his limitation. In him imagination is all but non-existent. What he could not see with his physical eye, his mind's eye was unable to envisage. His *Coronation of the Virgin* in the Prado gives us a faithful portrait of the models who posed for him, not visions of the Saviour's Mother and the Three Persons of the Trinity. The same is true of his mythological pictures, his *Apollo in Vulcan's Forge* (Prado), for instance, or the *Triumph of Bacchus,* called *"The Drunkards"* (Prado, Madrid): portraits of models and nothing more. His portraits of princes and princesses are no doubt excellent resemblances, but most of them are not endowed with the mysterious life we find in Rembrandt's and Goya's portraits, or in Ingres' or Holbein's. Never-

FRANCISCO DE ZURBARÁN · *St. Casilda*
Prado, Madrid

DIEGO VELAZQUEZ · *The Triumph of Bacchus,* called *The Drunkards*
Prado, Madrid

159

theless, Velazquez stands high for two reasons. First of all because of his immense care in rendering values, that is to say, in the exact degree of light appropriate to every gradation of color from black to white. This can be seen in the two small views of the Villa Medici in the background of the vast *The Surrender of Breda* (Prado), as well as in the portraits of *Innocent X* (Palazzo Doria, Rome), *The Infanta Margherita* (Kunsthistorisches Museum, Vienna), and in those two huge canvases *The Maids of Honor* and *The Spinners* (both in the Prado). In the latter, it is particularly interesting to see the marvelous amplitude and ease with which he handles subjects which were also treated by the lesser Dutch masters such as Metsu or Pieter de Hooch. In fact there is not a single picture by Velazquez which does not

BARTOLOMÉ ESTEBAN MURILLO · *Mater Dolorosa*
Prado, Madrid

DIEGO VELAZQUEZ · *Crucifixion*
Prado, Madrid

delight us by the exact gradation of its colors and the feeling of space they create between his figures.

The other factor which stamps Velazquez as a great painter is his astonishing assurance, the ease with which he solves all the problems involved in the act of painting. In front of one of his pictures we are tempted to believe that painting is easy – simply a matter of putting paint on canvas. In his works there is no attempt to experiment with new techniques, as we find in Rembrandt and Vermeer; nor do we see in them Titian's wealth of color or Goya's cursiveness. But if Velazquez' color is natural and without any great subtlety, he nonetheless knows very well, when painting costumes, how to bring out the harmonies of blacks, vermilions, purples, and pinks. The major qualities of his painting are directness, simplicity, and truth.

Because of these qualities, his painting reveals little of Velazquez himself, who in fact took as much trouble to keep himself in the background as others take to thrust themselves forward. He painted precisely what he was commissioned to paint, whether is was the surrender of a fortress, a hydrocephalous court jester, an *infanta*, or a crucifixion. Like an actor, he could play many different parts. For the exact opposite to Velazquez, we might

mystical Spanish people produced the matter-of-fact Velazquez, the commercial and industrial Dutch produced one of the greatest of all religious painters, namely Rembrandt.

Of Velazquez' pupils the two that most merit attention are Juan Battista del Mazo (1610–1667) and Juan Carreno de Mi-

BARTOLOMÉ ESTEBAN MURILLO · *The Holy Family*
Prado, Madrid

point to Van Gogh, whose paintings are invariably projections of his own inner self. For Velazquez, to paint was an almost physiological necessity like sleeping and eating. Neither his heart nor his brain seems to have been involved. One last remark: it is interesting to note that in the seventeenth century, whereas the

randa (1614–1685). Of the first we have *The Artist's Family* (Kunsthistorisches Museum, Vienna), an interesting picture in which the painter shows how intelligently he has learned the lessons of his master. Miranda's portraits are both truthful and distinguished; witness *Maria Anna, Dowager Queen of Spain* (Kunsthistorisches Museum, Vienna, and another one in the Old Pinakothek in Munich) and *The Infant King Charles II* (State Museums, Berlin-Dahlem).

Compared to the painting of Velazquez and his pupils, that of Alonso Cano (the *Dead Christ* and the *Madonna and Child*, both in the Prado) seems a pale reflection of the Italian masters. Bartolomé Esteban Murillo (1618–1682) quickly made a name for himself in Seville and received many commissions from churches and convents. His reputation kept on growing down to the end of the last century, when it dropped sharply; in fact, the pendulum has now swung too far the other way. Like his predecessors, Ribera, Zurbarán, and Velazquez, Murillo turned away from the idealism of the great Italian masters of the Renaissance, preferring to place his religious subjects in a familiar contemporary setting. In his *Holy Family* and *Rebecca and Eliezer* (both in the Prado), the actors in the Biblical scenes are Andalusian peasants. No doubt, he sought to make his Madonnas, Infant Christs, and youthful St. John the Baptists beautiful, but the beauty he had in mind was always an earthly one. Murillo also painted a number of portraits, which are robust and faithful, as well as innumerable pictures of ragged gypsies and beggar boys. In these, as in the others, he shows a taste for silvery harmonies and pale delicate colors, which, with his desire to please, make him something of a precursor of eighteenth-century painting. Since he painted a great deal, many of his works are conventional, but there are some, like *The Nativity of the Virgin* in the Louvre, which have affinities with Fragonard, with the best of Greuze, and even with some of Goya's paintings.

The name of Valdes Leal (1622–1690) is always associated with his famous *Triumph of the Cross* (in the Caridad at Seville), which has many decomposing corpses, and people are inclined to as-sume he specialized in gruesome subjects. This is far from being the case: in fact this is the only gruesome picture he ever painted. On the other hand, there are pictures of his in the Seville Provincial Museum which are full of movement and liveliness, such as the one of the Moors attacking a convent. Claudio Coello (1642–1693) looked for guidance neither to Velazquez nor to Murillo, but to Rubens. His *Christ with St. Francis of Assisi*, *Orlande Catteneo*, and *The Holy Family with St. Louis* are large canvases painted with well-saturated colors and achieving a beautiful play of light.

DECLINE IN GERMANY

The poverty of German painting during the seventeenth century is often accounted for by the ravages of the Thirty Years War and the insecurity it created. Perhaps that did contribute, but why do we find the same sterility in Switzerland, which was spared the war and which, to judge by pictures of interiors at the time, was prosperous?

Certainly there were painters enough in Germany and Austria who slavishly followed the Italians (like Johann Rottenhammer, 1564–1623) or the Dutch (like the flower painter Abraham Mignon, 1640–1679); but the only one to have any real interest is Adam Elsheimer (1578–1610). Born at Frankfurt, he went to Rome in 1601 and died there. On his way he must have stopped in Venice, as we can see from his *Tobias and the Angel* (National Gallery, London), for only in Venice could he have acquired his taste for color and light. In Rome he discovered Caravaggio and such classicists as the Carracci, and made the acquaintance of a young Flemish painter, named Rubens. Elsheimer painted small pictures on copper. His technique was rigorously precise but without stiffness. His subjects were Biblical or mythological episodes a forerunner of Poussin's and Claude Lorrain's historical landscapes.

ANTOINE WATTEAU · *Gilles*
Louvre, Paris

set in landscapes, as in his *Nymph Emerging from a Wood* in the State Museums, Berlin-Dahlem, *Moses and Jethro* in the State Picture Gallery in Cassel, and *The Good Samaritan* in the Leipzig Museum. With the importance he gave to scenery, which he took from the Italian countryside, Adam Elsheimer can be regarded as

THE ENGLISH PORTRAIT PAINTERS

So far England's only really gifted painters – Holbein and Van Dyck – had come from abroad. Holbein had his English imitators, but their work has no more than documentary value, and much the same can be said of those who followed Van Dyck. One exception must be made, however: the *Portrait of Endymion Porter* by William Dobson (1610–1646) in the National Gallery, London, is one of the best works of the period.

Sir Peter Lely (1618–1680) has generally been thought of as an English painter, though he was born in Holland, which he did not leave till the age of twenty-three. Like Dobson, he worked for Van Dyck, whose place he took after his death. Lely painted numerous portraits of the great ladies and gentlemen of the court of the pleasure-loving Charles II. His *Lady Bellasys* and his *Comtesse de Gramont,* both at Hampton Court, are typical examples of court paintings. Lely's portraits were intended to please and they succeeded in doing so, but they had neither Van Dyck's distinction nor his technical supremacy.

V

THE EIGHTEENTH CENTURY

In 1765, Pierre Patte, a French architect who worked in the Rhineland for the duke of Zweibrücken, wrote: "Paris is to Europe today what Greece was at her height: she supplies it with artists." This is not a patriotic overstatement, but the bald truth. For, during the eighteenth century, not only Germany – that is to say, Prussia, Württemberg, Bavaria, the Rhineland, and the Palatinate – but also Russia, Poland, and Italy, all had recourse to French artists and gave them the most important jobs. As well as an ambassador, nearly every foreign court had an artistic advisor in Paris, who reported, placed orders, made purchases, and chose artists. Also a great number of foreign artists went to Paris either for their initial training or for a final polish.

There were a number of reasons for this generally admitted supremacy of French art. First, the reputation of Louis XIV and of that unique monument, the château of Versailles. Second, the fact that the royal house of Bourbon had branches in Naples, Parma, and Spain. Finally, French artists were best able to express the spirit of the time. All through Europe, the eighteenth century was a period of prosperity, and even its wars never really disrupted the nations engaged. Life had become easier, pleasanter, more comfortable, and more refined. The stiffness of the previous century had given way to more sociable and more courteous exchanges; etiquette and protocol had given way to more general and easier good manners. Social life required qualities of friendliness and amiability, but above all the disposition never to bore those around you. The emphasis is not on personal life, let alone a personal cut-off from others: not until Romanticism did solitude become fashionable. Nonetheless, toward the middle of the century the more sensitive began to grow tired of this rather elaborate sociability, and began to appreciate the peace and calm of the countryside.

In this wordly life, woman reigned supreme, and it was very largely to glorify women and to give them pleasure that the artists worked. The theater, too, had a great influence on painting: Watteau's pictures hark back to his memories of Italian comedy; Boucher's and Tiepolo's mythological scenes look almost like episodes from an opera; Greuze, with his exaggerated pathos and forced sentimentality, could easily be illustrating the tearful dramas of Diderot and Nivelle de la Chaussée. And what could be more theatrical than the emphasis on gesture in the work of David and his school?

And yet despite the great charm of this art, we have to admit that it is incomplete. It has no feeling for the sacred or the supernatural, no sense of grandeur or of true poetry. Religious painting scarcely existed; the great myths of antiquity were usually mere pretexts for showing half-dressed or undressed women against painted backdrops. The commonest types of picture were those which complimented a pleasure-loving society's view of itself: graceful, sensuous interior decorations; *scènes galantes*; portraits, all-important to a society of this kind; finally, pleasing genre scenes. It is true that a few painters struck a personal and lyrical note: Watteau, Tiepolo, Fragonard. But charming as these painters are, their appeal is confined to the senses, and nothing more.

French art in this period was so rich in gifted painters that it is tempting to forget the rest of Europe. Yet, even if painting in Spain and the Low Countries was in complete lethargy, there were a number of interesting artists elsewhere.

FROM WATTEAU TO FRAGONARD

The French Regency—i.e., the beginning of the eighteenth century—was a period of reaction against the austerity and narrow piety that marked the closing years of Louis XIV's reign. The Regent and his circle set the tone for an utter looseness of morals; unrestrained pleasure was the only aim. It is odd that the chief painter of such an age should have been a subtle artist like Watteau, who preferred delicacy of feeling to the unleashing of instinct. At the time, only a handful of friends understood his work; his deeply mysterious and poetic canvases

were considered to be nothing more than charmingly pleasant scenes.

Admittedly, his art fell into no known category. He avoided mythological subjects, and where he did paint them it was in a wholly personal way; with few exceptions he left the life of his time alone. He took his own recollections of the theater, or of walks in gardens and woods, and transformed them into an imaginary world expressive of his dreams. The Italian comedies from which he took the figures that move through his work —Harlequin and Isabella, Scapino and Zerlina—were the crudest of farces. Out of this crude material he produced wonders.

Watteau's paintings have neither action nor clearly defined subjects; their titles are interchangeable. He drew continually, using both models and his friends, and would then choose a few of these figures and arrange them in a group. His re-

JEAN BAPTISTE PATER · *The Toilet*
Louvre, Paris

ANTOINE WATTEAU · *The Embarkation for Cythera*
Louvre, Paris

markably precise sense of composition, of balanced light and shadow with splashes of color, is all the justification there is for the arrangement. The real subject of Watteau's painting is a delicate sensibility which cannot be defined in words. Instead of bearing their present vague titles, his pictures ought to be designated by musical terms such as *dolce, allegretto, appassionata,* etc.

It is only since the middle of the nineteenth century that Watteau has been given the place in French art which is his due, and since then, all who have

spoken of him have claimed to catch an undertone of sadness in his work. It is much more natural to suppose that Watteau got rid of his black moods by creating a world where all was "luxury, order, and beauty" and no anxieties to disturb. This imaginary world seems an Arcadia where lovers and their mistresses murmur words of love to the sound of lute or guitar. Yet it is a world saturated with reality, full of all those elements that delighted the artist in the real world: women more graceful than beautiful, the sheen of silken fabrics, the reddish tinge of autumn leaves. Once, not long before his death, Watteau made a rapid sketch of a scene from everyday life, showing the shop of his friend Gersaint, an art dealer. The exactness of the observation and the exquisiteness of color put *The Shop Sign of Gersaint* (in the former Prussian state collection) on a level with *The Embarkation for Cythera* (in the Louvre) as the two masterpieces of French eighteenth-century painting. Other works of Watteau's include *The Music Party* and *Harlequin and Columbine* in the Wallace Collection, *Rustic Pleasures* in the Musée Condé at Chantilly, *The Faux Pas* in the Louvre, and *The Italian Comedy* in the State Museums, Berlin-Dahlem.

Watteau was a disciple of Rubens, but he had an incomparably lighter touch than his master. He had two pupils himself: Nicolas Lancret (1690–1743) and Jean-Baptiste Pater (1695–1736), whose elegant pastoral scenes are not without charm. All they did, however, was to repeat at a lower level of accomplishment what their teacher had already said: Lancret with a certain distinction, Pater with a more plebeian vitality.

Bridging the seventeenth and eighteenth centuries, Nicolas de Largillière (1656–1746) and Hyacinthe Rigaud (1659–1743) were two excellent portrait painters in the Flemish tradition. Rigaud portrayed Louis XIV and the great nobles, De Largillière the cream of the Parisian middle

FRANÇOIS BOUCHER · *Diana Resting after Her Bath*
Louvre, Paris

NICOLAS DE LARGILLIÈRE · *Marie-Anne de Bourbon*
Prado, Madrid

much sought after by society ladies, because, as a contemporary of his put it, he had found the way to make any woman look pretty, at the same time giving a good likeness. He did undoubtedly leave us charming if somewhat superficial portraits of Louis XIV's daughters, who are well known to have been no beauties. Nonetheless his big portrait of *Madame Adélaïde de France* in the Louvre has great style and is extremely pleasant, even if we ourselves prefer works of greater intimacy and less ostentatious appeal, such as the *Unknown Woman* in the Wallace Collection or the *Portrait of a Woman Painter* in the Besançon Museum of Fine Arts.

Tocqué was equally anxious to please his sitters, but rather more devoted to the truth. He left some very lively portraits of the men and women of his day: for instance, *Madame de Graffigny* (Louvre) or *Mademoiselle de Coislin*, or the singer *Géliotte* in his richly embroidered coat. There were also skillful, quick-working painters who would cover the walls and ceilings of the royal palaces, the theaters, and the town houses of the aristocracy with pink and white nudes against a turquoise sky: allegorical figures or clas-

class. As a result, De Largillière's work is much more characteristically eighteenth-century than Rigaud's: less reminiscent of a world governed by outward display and a rigid social code. But although Rigaud painted such highly official portraits as those of *Louis XIV* and *Bossuet* in the Louvre, his *Portrait of Fontenelle* (Hermitage, Leningrad) has a charming vividness. De Largillière's *Voltaire as a Young Man* and *Two Magistrates* (Musée Carnavalet, Paris), his *Belle Strasbourgeoise* (Meyer-Sassoon Collection, London), and his *Self-Portrait with Wife and Daughter* (Louvre) show his pleasure in depicting life, youth, clear complexions, bright eyes, and the shimmer of silks and velvets.

These two artists were succeeded as portrait painters by Jean Marc Nattier (1685–1766) and Louis Tocqué (1696–1772). Nattier was a fashionable painter

JEAN MARC NATTIER · *The Penitent Magdalen*
Louvre, Paris

MAURICE QUENTIN DE LA TOUR
Count Maurice de Saxe, Maréchal de France
State Picture Gallery, Dresden

sical gods. Among such painters were Antoine Coypel (1661–1722) and his son Charles (1694–1752), François Lemoyne (1688–1737), Jean François de Troy (1679–1752), and Carle van Loo (1705–1765), whose brother and two sons were also painters, and who seemed to the public of the time to be first-rank masters. Their art succeeded admirably in fulfilling its function, which was to build up an atmosphere of elegant sensuality, but it was never profound. Yet as soon as these same painters turned for their subjects to the life around them, their work gained greatly in vitality for being based on nature. This can be seen from Carle van Loo's *Hunt Breakfast* (in the Louvre), from *La Lecture de Molière* (in Sir Philip Sassoon's Collection), and from the *Hunt Breakfast* by De Troy (Baron Maurice de Rothschild's Collection, Paris). The artist most representative of eighteenth-century painting, the artist who was universally approved, was François Boucher (1703–1770). He undertook everything: mythological episodes, which he reduced to groups of unclothed young beauties (*Diana Resting after her Bath* in the Louvre); genre scenes (*Breakfast* in the Louvre); pastoral scenes (*Rustic Charms* in the Louvre); portraits (*Madame Boucher* in the David-Weill Collection, Paris); landscape (*The Windmill* in the Louvre). His whole output is that of a hard, quick worker who exploited his natural facility to the full, but who learned almost at once to do without nature, and thereafter gave it only an occasional absent-minded glance. We must not be afraid of being hard on Boucher, because he left some very beautiful drawings of nudes done from the life which show that he could have been a much better artist if only he had taken more trouble, and pandered less to public taste.

Two other painters, François Desportes (1661–1743) and Jean Baptiste Oudry (1686–1755), showed great energy and considerable exactness of observation in their still lifes and hunting scenes. We may mention Desportes' *Fowl, Game, and Vegetables* (Louvre), together with Oudry's *Hallali au Loup* (Nantes Museum of Fine Arts) and his extraordinary *White Duck* (Sir Philip Sassoon Collection), a painting in which every object is white. Both these artists painted landscapes: an unusual habit for the time. At the château of Compiègne there are a number of such studies made by Desportes in the countryside round Paris. They are so accurate, and the paint is so boldly handled, that they could have been painted a century or more later.

The eighteenth century also saw a considerable vogue for pastel in France. The Venetian painter Rosalba Carriera had introduced the new technique, which favored the clear, fresh colors that the public then liked, and blended very well with the decorations among which that public lived. Pastel was used almost exclusively for portraiture, and the two artists who made their name by it were Perronneau and La Tour.

Maurice Quentin de La Tour (1704–1788) has left us many portraits of the high society of his day, for he was much sought after in spite of his conscious independence, and his abrupt and offhand manner. Among others we may mention *D'Alembert* and *The Dauphine Maria Josepha of Saxony* in the Louvre, and also *Count Maurice de Saxe, Maréchal de France* (State Picture Gallery, Dresden). But La Tour himself admitted that he often spoiled his portraits by working too long on them. That is why the finished pastels are often inferior to the large number of preparatory studies in the museum at Saint-Quentin, where the sitter's face alone is shown, standing out from the blue-tinted paper. This can be conclusively proved by comparing the study of Madame de Pompadour with her portrait in the Louvre.

La Tour got astonishing results from the

JEAN BAPTISTE PERRONNEAU
Portrait of Madame de Sorquainville
Louvre, Paris

pastel medium, a medium which can convey both the nebulous and the exact. When one visits the rooms devoted to his studies in the Saint-Quentin Museum all these heads of nobles, actresses, painters, bankers, dancers, and literary men seem so alive, their features and their expressions seem so accurately caught, that one has the feeling that one is interrupting a private conversation.

While La Tour's patrons were mostly aristocrats, those of Jean Baptiste Perronneau were of the upper middle class. La Tour set out to capture transient facial expressions; but Perronneau was less interested in pinning down the ephemeral

than in showing more permanent human traits. He was a subtle colorist, with a more highly developed sense of color than La Tour. Certain of his portraits show him concentrating apparently on an exact reproduction of the sitter's appearance: that of *Madame Chevotet* in the Orléans Museum, for instance, or *Charles Lenormant du Coudray* in the Musée Cognacq-Jay in Paris, or two portraits in private Paris collections: *Madame Desfriches* in that of Mme. Ratouis de Limay, and *The Engraver Gabriel Huquier* in that of André Lazard. In others (such as the excellent *Unknown Woman* in the Jean Pierre Durand Collection in Geneva), the

JEAN BAPTISTE SIMÉON CHARDIN · *Still Life with Loaf*
Louvre, Paris

sitter seems to have been a mere pretext for subtle poetic harmonies of blues, greens, and gold. If La Tour dealt in prose, and often in rather trenchant prose, Perronneau was an exquisite poet.

It is worth noting that Perronneau also painted portraits in oil, and that the color in these is no less remarkable than in his pastels. He made a masterpiece out of the unpromising features of the *Duchesse d'Ayen* (David-Weill Collection), and is able to persuade us that *Madame de Sorquainville* (Louvre) must have been a charming woman for all her facial irregularity.

Certain other painters portrayed a middle class other than that of the bankers and high dignitaries. Rather than such bloodless artists as Ducreux and Drouais, we should here mention Joseph Duplessis (1725–1802) from Provence, whose portraits of *Gluck at the Harpsichord* in the Kunsthistorisches Museum in Vienna and *Madame Lenoir* in the Louvre are the work of an artist keen to show reality as he saw it, without any flattery or watering-down. Gluck's expression, as we see him apparently seized by an inspiration, is no less exactly conveyed than the mixture of goodness, insight, and amiable maliciousness which we can read on the delicate features of Madame Lenoir.

This urge to reproduce reality rather than to prettify it had been characteristic of the Dutch seventeenth century, and we can see it also in the works of Jacques Aved (1702–1766), who spent his youth in Amsterdam. Among his portraits, those of the *Marquis de Mirabeau* in the Louvre and *Madame Crozat* in the Musée Fabre, Montpellier, should ensure him an honorable place among French eighteenth-century painters. They show that he deserves a higher reputation than he at present enjoys.

Aved was a friend of Jean Baptiste Siméon Chardin (1699–1779), who, with Watteau and Fragonard, was one of the great French painters of his age. After a relatively short professional training he began to paint still lifes, for which he could find an immediate sale. He had no imagination; he worked extremely slowly, and spent a long time over each canvas. A remark of Aved's led him to give up still life for scenes of everyday life of the kind painted by Metsu, Terborch, and Pieter de Hooch. He never painted scenes that involved movement; the figures in his genre paintings are as motionless as the objects that feature in his still lifes. His mothers and children, like his china, wineglasses, and bottles, are nothing more than excuses to paint. The great merit of his work lies in the quality of his painting: in its precision of tone, its range and accuracy of color, and also in the rich pigment laboriously built up in countless small brush strokes. By such means Chardin was able to convey the softness of fruit, the brilliance of metal, the transparency of glass, as accurately as the warmth of flesh, the whiteness of a napkin, or the sheen of silk. In this way he taught us to appreciate the beauty of the objects that we see every day. The *Kitchen Maid* in the Liechtenstein Collection, the *Child with Whirligig* and *La Pourvoyeuse* in the Louvre give the same visual delight as the Stockholm National Museum's *Hare* or the Louvre's *Pipe and Drinking Glasses*.

At the end of his life Chardin fell ill and no longer had the strength for the many sittings he needed when he worked in oil. After 1770, in his seventies, he turned to pastel, producing several works of which his *Self-Portrait* (former Baron Henri de Rothschild Collection) and his *Portrait of the Artist's Wife* in the Louvre are the best known. With a boldness far in advance of his time, he used a technique of small strokes of different colors – Degas, much later, was his only follower along this path – and showed the varying effects of light by means of cleverly contrasted tones.

A legendary image has grown up of

173

HUBERT ROBERT · *The Gardens of Versailles
in 1775*
National Museum, Versailles

Chardin, as a very pleasant fellow, tolerant, disinterested, and unpretentious. It has, however, been conclusively shown that he was not at all like this. Chardin was touchy, violent, avaricious, and unfair to his fellow painters, interested only in his own career. But he was a marvelous painter.

The eighteenth century saw artists turning away from historical landscape in the style of Claude Lorrain to paint more straightforward and matter-of-fact landscapes. Joseph Vernet (1714–1789), for instance, has one very unforced and naturally lit canvas to his credit in the *Ponte Rotto* in the Louvre, which seems like an anticipation of Corot's Italian landscapes. Other works of his, however, such as his big views of French harbors (*The Port of Marseilles*, in the Louvre), are made up of a jumble of admittedly amusing anecdotes mechanically translated into paint.

Hubert Robert (1733–1808) realized that although the historical landscape as conceived by Claude Lorrain and Poussin might now be outdated, it could be made more attractive and picturesque. He rejected the huge ceremonial settings in the Roman countryside, which his predecessors had viewed as evocative of great historical events, in favor of scenes where overgrown classical ruins tower above the humble Italian folk who populate them. He painted some delightful pictures, whose refined luminosity made them highly suitable for drawing-room decoration. The pastoral subjects which he treated had a certain element of the idyllic, and were not so rustic as to offend the collectors of the day. After living for a long while in Rome, he went back to France, worked for a time in Provence, and then returned to Paris and painted views of that city. In all his work – in *The Terrace in Ruins* in the Hermitage, Leningrad, *The Gardens of Versailles in 1775* in the National Museum, Versailles, and *Le Décintrement du Pont de Neuilly* in the Musée Carnavalet – he emerges as an intelligent, subtle artist with a delicate sense of color. Occasionally he strained after effect, but he proved at the same time to be a patient observer, who took pains to give a truthful account of what he had seen.

Louis Gabriel Moreau (1739–1805) was known as Moreau the Elder to distinguish him from his younger brother, the draftsman Jean Michel Moreau, or Moreau the Younger. He painted small pictures of the country around Paris, bathed in a pale but natural light. He was a lesser master, but his *View of the Bellevue Hill* in the Louvre and his *Outskirts of Paris near Montreuil* both show that he was impelled towards landscape painting by

JEAN BAPTISTE GREUZE · *Child with an Apple*
National Gallery London

a genuine feeling for the countryside.

There have been few artists as uneven as Jean Baptiste Greuze (1725–1806). It was not that he lacked talent, for in fact he had more than enough, but he was unbearably conceited and greedy for success. He was indeed successful with paintings which either made a crude appeal to the sentimental (*The Father's Curse* and *The Village Bride,* both in the Louvre), or else tickled jaded tastes by showing adolescent girls rolling great innocent eyes as they coyly disclosed their immature breasts (*The Broken Pitcher* in the Louvre and *The Morning Prayer* in the Musée Fabre, Montpellier). Greuze the champion of virtue is as poor a painter as Greuze the insidious erotic: his color is washed out, his drawing flabby and stereotyped. It is hard to believe that the same man could have painted such strong and vivid canvases as the *Portrait of Wille the Engraver* in the Musée Jacquemart-André in Paris, the *Child with an Apple* (National Gallery, London), or that charming sketch *The Happy Mother* in the Boymans Museum in Rotterdam, with its fluid, transparent shadows.

Jean Honoré Fragonard (1732–1806) was the last artist of this century to reflect its spirit, and his work seems to sum up all that his predecessors had achieved. He painted *scènes galantes* like Watteau, sensual mythological scenes like Boucher, everyday family life like Chardin, landscapes like Joseph Vernet and Hubert Robert. He borrowed largely from Dutch, Flemish, and Italian masters, yet all that he borrowed was transformed into genuine Fragonard. He had prodigious skill, but also infinite variety. Some of his paintings are executed with precision that verges on the impersonal, others are dashed off with bold freedom of technique. He could be by turns sensual (*La Chemise Enlevée* and *The Bathers* in the Louvre), sensitive (*Invocation to Love* in the Schiff Collection, New York), roguish

175

ahead of their time, and seem to anticipate the experiments on which many nineteenth-century painters were to embark.

THE RISE OF ENGLISH PAINTING

Ever since Holbein and Van Dyck, the English had become accustomed to treating painting as a job for foreigners, and seeing the foreigners' success as proof that the native artists had no choice but to imitate them. It was here that Hogarth, quite apart from having been one of the most remarkable of all English painters, did a great service both to the public and to his fellow artists. For his example convinced them that there was no necessity to work from formulas imported from abroad: that they could perfectly well take as their subjects the things and

(*The Swing* in the Wallace Collection), a pure virtuoso (the *Portrait of the Abbé de Saint-Non* in the Barcelona Palace of Fine Arts), a conscientious observer (*Les Lavandières* in the Picardy Museum, Amiens), a charming poet (*Les Marionnettes* in A. Veil-Picard's Collection, Paris), and even a forerunner of Romanticism who seems to anticipate Delacroix (*Renaud and Armide* in the same collection). He was the painter of happy, untroubled sensuality with none of the ambiguity to be found in Greuze; at the same time he celebrated the joys of maternity, childhood, and the family. Some of his more hastily sketched and thinly covered canvases fail to satisfy for all their virtuosity, because the painter seems to have let his brush go. In others, the exceptionally free technique and bold color relations are far

people with which they came into contact every day. Hogarth and his successors–portrait painters, genre and landscape painters–chose to paint reality, although an occasionally improved or prettified reality in the case of the fashionable portraitists. The only artists who reacted against this principle were Fuseli and Blake.

William Hogarth (1697–1764) made his reputation by his scenes of everyday life, but was also known as a portrait painter. Like Greuze, he set out to preach moral sermons and to chastise the vices of his day in sequences of paintings on single themes. These were like novels divided into chapters: *The Harlot's Progress* (known only from engravings), *The Rake's Progress* (in the Sloane Museum), *Marriage à la Mode* (National Gallery, London). But where Greuze's moralizing works suffer from rhetorical sentimentality and drabness of color, Hogarth's sequences show him as a vigorous artist fond of a rich palette: a descendant, it would seem, of the seventeenth-century Dutch artists, and particularly of Jan Steen. One of his best genre pictures is *A Scene from the Beggar's Opera* in the National Portrait Gallery, while portraits worth mentioning include *The Vicomtesse de La Valette* in the Geneva Museum of Art, *Hogarth's Servants* in the National Gallery, and, in the same gallery, the delightful *Shrimp Girl*, all golden browns and salmon pinks.

For nearly a hundred years after Hogarth there was a remarkable school of British portraitists, deriving from Van Dyck but largely inspired by Rembrandt and Titian, too.

Sir Joshua Reynolds (1723–1792) went to Italy in 1749 and remained there for three years. Back in London, he was quickly successful and was made the first president of the Royal Academy at its foundation in 1768. His portraits of the British aristocracy and of the principal figures of his day are at once faithful and full of dignity: for instance, his *Self-Portrait* in the Uffizi; *Samuel Johnson* and *Lord Heathfield* in the National Gallery, London, the former realistically uncouth, the latter with a brilliant red coat set off against a stormy sky; or *Laurence Sterne* (in the Marquess of Lansdowne Collection, London) with his enigmatic smile. Of his portraits of women the most interesting are those in which the model, instead of playing to the gallery, is apparently content to be herself: for example, *Countess Spencer and Her Daughter* (Althorp Park, Earl Spencer's Collection) and *Kitty Fisher* in Granville Proby's collection at Elton Hall. Reynolds learned a good deal from his great Dutch, Flemish, and Venetian predecessors; he absorbed their lessons and evolved a personal style.

Thomas Gainsborough (1727–1788) began with small portraits in which both the figures and the landscape background are painted with scrupulous care: such as the *Portrait of Mr. and Mrs. Andrews* (in the possession of G. W. Andrews, Redhill, Surrey) and *The Artist with His Wife and Daughter* in the collection of Sir Philip Sassoon. In 1760 he settled in Bath, then at the height of its fashion, and was soon sought after and taken up. His technique, though competent, is often superficial, but he has left us paintings which immortalize the charm of their sitters: *Mrs. Robinson ("Perdita")* in the Wallace Collection, *Miss Elizabeth Singleton* and *Miss Margaret Gainsborough*, both in the National Gallery, London. He also painted landscapes and rural scenes in a rather loose technique that shows complete absence of feeling for the pastoral life.

These were the two leaders of a school of English portrait painters that included George Romney (1734–1802), an undistinguished colorist with a gift for improvisation, who strove above all for elegance and charm (*Miss Willoughby*, National Gallery of Art, Washington);

GEORGE ROMNEY · *Self-Portrait*
Uffizi, Florence

John Opie (1761–1807) (*The School-mistress*, A. T. Lloyd Collection, London); and John Hoppner (1757–1810) (*Mrs. Williams*, O. S. Ashcroft Collection, London). Rather more talent and individuality are to be found in two Scottish painters. Henry Raeburn (1756–1823) was an artist of solid skill and adaptability who managed to convey the freshness of childhood and the healthy beauty of Scottish women quite as successfully as the unaffected self-confidence of an officer wearing the national dress. However, again and again his lighting effects bring to mind modern theatrical lighting (*Sir John Clerk and His Wife* in the Lady Boit Collection, London; *William Ferguson of Kilrie* in the possession of Viscount Novar, London; *Colonel Alastair Macdonnell of Glengarry* in the National Galleries of Scotland, Edinburgh). Widely different but extremely likeable, Allan Ramsay (1713–1784) was the author of tightly drawn portraits with realistic lighting and delicate colors (*Grisel,*

Countess Stanhope in the possession of Earl Stanhope, Chevening, and *The Painter's Wife* in the National Galleries of Scotland). He seems to have relied less on technical proficiency than his colleagues, and to have studied nature with greater care.

The last of these English portrait painters was Sir Thomas Lawrence (1769–1830), who enjoyed a European reputation in his day and, as a spectator at the various diplomatic conferences of that period, had opportunities to paint a number of the leading statesmen. He was equally popular with ladies of fashion, thanks to the skill with which he could reproduce their attractions. Some of his portraits are pure showpieces, but others (such as *The Archduke Charles of Austria* and *Pope Pius VII* in the Royal Collection, or *Mrs. Siddons* in the National Gallery, London) show that he could make spectacular use of his great technical skill.

Rather apart from these men was Johann Zoffany (1735–1810), a German who came to work in London at the age of twenty-three. Besides individual portraits he

SIR THOMAS LAWRENCE · *Portrait of Mrs. Siddons*
National Gallery, London

THOMAS GAINSBOROUGH · *Portrait of Mrs. Siddons*
National Gallery of Art, Washington

painted little pictures known as "conversation pieces": tiny group portraits of a family or of a circle of friends, much as the Dutch used to paint in the preceding century (*The Dutton Family* in Viscount Bearsted's Collection, *Mrs. Oswald* in that of the late Lord Lee of Fareham). Zoffany's paintings are sometimes scrupulous to the point of lifelessness, and his light is metallic; but they hold the eye by their keen pursuit of the truth and by often quite original color relations.

Hogarth's genre painting in the tradition of Metsu and Terborch found no followers. George Morland (1763–1804) painted a number of episodes from country life (Lord Swaythling's *The Postboy's Return*, or Mr. Granville Proby's *Rustic Conversation*, Elton Hall) but he

was an unsubtle observer. George Stubbs (1724–1806), on the other hand, showed the most relentless accuracy and meticulous technique in a number of small canvases depicting people and animals in a landscape setting: *The Third Duke of Portland on a White Horse* (Welbeck Abbey, the Duke of Portland Collection), *The Reapers* in the Lord Bearsted Collection, *Sir John Nelthorpe, Sixth Baronet, Partridge Shooting with Two Dogs* in that of Mr. R. N. S. Nelthorpe at Scawby.

The one true English genre painter of the late eighteenth century was Thomas Rowlandson (1756–1827). There are no oil paintings among his work, only watercolor drawings which cheerfully and ferociously satirize the life of the time; but his great verve, and the liveliness and freedom of his draftsmanship, are such that he cannot be left out. Compared with Rowlandson's, the drawing of Reynolds or Gainsborough seems academic and tame.

English landscape painting, which was to become so important in the nineteenth century, started with Richard Wilson (1714–1782). After he had begun by painting portraits, he set out for Italy at the age of thirty-five. He was advised to take up landscape by Joseph Vernet in Rome, and on his return to England began to recall the Italian scene in small pictures whose technique was rather tentative (*Lake Avernus* in the National Gallery, London). Then he went to work in his native Wales (*Snowdon* in the Nottingham Museum, *A Welsh Valley* in the Manchester City Art Gallery, *Holt Bridge* in the National Gallery, London). There is still an element of conventionality in Wilson's landscapes, but his skies and water give evidence of a very delicate feeling for nuances of light.

John Crome (1768–1821), owing nothing to Italy, chose to learn only from the Dutch landscapists and from nature itself. He painted naturalistic pictures of

180

the heaths around Norwich, where he was born, and of the fishing ports: *Mousehold Heath* in the Victoria and Albert Museum, London; *Yarmouth Jetty* in the Castle Museum at Norwich; *Moonlight on the River Yare* in the collection of Captain the Hon. Arthur Howard, London.

Watercolor played such an important part in nineteenth-century English painting that we must name two men who became significant figures as soon as it grew into a separate branch of art. They are Alexander Cozens (1715–1786), whose shorthand notation of landscape is suggestive of Chinese painting, and his son John Robert (1752–1797), whose delicately colored Swiss and Italian views are not so much accurate representations of the scene as poetic transcriptions of a particular light effect.

Romanticism makes its appearance in the Cozens's watercolors and is clearly to be seen in the work of two other artists of the time: the Swiss artist Füssli or Fuseli, and William Blake. But although Fuseli spent almost all his working life in London we shall reserve him for the section dealing with Swiss eighteenth-century painters; for in spite of his emigration to England, he remained essentially Germanic at heart.

William Blake (1757–1827), who was as much a poet as a painter, led a precarious life for all that he received some support. He claimed to see visions and to have frequent conversation with figures from the past; and in his lifetime many people looked upon him as a madman. At first he worked as an engraver; at about the age of forty he began publishing his own poems, and illustrated them himself, often in color. The English regard Blake as a very great artist; it is hard to understand how they can fail to realize that despite the richness of his imagination, the pictorial vocabulary which alone could have given substance to his visions is feeble in the extreme. Whether he is illustrating the Bible or his own poems, his human figures are rendered in the most banal visual terms, derived from the anatomical conventions of mediocre Italian engravings after Michelangelo and Raphael. To treat Blake's drawings in terms of literature, it is as if the Book of Revelations had been rewritten by an utterly pedestrian writer.

THE SETTECENTO

In the early nineteenth century it was thought that the decline of Italian painting, which had set in during the seventeenth century, had simply become accentuated in the eighteenth. Even Tiepolo and Canaletto barely escaped this general censure. More recently, however, judgment has been revised. We realize that even if eighteenth-century Italian painting had no great masters apart from Tiepolo, it had a number of interesting painters.

WILLIAM BLAKE · *The Great Red Dragon and the Woman Clothed with the Sun* National Gallery of Art, Washington

Venice was at that time the only really productive center of the arts in Italy. Later, in the second half of the century, Rome came to serve as a meeting-place for artists, connoisseurs, and critics from all over Europe. But the important figures there were all foreigners. Winckelmann, Mengs, Tischbein, and Goethe were Germans; David was French; Fuseli and Angelica Kaufmann, Anglo-Swiss. Admittedly, Piranesi lived in Rome, but he was a Venetian, and apart from him the Roman artists were second-rate.

The Neapolitan Francesco Solimena (1657–1747) covered the walls of Naples' churches with huge frescoes showing immense architectural structures within which stood contrasting groups of figures, placed now in light, now in shadow: e.g., *The Fall of Simon Magus* and *The Conversion of St. Paul* in San Paolo Maggiore, Naples, and *The Battle of the Centaurs and the Lapiths* in the National Gallery of Capodimonte, Naples. Undoubtedly Solimena is a pretentious artist, but it cannot be denied that he is a brilliant improviser, with a fertile mind and a gift for conveying movement. Another Neapolitan, Giuseppe Bonito (1707–1789), began by following Solimena closely, as in his *Dedication of the Temple* (Naples). After that he struck out in a different direction. In *The Wounded Man* (Italo Brass Collection, Venice) and the *Genre Scene* in the collection of Achillito Chiesa, Milan, he set himself to apply his exceptionally acute eye and fine sense of color to the painting of subjects from everyday life.

This was a period when northern Italy was richer in artists than Florence or Rome. The Genoese painter Alessandro Magnasco (1667–1747) has been rescued from oblivion during the past forty years – which is all to the good – but has been grossly overrated. He used a palette loaded with browns, blacks, and ochers, and a lively if somewhat monotonous style to conjure up gypsy encampments, monasteries inhabited by scraggy, half-starved monks, and Pulcinella's family life. Critics have tried to make him into a poet of the fantastic, but unfortunately his fantasy is unconvincing. He exploited the picturesque aspects of poverty, and did so with a technique whose fluency should not blind us to the fact that it is extremly limited. Paintings like *The Refectory* in the Museo Civico in Bassano, *The Market* in the Castello Sforza, Milan, or *The Banquet* in the Louvre attract us by their originality and vigorous treatment; but Magnasco is nevertheless one of those artists who are best appreciated if only a few of their pictures are seen at a time.

Giuseppe Bazzani (1690–1769) lived and worked at Mantua. In view of his immoderate fondness for the elegant and charming, and the hazy sensuality of his color, he should have confined himself to *scènes galantes* or mythological subjects. Instead, he chose religious subjects e.g., *St. Louis and a Cherub* in Professor Publio Podio's collection at Bologna, and *The Annunciation* in that of Italo Brass at Venice, whose oversweet piety leaves a disagreeable aftertaste.

Vittore Ghislandi (1665–1743) of Bergamo divided his interests between art and monastic life; hence his other name, Fra Galgario. He painted nothing but portraits: vigorous, immensely alive, rich in color, and thick in paint. Such are his *Paolo Gufrini* in the Palazzo Vecchio in Florence, with its austere features under a capacious wig; the excellent *Portrait of a Man* in the Poldi-Pezzoli Museum in Milan; and the *Portrait of Isabella Camozzi di Gherardi* in the collection of Count Camozzi Vertova at Costa di Mezzade (Bergamo).

Of Giacomo Ceruti nothing is known except that he was born about the middle of the eighteenth century and worked at Bergamo and Padua, painting chiefly still lifes and genre scenes. In his light-toned paintings – e.g., the *Washerwoman* in the

GIOVANNI BATTISTA TIEPOLO · *The Last Supper*
Louvre, Paris

Pinacoteca Martinengo at Brescia, the glum-looking *Dwarf* in Count Salvadego's Collection at Padernello, or the *Girl with a Fan* at the Accademia Carrara (Bergamo), where he has so exactly caught a redheaded girl's pale complexion – he portrayed the humble workpeople of his own time with a restrained realism, in a limited range of delicate grays. Ceruti, who rejected the theatrical effects and the strong contrasts of light and shadow of the Baroque and painted the everyday life around him with truth and simplicity, is an exceptionally original artist who deserves to be better known.

Giuseppe Maria Crespi (1665–1747), a native of Bologna, also deserves to be better known, to judge from his highly individual frescoes in the Palazzo Pepoli at Bologna, his series of *The Seven Sacraments* in the Dresden State Picture Gallery, which soberly and accurately depicts the chief events of the religious life, his *St. John Nepomuk Confessing the Queen of Bohemia* in the Pinacoteca Reale in Turin, and his *Cupid and Psyche* in the Uffizi. Crespi adopted the shadows introduced by Caravaggio into Italian painting, but instead of leaving them hard and opaque he tried to make them transparent, so as to allow the forms gradually to feel their way into the light. He is as subtle a master of chiaroscuro as Terborch or Velazquez, and there are times when his thickly laid colors, applied with great freedom, remind us of Chardin's "buttery" texture. Some of his canvases have darkened because the brown underpainting has come through; in others he seems to have been unduly hurried or tired.

In Venice the art of Sebastiano Ricci (1659–1734) and Giambattista Piazzetta (1683–1754) precedes and seems to clear the way for that of Tiepolo. Ricci is a competent but superficial illustrator of scenes from religion and mythology *(The Rape of Europe* in the Venice Accademia). Piazzetta painted rural subjects in light colors over a red-brown underpainting which gives a reddish tinge to all his shadows *(Eliezer and Rebecca* in the Brera, Milan; *Idyll* in the National Gallery, Dublin).

Giovanni Battista Tiepolo (1693–1770) is an artist of much wider scope, an ex-

quisite colorist and a prodigious inventor of forms. In his frescoes for the walls and ceilings of churches and palaces *(Scenes from the Old Testament* in the Archbishop's Palace at Udine, *The Triumph of Apollo* in the Palazzo Clerici in Milan, *St. Dominic Instituting the Rosary* in the church of the Gesuati in Venice, and the decorations in the Archbishop's Palace at Würzburg and the Royal Palace in Madrid) and in his small canvases illustrating sacred subjects *(The Education of the Virgin* in Santa Maria della Consolazione, Venice, or *The Last Supper* in the Louvre), or incidents from classical history *(The Magnanimity of Scipio* in the Stockholm National Museum), or from Tasso *(Rinaldo and Armida* in the Art Institute of Chicago), his imagination never runs dry or gets short of breath. His talent seems inexhaustible. He cares little about verisimilitude: Abraham's wife Sarah wears a farthingale and a huge sixteenth-century collar, while the angel visiting her is draped in material that might have been specified by a modern stage designer. He

CANALETTO · *View of Dresden*
State Picture Gallery, Dresden

inserts turbaned Turks here, there, and everywhere: in *The Beheading of John the Baptist* in the Colleoni Chapel at Bergamo, and also in one of his masterpieces, the *Anthony and Cleopatra* frescoes in the Palazzo Labia at Venice. Whatever subject he chooses, he wraps it in a festive atmosphere, in which his iridescent colors, his turquoise blues, his straw yellows, his pinks all play their part. At the same time, he knows how to rise to the dramatic occasion, as in his altarpiece in the Chiesa delle Grazie at Este, *Saint Thecla Delivering the City from the Plague,* and in his *Road to Calvary* in the church of Sant'Alvise at Venice. His inventiveness never flags, for the good reason that, with him as with all great visionaries, it draws its material from real life. Certainly Tiepolo must have seen with his own eyes the insolent attitude of his *Danae* (in the Stockholm University), just as he must have seen the sleeping child in *Hagar and Ishmael* in the Scuola di San Rocco in Venice; and it was from such seeds picked up from the real world that his pictures grew. There are moments when the magic world of Tiepolo begins to exhaust the spectator, and even to put him off by its eternally *allegro* mood. There are many others when its optimism is a comfort it would be wrong to despise.

Already in the eighteenth century Venice had attracted crowds of foreigners, both by her unique character and by the variety of pleasures which she could offer: concerts and *fêtes,* gambling dens and courtesans. Some of the visitors wanted to have views of this incomparable city to take "back home" with them. Thus a school of Venetian landscapists sprang up, of whom Canaletto and Guardi are, quite rightly, the most famous.

Displaying great accuracy, particularly in the rendering of light, Canale, known as Canaletto (1697–1768), worked without respite to record the finest views of

FRANCESCO GUARDI · *Portico and Small Square*
Musée Jacquemart-André, Paris

his native town; e.g., *A Stonemason's Yard in Venice* in the National Gallery, London, *The Grand Canal* in the Louvre, the *Riva degli Schiavoni* in the State Museums, Berlin-Dahlem. Anticipating his customers' wishes he took care to get every detail right. Compared with him, Francesco Guardi (1712–1793) seems to have been more drawn to the picturesque, and at the same time to be more personal in his use of color. His range is extremely limited – greenish browns, whites with a tinge of gold, dull pinks, and turquoise blues tinged with green in his skies – but with it he obtains subtle effects. Less meticulous than Canaletto, he paints with tiny strokes and fills his townscapes (such as *La Salute* in the Boymans-van Beuningen Museum in Rotter-

185

dam, *Gondola on the Lagoon* in the Poldi-Pezzoli Museum in Milan, or *A Balloon Ascension* in the State Museums, Berlin-Dahlem) with tiny figures whose attitudes, seized from life, are astonishingly accurate.

Venetian eighteenth-century painting is rounded off by a minor master, Pietro Falca, known as Longhi (1702–1785). His clumsily extended canvases (such as *The Dancing Lesson* and *The Apothecary*, in the Venice Accademia) are primarily of documentary interest; his sketches from nature are a good deal better.

Finally we must mention Rosalba Carriera (1675–1757), who made a very large number of portraits and character studies in pastel. Her works are pleasant enough, though striving after hazy effects, she often lapses into flabbiness. Perhaps her greatest achievement was to have carried the fashion for pastel portraits to Paris, where she was enthusiastically received.

WILHELM TISCHBEIN · *Portrait of Goethe in the Campagna* (detail) Staedelsches Kunstinstitut, Frankfurt am Main

FRENCH AND ITALIAN INFLUENCES IN GERMANY

The German and Austrian eighteenth-century painters modeled themselves sometimes on Italian painting, sometimes on French. The former inspired the decorators of churches and palaces during the Rococo period; the latter, the portraitists of the nobility.

The best portraitist of this period was J. G. Ziesenis (1716–1777), who was painter to the court of Hannover. His *Portrait of the Duchess of Saxe-Gotha* (State Museums, Berlin-Dahlem) is a work where the artist conveyed the sitter's elegance and charm while remaining true to life.

Daniel Chodowiecki (1726–1801) was an artist of Polish origin who settled in Berlin. He concentrated less on painting than on drawing, engraving, and illustration. French influence is clearly to be seen in his works, the technique of which is rather constrained. Not lacking in personality, he was an acute observer with a good sense of humor (*Entertainments in a Park* and *Calas's Farewells* in the State Museums, Berlin-Dahlem).

Friedrich August Tischbein (1750–1812) studied in Italy and in Paris, but he chose to model himself on the English portraitists and to surround his sitters with a poetic atmosphere, as in his *Herr von Chatelain* in the New Pinakothek at Munich. His cousin Wilhelm Tischbein (1751–1829) was an inconsiderable artist whose reputation is due mainly to the fact that he was a friend of Goethe's and lived with him in Rome. His *Portrait of Goethe in the Campagna* (Staedelsches Kunstinstitut, Frankfurt) is interesting on account of its subject.

Winckelmann's writings, which were received with keen interest, formulated the concept of "ideal beauty." This started a fresh revival of classical art. One of Winckelmann's followers was his friend and are not without merit, e.g., the *Portrait of a Spanish Infanta* (Louvre).

Anton Graff (1736–1813), a native of Winterthur, went to Dresden at the age of thirty and became the fashionable portrait painter there. His carefully executed portraits, without pretense of originality or display of virtuosity, are superficial because he was mainly anxious to please his sitters.

Jean Étienne Liotard (1702–1789) was born in Geneva, studied in Paris, went to Italy and thence to Constantinople. He found admirers in Vienna, Paris, London, and Amsterdam, and then settled in his native Geneva, making occasional visits to Paris, Vienna, and London. He

ISMAEL MENGS · *Self-Portrait*
State Picture Gallery, Dresden

Raphael Mengs (1728–1779), a painter who also wrote on art. During the second half of the eighteenth century, it was thought that Rome, with its great influx of artists and connoisseurs from every corner of Europe, was about to become the birthplace of a new Renaissance in which Mengs would play the part of Raphael. Winckelmann did not hesitate to proclaim Mengs the greatest painter of his time: in fact, of all time. Unfortunately, the second Renaissance never materialized, and Mengs's work, as instanced by his *Parnassus,* a ceiling in the Villa Albani, or his decorations for the Papyrus Room in the Vatican, is bad. Far from drawing its inspiration from classical art, it is a copy of seventeenth-century Bolognese painting at its worst, the most mediocre paintings of Albani and Guido Reni. Subsequently Mengs made several trips to Spain, and his unevenness is proved by the fact that the court portraits he painted in Madrid have nothing in common with the pseudo-classical paintings of his Rome period,

JEAN ÉTIENNE LIOTARD · *Francesco Algarotti*
Rijksmuseum, Amsterdam

acquired his reputation by his Levantine figures, and by dressing in oriental style, and he was nicknamed "the Turkish artist." His portraits and his genre scenes in pastel are rigorously drawn and render nature most faithfully, unlike the pleas-

FRANCISCO DE GOYA · *Doña Tadea Arias de Enríquez*
Prado, Madrid

FRANCISCO DE GOYA · *The Nude "Maja"*
Prado, Madrid

ant and brilliantly executed kind of painting then fashionable in France. Some of his works are mediocre, but others, with their realistic lighting, their original color schemes, and their acute psychology, secure him a place among the European painters of his time. Among his most accomplished works we may mention the *Count Francesco Algarotti* in the Rijksmuseum, Amsterdam, and, in the Geneva Museum of Art, *Madame d'Epinay* and *Portrait of the Aged Artist*. Johann Heinrich Füssli or Fuseli (1741–1825) was born in Zurich. At the age of twenty-two he settled in London, where he both painted and wrote. On Reynolds's advice he went to Rome, where he made friends with David and Winckelmann. Back in London he soon became known as "the wild Swiss." Fuseli took his subjects from Homer and Shakespeare and old Germanic legends. His vast and violently romantic canvases show his

strong bent for the fantastic, the horrible, and the macabre. What he lacks above all is individual character. While the anatomy of his figures is obviously inspired by Michelangelo, his treatment derives from the Flemish school, from Rubens and Van Dyck. In addition, he was strongly influenced by the theater: his heroes of primitive and medieval legend decked out in fancy dress are quite implausible. Fuseli is less interesting as a painter than as a representative of Romanticism, which he carried further than any other Romantic painter in works such as *Amanda-Rezia in the Arms of Huon*, a work inspired by Wieland's *Oberon* (now in a private collection at Wädenswil near Zurich), *Titania Finding the Magic Ring* (Art Gallery, Zurich), and *Mad Kate*, inspired by a poem of Cowper's (now in a private collection at Oberhofen in the canton of Bern).

GOYA AND SPAIN

In the eighteenth century, Spain's situation was very different from Great Britain's, so far as painting was concerned. The British had a school of painters, that is to say, they had two outstanding portraitists in Reynolds and Gainsborough, and a group of artists whose work was more or less related to theirs. But in the Spain of that time Goya was a solitary figure–a single brilliant meteor. There was no one to rival him. Luis Paret y Alcázar (1747–1799) was an imitator of Ollivier and Traverse, French painters working in Madrid; Luis Menéndez (1716–1780) was a worthy and respectable painter of still lifes.

Francisco de Goya y Lucientes (1746–1828) started out as a fashionable artist designing cartoons which recorded the life of the day for the tapestry industry of Santa Barbara, painting portraits for the court and pictures for churches. For many years his life was all that an artist could hope for, but it was marred by two unfortunate events. When he was almost fifty, he became deaf and isolated from contemporary society. A few years later, the French armies invaded Spain, exiled the king, and placed one of Napoleon's brothers on the throne. At first Goya, with his liberal views, thought that the French were going to apply the principles of their own Revolution to Spain, and would reform the old regime. But soon his patriotism got the upper hand, and in paintings and aquatints alike he denounced the horrors for which the invaders were responsible. At the restoration of King Ferdinand, the aged painter left Spain, for reasons that have remained obscure, and settled in Bordeaux, where he died.

Unlike Velazquez, Goya as a portrait painter took sides. While faithfully reproducing the model before him, he pursues truth to the point where it verges on caricature, as in his *Family*

FRANCISCO DE GOYA · *Self-Portrait*
Prado, Madrid

of *Charles IV* or in the portrait of his father-in-law, *The Painter Bayeu,* whose dessicated face is a mask of boredom (both in the Prado in Madrid). There is also the *Portrait of an Unknown Statesman* (former Enrique O'Shea Collection in Madrid), where the sitter's bloated, loutish features contrast oddly with his embroidered jacket and the broad sash over his chest. But when his sitter is a young and attractive woman, Goya paints her as though he were a lover ravaged by desire (*The Countess of Chinchon* and *Doña Antonia de Zarata,* both in the Metropolitan Museum of Art, New York). Even in the Louvre's *Unknown Woman,* whose face is pasty and swollen, he rendered the contrast between black curls and pink cheeks, and the silky grays of the dress.

His genre paintings include scenes from popular life, such as *The Burial of the Sardine,* and scenes of violence which reveal a bent for the macabre, such as

A Madhouse (both in the Academia de San Fernando in Madrid). His patriotic fury inspired *May 2, 1808* and *May 3, 1808* (both in the Prado). These magnificent works castigate the brutality with which the French troops put down a revolt that had broken out in Madrid. The climate of our own time has led us to emphasize the dramatic aspects of Goya's art: e.g., the two works we have just mentioned, and the boldly executed paintings in blacks and browns with which he decorated his own house, known as *La Quinta del Sordo* or "The Deaf Man's House." But we should not overlook the many canvases in which he immortalized beauty, youth, and elegance: paintings such as the London National Gallery's *Doña Isabel de Porcel* or *The Duke of San Carlos* in the collection of the Marquis de la Torrecilla, Madrid.

His painting links the two centuries in which he lived. Some of his works, like the two *Majas* in the Prado, one nude and one clothed, are in the tradition of Watteau and Fragonard. Others are so free in their treatment, so novel in their color schemes as to anticipate Daumier, Monet, and Renoir; e.g., *The Pilgrimage to San Isidro* in the Prado, with its fresh, true light, *A City on a Rock* in the Metropolitan Museum of Art and *The Bordeaux Milkmaid* in the Prado. A few years before his death, this man, who had so attacked the church in his aquatints and who, in decorating the church of Sant' Antonio de la Florida in Madrid, thought only of displaying his own powers, painted one small picture which expresses the deepest religious feeling: *The Last Communion of St. Joseph Calasanz* (Musée Bonnat at Bayonne).

Goya was an immensely productive but uneven artist. Some of his portraits appear to have been hurriedly done. He could not do without reality; when he executed *The Allegory of Madrid* in the Madrid Town Hall he painted three charming women, without bothering to indicate what they were meant to represent. But when a subject gripped him, when he was moved by a strong emotion – love, hatred, or horror – he showed himself to be a prodigious artist, startlingly original, and a skillful and resourceful technician.

CLASSICAL REVIVAL

The French Revolution, with its political and social transformations, was preceded by another revolution of a purely artistic kind, which was no less radical and destructive than the other. As early as the middle of the eighteenth century a number of artists – a draftsman (Cochin), an architect (Soufflot), and an archaeologist (the Comte de Caylus) – had risen against the exaggerations of the Rococo style, with its emphasis on the bizarre and the asymmetrical. They set out to lead the visual arts back to simplicity, moderation, and order, and took their models from surviving examples of Greek and Roman art. This first attempt to revive classicism had only limited results. A second, more vigorous attempt was inspired by the excavations which began at Herculaneum in 1738 and at Pompeii in 1755, and which aroused great interest among artists and scholars. Later in the century the German aesthetician and archaeologist Joseph Winckelmann published a number of writings in which he celebrated classical sculpture. They were soon translated into French and English, and had a considerable effect.

Previously, the painter Joseph Vien (1716–1809), prompted by Caylus, had attempted to react against the sensual, over-elegant art of his time. But his paintings, for instance, *Daedalus Attaching Wings to Icarus* (École des Beaux-Arts, Paris), in which he tried to recapture classical dignity and simplicity, are colorless and cold. Vien was not a strong

JACQUES LOUIS DAVID · *Madame Récamier*
Louvre, Paris

enough personality to carry the new ideas to victory and ensure the radical transformation of art.

Jacques Louis David (1748–1825), a pupil of Vien's, won the Rome Prize in 1774. During his stay in Rome he was converted to the new ideas by his friend Quatremère de Quincy, a sculptor who later became an archaeologist and aesthetician and who explained Winckelmann's theories to him. Back in Paris, David exhibited his *Belisarius* (Palace of Fine Arts, Lille) with great success; it was closely modeled on Poussin. Then, back again in Rome, he completed his *Oath of the Horatii,* which was greatly admired at the Salon of 1785. David benefited from the fact that his paintings, allegedly inspired by the austere grandeur of classical art and extolling civic virtues, coincided with the French Revolution, whose champions, nourished on Plutarch and Tacitus, took the Roman republic as their ideal.

Elected to the Convention, David was a fanatical Jacobin who helped vote the death sentence for Louis XVI. He was the short-lived Republic's artistic dictator. Later, he was First Painter to Napoleon, who made him a baron. After the fall of the Empire, fearing reprisals, David emigrated to Brussels, where he died.

David's paintings fall into two distinct groups. There are, first, his doctrinaire works—large canvases treating Greek and Roman subjects, such as *The Oath of the Horatii, The Death of Socrates, The Rape of the Sabines, Leonidas at Thermopylae* (all of them in the Louvre)—in which he strained to recapture the grand style. These works are undeniably competent, eloquent in a theatrical way, and occasionally not without grandeur; but they lack warmth, and the composition is laborious. Although David wants to convey movement, his figures seem frozen for all time. All he cared about was composition and line: color was a seductress whose blandishments any virtuous republican ought to shun. Not only are color harmonies cruelly absent from his paintings, but also the pigment itself, which is reduced to one thin, opaque coat, is applied with a nearly dry brush.

The second group – paintings done from nature – is very different. When David forgot his theories, he was a powerful, altogether admirable realist. He painted a number of very large canvases treating topical subjects – *The Tennis Court Oath, The Consecration of the Emperor Napoleon I* (both in the Louvre), *The Distri-*bution of the Eagles on the Champ-de-Mars* (in the Versailles National Museum). Here his coldness is gone, as though thawed by contact with reality. The *Consecration*, in particular, is admirable for the sure skill with which David has composed so vast a scene, arranged the various groups, and rendered both the faces of the participants and their heavily embroidered jackets and spangled dresses. The same qualities can be seen in his portraits, such as that of *Pope Pius VII* with his fine features, and the smiling, elegant *Madame Récamier* (both in the Louvre), or the extraordinary, implacable figures of the *Three Ladies of Ghent,* who seem to have stepped out of Balzac's pages in their Sunday best. Finally, there is one painting by David which grips us by its austere and brutal realism: the Brussels Musées Royaux's *Marat*, shown dying in his bathtub, just after having been stabbed.

VI

FROM CLASSICISM AND
ROMANTICISM TO REALISM

At the beginning of the nineteenth century neo-classicism, under David's undisputed leadership, was triumphant in France. Grouped around their master, his followers and pupils produced large canvases, treating subjects drawn from the poets and historians of Greece and Rome; classical sculpture inspired them to "improve" upon nature, to idealize her. But although Anne Louis Girodet (1767–1824) painted a work like *Endymion Asleep*, in the Louvre, his rhetorical *The Flood* (Louvre) brings to mind Michelangelo rather than classical art; he also drew upon popular authors of the time, in paintings such as *Ossian Receiving the Shades of the French Warriors* and *The Burial of Atala* (both in the Louvre). Pierre Guérin (1774–1838) followed the doctrine of "ideal beauty" more faithfully, and he came close to David in his theatrical *Phedra and Hippolytus* and *The Return of Marcus Sextus* (both in the Louvre). Girodet and Guérin have left us a number of competent portraits, such as the former's *Murat* (Comtesse A. de Ganay Collection) and the latter's *Portrait of One of the Artist's Daughters*

(Museum of Fine Arts at Boulogne). François Gérard (1770–1837), whose *Psyche Receiving Cupid's First Kiss* (in the Louvre) is wholly lacking in warmth, worked primarily as a fashionable portraitist. In *The Countess Regnault de Saint-Jean d'Angély* (Louvre), *The Countess Abel Hugo* (Montferrier Collection, Paris), *The Baronne de Pierlot* (Baronne de Pierlot Collection, Paris), and other portraits, he successfully avoided monotony and captured the youth and charm of his sitters.

Antoine Gros (1771–1835) was a pupil of David, but he soon shook off his master's influence. Commissioned to illustrate the French victories in the Napoleonic wars, he displayed his fondness for movement and color. A great admirer of Rubens, he did not try to conjure up Greek and Roman warriors, but to record modern battle scenes with brilliantly uniformed, picturesque soldiers, including Arabs, Negroes, and Cossacks. His *Battle of Aboukir* (Versailles National Museum), which is most skillfully composed, and his *Napoleon at Eylau* (Louvre), where the dead and wounded lie covered with snow under a leaden winter sky, are vigorous without being rhetorical. After

the restoration of the Bourbons he painted a large canvas, *Louis XVIII Leaving
the Tuileries* (Versailles National Museum), in which there is a Goya-like element of fantasy. We also owe Gros a
number of portraits expressive of feminine
sensibility and charm: *Madame Poussielgue* (Poussielgue Collection, Paris), *Madame Bruyère* (Alby Collection, Paris),
and *Madame Durand* (Lessert Collection,
Paris). The end of his life was tragic.
Badgered by David, who reproached him
for having confined himself to "trivial
subjects" and urged him to produce at
last a truly "historical painting," he spent
the last fifteen years of his life treating
classical themes in a hollow, rhetorical
style. Realizing that he was on the wrong
track, and tormented by his shrewish
wife, he drowned himself in the Seine.
While "historical painting," which David

ANNE LOUIS GIRODET · *Burial of Atala*
Louvre, Paris

and his followers considered the only
kind worth a serious artist's time, held
the center of the stage, there were genre
painters who treated scenes of everyday
life and who drew inspiration from the
seventeenth-century Dutch school, e.g.,
Louis Boilly (1761–1845), whose *Arrival
of the Stagecoach* and *Print Collectors*
are in the Louvre. François Granet (1775–
1840) studied under David, but soon
realized that large canvases and classical
subjects were not for him. After spending
seventeen years in Rome, he devoted himself to the portrayal of church and monastic interiors, in which he showed an
exact appreciation of contrasts between
light and shadow.
Pierre Paul Prud'hon (1758–1823) was
not in the least affected by David's
theories. He had taste and a feeling for
classical antiquity, but he was inspired
by the elegiac poets rather than by the
historians; he also admired Leonardo da
Vinci and Correggio. He liked to surround his figures with transparent and
delicately graduated shadows and to bathe

FRANÇOIS GÉRARD · *Countess Régnaud
de Saint-Jean-d'Angély*
Louvre, Paris

JEAN AUGUSTE DOMINIQUE INGRES
Vénus Anadyomène
Musée Condé, Chantilly

them in a lunar light. Above all, he was interested in a definite human type, which he sought to embody in his painting. His themes were simply pretexts for creating infinitely graceful women and children, and even the most abstract allegories come alive in works such as *Love Seduces Innocence, and Repentance Follows* (Bisaccia Collection, Paris), *The Abduction of Psyche* (Louvre), *Psyche Asleep* (Musée Condé at Chantilly). Two of his portraits in the Louvre are very fine: *The Empress Josephine* and *Madame Jarre*.

Another pupil of David's, Jean Auguste Dominique Ingres (1780–1867), soon proved himself a master and one of the most original artists of his day. For a long while he was misunderstood, but by the time he was fifty he began to be showered with honors and acclaimed as the leader of the classical school. In fact, his reputation rests on a misunderstanding, for there is nothing necessarily classical about his work, which is the product merely of an artistic temperament that unconsciously followed its deepest instincts, whatever the theories he invoked. Having been brought up in David's studio on the dogma of "ideal beauty," Ingres always professed to be a passionate admirer of Raphael and of classical art, and claimed to be giving an exact account of nature, corrected where necessary by imitation of ancient art. But in practice he distorted what he found in nature in order to obey the dictates of his unconscious needs: hence such deformations of the human anatomy as the arms of his *Thetis* in the Aix-en-Provence Museum, or the unbroken curve formed by the back and thighs of his *Grande Odalisque* in the Louvre; and there are many other examples. Ingres the aggressive theoretician was very different from Ingres the painter.

There is no reason why we should not admit Ingres's limitations. He was wholly lacking in imagination, and had no sense of poetry; he was incapable of composing a picture, and was out of his depth as soon as he had to group a number of figures together; he was at ease only when dealing with one or two. His *St. Symphorien* (in the Louvre) was sharply criticized when he first showed it, and rightly so. Some of his works reveal his passion for the female body, in which he curiously combines the most admirable observation of nature with arbitrary distortions: *The Odalisque with the Slave* (Walters Art Gallery, Baltimore), *The Turkish Bath* (Louvre), and the *Vénus Anadyomène* (Musée Condé, Chantilly). There are historical costume pieces that seem laboriously detailed mosaics *(Molière and Louis XIV*, Wildenstein Collection, New York). There are also portraits of men and women, in which he applied himself to put down exactly what he saw, and succeeded in expressing his sitters' characters: *The Painter Granet* (Museum, Aix-en-Provence), *Portrait of Joseph Antoine Moltedo* (Metropolitan Museum of Art, New York), *Monsieur Cordier* (Louvre), *La Belle Lélie* (Museum of Fine Arts, Rouen), *Mademoiselle Rivière* (Louvre), *Madame de Senone* (Museum of Fine Arts, Nantes). Critics have often jeered at Ingres's color, claiming that he was no colorist; if you define a colorist as a painter who makes his colors sparkle, they are right. But although Ingres used a very smooth and meticulous technique, and shunned variations of tone, he was a refined and daringly original colorist, as can be seen in the contrasts between Madame Rivière's hair and the golden whites of her shawl and dress, and the pure ultramarine of the divan on which she rests, or from the Grande Odalisque's harmonies of blue and pink. Ingres was misunderstood at least twice: first, when his earliest works led the champions of "ideal beauty" to call him "Gothic," and second, when the academic painters of the Institute de France saw him as a successor to Raphael, and a champion of "sound" theories. Ingres did indeed make a cult of Raphael, as he proved on many occasions, e.g., the figures of the Madonna and the cherubs in *The Vow of Louis XIII* in the Louvre. But this is the least valuable aspect of his work.

Ingres trained a number of pupils in his studio, but the most gifted of them failed to live up to their initial promise, apart from Chassériau, who will be dealt with below, and who, in any case, soon broke away. Ingres's art was too personal for him to have made a good teacher, and he was incapable of forming a coherent body of ideas on which to base a school.

ROMANTIC PAINTING

If we knew Théodore Géricault (1791–1824) only from his painting, we would think of him as a virile and energetic man, in love with grandeur and power. And yet those glimpses of him which emerge from his letters and from the accounts given by his contemporaries (which are less numerous and less explicit than we should like) disclose a tormented, anxiety-ridden, easily discouraged man, prone to curious changes of mind. At an early date he attracted attention with vigorous paintings of soldiers of the Napoleonic armies (such as *Mounted Officer of the Imperial Guard* and *The Wounded Cuirassier*, both in the Louvre), which show his liking for horses and movement; but as a result of an unhappy love affair he was forced to leave Paris. He went to Rome, where he was deeply disturbed by classical art and by the great Italian masters, and painted several studies for a large canvas, which he never executed: *Riderless Horse Races*, in which he intended to show a familiar Roman scene, stripped of any element of the accidental.

In 1816 the frigate *La Méduse* was wrecked off the coast of Senegal; her passengers took to a raft; and nine-tenths

EUGÈNE DELACROIX · *Self-Portrait*
Louvre, Paris

of them died. This disaster deeply stirred the public at a time when it was already inflamed by political events. Géricault then painted his huge canvas *The Raft of the Medusa* and exhibited it in the Salon of 1819, where it was unfavorably received on account of the horror of the theme and the harsh treatment by the artist. The painter was disheartened and left for England. In his last four years he planned several large pictures, but painted only small ones. He died after a fall from a horse.

Géricault's art is as complex as was his personality. His subjects are taken from real life, but he eliminated everything inessential. Although based on an actual newspaper report, his *Raft of the Medusa* might depict a scene taking place in any period; it might even illustrate an incident of the Flood. His concern with reality is combined with a marked taste for the monumental, for oversized forms and dramatic effects—which, in conjunction with his preference for somber colors, brings him close to the great Baroque painters of the seventeenth century, to Caravaggio and Ribera. Here, at the beginning of the century that was to see the battles fought by classicism, romanticism, and realism, the first preliminary engagement seems to be taking place within Géricault's mind. Some of his paintings, in which he sought to render reality, no matter how horrible, with the utmost accuracy (e.g., those depicting madmen, such as *The Mad Kidnaper* in the Museum of Fine Arts at Springfield, Massachusetts, or his anatomical studies), make him a forerunner of realism.

It would give a false and incomplete picture of Eugène Delacroix (1798–1863) if we were to treat him simply as the leader of the Romantic school, as against the classical school led by Ingres. Apart from a trip to Morocco, which only lasted six months but left a lasting impression on him, his life was uneventful, and was entirely devoted to painting. In addition to works which evoke the people and scenes of North Africa he treated historical subjects taken from Shakespeare, Byron, Goethe, and Walter Scott. This was not merely to conform with the conventions of the time; only subjects remote from everyday reality inspired him, for only then did his imagination have full scope. Even when he treated an incident from the 1830 Revolution, in *Liberty at the Barricades* (Louvre), he weakened its contemporary character by putting an allegorical figure in the midst of modern rioters.

As a young man he was nevertheless strongly influenced by such contemporary English painters as Lawrence, Constable, and Bonington, as well as by Rubens and the Venetian school. The result can be

THÉODORE GÉRICAULT · *The Raft of the Medusa*
Louvre, Paris

EUGÈNE DELACROIX · *Algerian Women*
Louvre, Paris

seen in his bold and sensitive brushwork, and in the contrasts between impasto highlights and transparent glazes we find in the *Algerian Women* and the *Still Life with Lobsters* in the Louvre. From about 1840 on, he began to cover his canvases with small fluent strokes which allowed him to vary and contrast his colors, as in the *St. George and the Dragon* and the *Odalisque* in the Louvre, *The Lion Hunt* in the Bordeaux Museum of Painting and Sculpture, and *Herminia and the Shepherds* in the Stockholm National Museum. At first Delacroix looked for the picturesque; later he came to prefer the classic virtues of order, simplicity, and grandeur. It was he who wrote the sentence that contradicts all romantic theories: "The greatest genius is but a more highly rational being."

Delacroix was a skillful colorist, who enjoyed contrasting the richest shades of his palette: something we would be better able to appreciate if his work had not suffered so much from the poor quality of the paints he used and unwise mixing methods. It has repeatedly been said that he could not draw, but this is a superficial judgment. Certainly it is easy to find inaccuracies in his work, yet despite this his line is perfectly expressive of life and movement. Not one of his pictures is painted with mere mechanical professionalism, and they never leave the viewer cold. Furthermore, he was the only artist of his time capable of executing vast murals and portraying great historical scenes and figures in a way that goes beyond any mere student exercise. The decorations in the Luxembourg and Palais Bourbon libraries, the ceiling of the Apollo Gallery in the Louvre, and the paintings in the Chapelle des Saints-Anges in the church of Saint-Sulpice in Paris are first-rate works, which equal comparable paintings by the most highly esteemed Italian masters.

To appreciate the value of Delacroix's work we need only compare it with that of painters who were thought at the time to be his equals, if not actually his superiors: Paul Delaroche (1797–1856) (*The Children of Edward IV*, in the Louvre), or Eugène Devéria (1805–1865) (*The Birth of Henry IV*, ditto). Their pictures are merely anecdotal illustrations which have little visual appeal.

Théodore Chassériau (1819–1856) made

HONORÉ DAUMIER · *Don Quixote*
New Pinakothek, Munich

THÉODORE CHASSÉRIAU · *The Toilet of Esther*
Louvre, Paris

a spectacular debut. The first works by this child prodigy (*Vénus Anadyomène, Esther before Ahasuerus*, both in the Louvre) amazed his contemporaries. Unfortunately his creative energies soon evaporated, and his later pictures, such as *The Tepidarium* in the Louvre, or those inspired by his visit to Algeria, lack the characteristics of his earlier work: style, a feminine type which is his own creation, and an elusive poetic quality with an exotic twist.

DAUMIER

Over a period of many years Honoré Daumier (1808–1879) published one spirited lithograph after another in various periodicals, satirizing the powers that be

201

and the customs of the time. Apparently he was nearly forty before he began to paint: little canvases in browns and dull reds that recorded scenes from everyday life, or took their subject matter from Molière, La Fontaine, and Cervantes. It was not until the early twentieth century that Daumier was recognized as one of the outstanding painters of his time. Other artists before him had found subjects in the life and customs around them, and had put them down with scrupulous truthfulness: Hogarth, for instance, or Chardin, or the seventeenth-century Dutch. Daumier's originality was to treat such subjects not as a conscientious realist, but as a visionary, a visionary of the real. By nature he was a poet, given to hyperbole; had he received a proper artistic training he would have painted powerful scenes from the Bible, or from the poets and dramatists. But because he was conscious of the limitations of his background, and at the same time an ardent democrat, he chose instead to treat such subjects as *The Third-Class Carriage* (Metropolitan Museum of Art, New York), *The Chess Players* (Petit Palais in Paris), *The Print Collector* (Esnault-Pelterie Collection, Paris), *Crispin and Scapin* (Louvre), and *Don Quixote and Sancho Panza* (C. Payson Collection, New York).

He transcribed his everyday subjects in accordance with his own vision. His bourgeois and lower-class Parisians were transformed into creatures of great formal power or into grotesque masks. Instinctively, he omitted the little details that date or locate a scene with too close accuracy – details that any genre painter would have tried to record – and treated such subjects as an excuse for exaggerating the forms of the human body, its gestures, and its facial expressions. When Degas paints a laundress he tries to be as accurate as possible, faithfully recording the shop with the wet clothes hung up to dry, or the gestures of the woman picking up her iron. But in the Louvre's *Washerwoman*, shown climbing up the steps from the Seine, the bundle of linen she carries might as well be a sack of potatoes, while the houses across the river have been simplified to the utmost.

Daumier often portrayed episodes from Molière's plays, and one of the finest pictures is *The Drama* (New Pinakothek, Munich), where we look past spectators crammed into a box, and see the stage on which actors are performing some somber play. It is easy to see how Daumier's taste for exaggeration led him to love the theater, where everything is larger then life. Like Victor Hugo and Alexandre Dumas Père, he amplified and simplified. He also loved to depict peaceful interiors, where collectors are examining paintings, or browsing through a portfolio of prints. Invariably, he drew and painted from memory. Whatever he had seen was filtered through his mind, and whatever was not essential was eliminated. Thus, by avoiding unnecessary detail and by exaggerating form he endowed the meanest subjects with grandeur and style.

THE LANDSCAPE PAINTERS

In the days when David reigned over painting, landscape was much more important in England than it was in France. Steeped in the dogma of "ideal beauty," the theoreticians of the time saw landscape as an inferior kind of painting and would only admit the "historical landscape," where a subject capable of "inspiring noble feelings" might allow the painter to "compose settings in accordance with the greatest splendors and beauties that nature might show." This meant that to stand any chance of being accepted by the Salon, a landscape had to be painted in the studio and illustrate a mythological or historical theme. A painter's studies from nature could only serve as raw material; their content must be duly ennobled, idealized, and rearranged.

Such was the situation about the year 1822, when Jean Baptiste Camille Corot (1796–1875), the son of a milliner in the Rue du Sac, began to paint. Exceptionally modest, a hard worker who had time for nothing but his art, as a young man he had some lessons with two well-known landscape painters, before going to Italy for the first of many extended stays there, mainly in Rome. It was his custom to paint a great many small studies from nature, out of which he would construct the pictures he sent to the Salons. These were not too badly received by the critics, and gradually Corot's life took on the same regular seasonal rhythm as that of a farm laborer or a worker in a vineyard. Every spring he would set out on journeys to the various regions of France, to Italy, or to French Switzerland, and paint the studies from nature which were to serve as a basis for his large Salon canvases. It is worth noting that, unlike most landscape artists, Corot had no favorite regions or sites. His choice of a place to paint was usually motivated by his hope of finding good friends and pleasant company.

In his earliest works, the "motif" or subject is set down with scrupulous care; not until about the middle of his career did he occasionally paint misty canvases in which the foliage is like a thin haze. But there was one point he consistently held to be of the first importance, as his works and writings alike bear out. He wanted the tones—that is, the different gradations of light and shadow, discounting color—to be captured as accurately as possible; the same task to which Piero della Francesca, Velazquez, and Vermeer had all previously applied themselves in their various ways. "The first two things to study," he wrote in one of his notebooks, "are form and tone. Color and technique give the work charm." But if color took second place with Corot, he did not despise it. He normally used a scale of delicate shades—browns, grays, ochers, and dull greens—but on occasion he was well able to strike a brilliant note, as in the windows of *The Cathedral of Sens* and the dress of the *Lady in Blue:* two works in the Louvre whose freshness is amazing when we remember that Corot painted them at the age of seventy-eight. Since we have to give some further examples of Corot's work let us name *The Bridge at Narni* (Louvre) and *Rome and the Trinità dei Monti* (Geneva Museum of Art) as representative of his Italian landscapes, while *The View of Marissel* (Louvre) and *The Cathedral of Chartres* (Louvre) may be representative of his French ones. *Homer with Shepherds* in the Saint-Lô Museum is one of the best examples of the "historical landscapes" he painted in the studio and destined for the Salon, while *Diana Bathing* (Bordeaux Museum of Painting and Sculpture) is

JEAN BAPTISTE CAMILLE COROT · *Self-Portrait*
Louvre, Paris

JEAN BAPTISTE CAMILLE COROT · *The View of Marissel*
Louvre, Paris

typical of the misty, poetic landscapes which used to be considered the best part of his work.

When the weather turned bad and Corot had to work indoors, he would sometimes paint a professional model as a change from landscapes, dressing her up in an Italian peasant costume to remind himself of his youth. The painters's contemporaries, except for a few far-sighted people like Degas, scorned these little figure paintings, and only in the last fifty years have their great qualities been recognized. They have been compared to works by Vermeer, and there is undeniably an affinity between such of Corot's works as *The Woman with the Pearl* (Louvre), the *Reclining Nymph* (Geneva Museum of Art), and *The Studio* (Lyons Palace of Art), and the works of the painter of Delft.

If Corot has come to be regarded as a great painter, beside whom many once more illustrious figures seem bombastic or stuffy, this is due above all to the accuracy of his eye, to his feeling for light and color, and to the simplicity of his technique. It is also due to the poetic atmosphere given off by his work, to the fact that he makes us share his love of the countryside, which, next to painting, was the great passion of his life. Corot, who wanted to be nothing but a painter, was also a great poet.

Gustave Courbet (1819–1877) was the son of a small landowner at Ornans in the Franche-Comté, and went to Paris as a young man in order to paint. His first pictures were naïvely romantic, but he soon realized that his vocation was to paint what he saw around him: peasants of Ornans and landscapes of his native

GUSTAVE COURBET · *The Artist's Studio*
Louvre, Paris

Jura. He made passionate enemies by his earliest Salon exhibits, but friends as well. He was sustained throughout many quarrels by a colossal, childish conceit. Twice, at the Paris Exhibitions of 1855 and 1867, he managed to get himself a special pavilion for retrospective selections from his works. In 1871 he supported the Paris Commune. The pro-republican forces at this time wanted to pull down the column in the Place Vendôme (which commemorates Napoleon's victories), and this was done. Later, Courbet was held personally responsible for the destruction of the column and condemned to pay the cost of restoring it, some 300,000 francs. Already a sick man, the aged painter escaped to Switzerland. He died at La Tour de Peilz on Lake Geneva.

Fired by the example of Géricault, Courbet, who proclaimed himself a realist, set out to paint great canvases of peasant life. Apart from the unfinished *Fire*, he never painted Paris scenes, although he spent a large part of every year in Paris. His *Young Women on the Banks of the Seine* in the Petit Palais (Paris) are stolid countrywomen, anything but Parisiennes. He painted straightforward pictures of country people at work *(The Stone Breakers* formerly in the Dresden State Picture Gallery, *The Wheat Sifters* in the Museum of Fine Arts at Nantes, *Siesta* in the Petit Palais), all of which possess nobility. A passionate hunter himself, he painted hunting scenes like *L'Hallali* in the Museum of Fine Arts, Boston. He also painted a number of well-fleshed nudes, of which the finest is that which figures in his huge canvas *The Painter's Studio* in the Louvre. His *Burial at Ornans* in the Louvre has the grandeur and solemnity of a classical bas-relief. Finally, he painted excellent portraits of himself, his family, and his contemporaries (*Man with Pipe* in the Musée Fabre, Monpellier, *Madame Boreau* in Paul Rosenberg's Collection in Paris); landscape views of the Jura and sea-

scapes (*Étretat* in the collection of David Rockefeller, New York); and opulent arrangements of flowers *(Vase of Flowers* in the Hamburg Museum). Instead of the brush, he often used the palette knife, by which he gave his work a close, smooth, veined texture like colored marble or agate. In his lifetime he was criticized for representing only the ugly, crude, vulgar sides of nature, but it was never suggested that he could not paint. He was master of his technique at an early age, and he scarcely evolved thereafter. At first glimpse, it might seem that an art which set out to do no more than give a faithful picture of reality would be a limited art; but the fact is that the artist selects and interprets even when he thinks he is giving an unvarnished report of what lies before his eyes. The best proof of this is that when looking at certain scenes or persons, we cannot help thinking that they might have been painted by Courbet, the marvelous technician born to cover canvas with paint. Jean François Millet (1814–1875) was not a landowner's son like Courbet, but was born of poor peasants in the Cotentin peninsula, where he learned as a boy to use the scythe and the spade. Sent to Paris on a grant from the Cherbourg municipality, he had a hard time. He gradually wearied of painting small genre

JEAN FRANÇOIS MILLET · *Spring*
Louvre, Paris

pictures for art dealers, and began to take his subjects from among the people he observed on trips to the countryside near Paris. In 1849 an outbreak of cholera induced him to leave the city. He settled at Barbizon, a small village frequented by artists on the edge of the Fontainebleau forest. He found himself in surroundings like those where he had spent his youth, and this fact determined the character of his art. For the next quarter of a century, he became the chronicler of peasant life.

Before him, artists who included peasants in their paintings treated them simply as picturesque elements, as a pretext for a startling splash of color. Millet wanted to show the peasant at work, sowing, reaping, cutting down trees, rather than the peasant in his free moments eating and drinking, as in Louis le Nain, or reveling and brawling, as in Van Ostade. Nor does Millet ever show us, like Bruegel, the peasant enjoying himself at fairs and the like. He knew from experience that work in the fields was hard, and he represented it as such. At the time, he was criticized for overstating his case, and for representing peasants exclusively as forced laborers; and it is true that this criticism is sometimes deserved. But it cannot be denied that in such works as *The Gleaners* and *A Girl Spinning* in the Louvre, *The Potato Gatherers* in the Museum of Fine Arts, Boston, and *The Return from the Fields,* formerly in the Dollfus Collection, he admirably renders the loneliness of the fields as they stretch away to the horizon; and the slow movements of the laborers whose joints have grown stiff from a lifetime of hard work. A great reader of the Bible, he realized that the work of the countryside had scarcely changed over the centuries. Like Daumier, he was accustomed to draw from memory, and took pains to eliminate unnecessary detail, to simplify and generalize. He was not a natural colorist; his color

CASPAR DAVID FRIEDRICH · *The Cross on the Mountain*
State Picture Gallery, Dresden

is often muddy and unsure. In his last years he executed a number of landscapes in pastel, such as *Spring* (Louvre).

GERMAN PAINTING IN THE FIRST HALF OF THE NINETEENTH CENTURY

In 1810 a group of German artists under the leadership of Peter Cornelius (1785–1867) and Friedrich Overbeck (1789–1869) banded together with the joint aim of regenerating art and of leading a godly life. Rather than basing their work on classical sculpture or painting from models, they studied the paintings of Perugino and other fifteenth-century Italian masters. They settled in Rome in the monastery of Sant'Isidoro, where they were commissioned as a group to paint a series of frescoes on the legend of St. Joseph in the villa of a consul named Bartholdi. A few years later they were commissioned to paint a sequence in the Casino Massimi in honor of the great Italian poets. The second series was never completed, because the group disbanded, and Cornelius returned to Germany. The Casa Bartholdi frescoes were moved to Berlin; they strike us as banal and cold.

One of Cornelius' pupils, Wilhelm von Kaulbach (1805–1874), founded the so-called Düsseldorf school, and painted large-scale works such as his *Defeats of the Huns* (Berlin and Munich) and his "philosophical" frescoes (Berlin and Munich). It is impossible to conceive anything emptier or more pretentious than these vast compositions; we feel that this painter must never have seen anything but engravings, not the real world. Art historians are generally agreed that the only artist of the Düsseldorf school who deserved the name of painter was Alfred Rethel (1816–1859), whose frescoes of the life of Charlemagne at the town hall of

Aix-la-Chapelle have an austere nobility. Caspar David Friedrich (1774–1840) chose to paint the natural beauties of North Germany rather than "historical landscapes" inspired by the Italian scene. But he did not restrict himself to literal representation, and he always managed to put into his carefully executed paintings some element calculated to arouse feelings of sadness, anxiety, or disquiet. If Friedrich had been less afraid of the sensual – that is, if only his small canvases showed more feeling for color and for paint – he would have been one of the best painters of his time. Even so, we can appreciate the delicate poetry of his *Landscape with Rainbow* in the Weimar Museum, or his *Cross on the Mountain* (State Picture Gallery, Dresden).

WILLIAM TURNER · *Venice, the Piazzetta from the Water*
National Gallery, London

JOHN CONSTABLE · *Salisbury Cathedral*
Museu de Arte, São Paulo

Karl Spitzweg (1808–1885) may only be a minor master, but he is not to be sneered at. The intriguing effects of light and enjoyable texture of his pictures make up for their anecdotal character and rather forced humor. He studied in Paris and paid special attention to the work of Diaz and Isabey (*The Poor Poet* in the Bavarian National Museum in Munich and *The Bookworm* in the Liechtenstein Collection in Vienna).

THE ENGLISH LANDSCAPE PAINTERS

One typical feature of the English art of this century was the great part played by landscape, particularly in watercolor.

Two of the most interesting representatives of this trend were Thomas Girtin (1775–1802) and John Sell Cotman (1782–1842). Before them, watercolorists would first make a brush drawing in sepia or India ink, and then tint it with transparent colors. Girtin and Cotman were the first to omit a monochrome groundwork, and to work entirely in watercolor from the start. The most original landscape artist of the period, however, was Joseph Mallord William Turner (1775–1851). A great admirer of Claude Lorrain, he undertook to give historical landscape a new lease on life by paying more attention to color and by handling it in a romantic spirit: thus

Aeneas and the Sibyl or *The Garden of the Hesperides* (both in the Tate Gallery, London). But for all his admiration for Claude Lorrain, he was influenced in his seascapes by the Dutch marine artists of the seventeenth century, as in *Calais Pier: An English Packet Arriving*, in the National Gallery, London. Today we are less impressed by his big compositions than by his studies from nature, such as *The Thames near Walton Bridge* and *Landscape with Cows* (both in the Tate Gallery). Later in his career he painted watercolors of Venice, the Swiss Alps, and other subjects, which are remarkable for their refinement of color and their shorthand notation; e.g., *Fire at the House of Parliament* in the British

Museum, and his various views of the Rigi. Transferring this technique of transparent colors from the watercolor medium to that of oil, he came to give more and more emphasis to color and to use an increasingly free technique, as in *Venice, the Piazzetta from the Water* (National Gallery, London).

John Constable (1776–1837) never left his native country, and strove only to give a scrupulously faithful account of the rural subjects that he knew. Like Corot, he had to satisfy his collectors by painting studio pictures based on sketches made in the open air. At first his style was rather dry and finicky, but he soon lost his constraint and painted landscapes which convey light and color

RICHARD PARKES BONINGTON · *Scene in Normandy*
National Gallery, London

with incredible accuracy and a most sensitive technique; see such works as *Shipping on the Orwell, Brighton Beach with Colliers, Hampstead Heath,* all in the Victoria and Albert Museum, and the *Salisbury Cathedral* in the Museu de Arte, São Paulo. Using small strokes, varying his colors, and often having recourse to the palette knife, he succeeded in creating an extremely elaborate and finely graduated network of color, which is wonderfully suited to reproducing the iridescent light of the English countryside and English skies.

Though his short working life was spent in France, Richard Parkes Bonington (1802–1828) was essentially an English painter. He painted small oils and watercolors of historical subjects (such as *Richelieu and Anne of Austria* in the Louvre), which serve him as pretexts for a sparkling display of color, as well as landscapes of Paris, Normandy, and Italy (*Versailles* in the Louvre, *The Institute Seen from the Quays* in the British Museum) that are miracles of free handling and careful observation.

About 1848 a few young English painters were drawn together by their dislike of academic formulas, and founded the Pre-Raphaelite Brotherhood. Their art is little known outside England, because none of their works is to be found in a foreign museum, while their intentions have been misrepresented. It is said that they came together on religious grounds, which is untrue; that they wished to seek inspiration in the art of the Italian fifteenth century, with which they were unfamiliar; and that their movement was launched by Ruskin, when that writer only came to their defense some time after they had begun to exhibit. The fact is that the P.R.B.'s (for they called themselves by the initials of their group) rejected the conventions of the academic painting of the day, and reacted against it by reproducing nature with the most niggling literalness. The leaders of the movement were Dante Gabriel Rossetti (1828–1882), the son of a Dante scholar who had settled in England, John Everett Millais (1829–1896), and William Holman Hunt (1827–1910).

VII

THE IMPRESSIONIST PERIOD

EDOUARD MANET

In the 1860's a number of young French painters who had grown sick of the falsity and flatness of academic painting sought to create a livelier and more truthful art. These were the men who gave birth to Impressionism. It was only natural for them to regard as their leader a painter of the older generation whose works shocked his contemporaries whenever they were shown. Yet Edouard Manet (1832–1883) had no intention of provoking scandal, and was surprised that his pictures should meet with so much hostility when his one object was to set down reality exactly as it was. His earliest pictures, like *Lola de Valence*, *The Luncheon on the Grass*, and *Olympia* (all three of which are in the Louvre), showed him to be a straightforward naturalist who used black to contrast with extremely light colors, and only hinted at the intermediate shades. He was likened to Frans Hals and Velazquez, although the only Velazquez that Manet knew were those in the Louvre, and he had not yet been to Spain. Revolutionary and barbaric as he may then have seemed, Manet was a very able tech-

nician who knew exactly what effects he wanted to get. He was not one of those artists whose works are produced by a slow laborious process: when he was dissatisfied with a canvas just completed, he would scrape off the paint and begin afresh. He wanted his painting to be spontaneous.

He painted figures, nudes, very few landscapes – he was above all a Parisian – portraits (one of the finest is that of *Emile Zola* in the Louvre), and admirable still lifes such as the Louvre's *Vase of Peonies*. All he asked of a subject was that it should be taken from contemporary life and be capable of being painted from nature. However, he flouted this principle by painting *A Bar at the Folies-Bergère* and *The Masked Ball* in the studio. He lacked imagination, and his work has been shown to contain flagrant borrowings from former masters; but it would be wrong to speak of plagiarism when an artist stamps the borrowed material with his own style. About 1866 he came into contact with younger painters such as Monet, Pissarro, Sisley, and Bazille; but Monet's influence on his work did not make itself felt until years later. From 1870 on, Manet lightened his

ÉDOUARD MANET · *A Bar at the Folies-Bergère*
Courtauld Collection, London

palette, began to employ smaller and smaller strokes, and set himself to capture fleeting effects of light. His gradual development can be followed if we examine successively *In the Garden* (J. Watson Webb Collection, New York), *Chez le Père Lathuile* in the Tournai Municipal Museum, and the *Bellevue Garden* (Ernest Rouart Collection, Paris). Manet's work thus falls into two groups. In the first, he follows the tradition, though disclosing his basic originality; in the

second, he is inspired by Monet, and proves to be an Impressionist. But throughout this shift from the one style to the other he always remains himself. There are some artists whose work is the result of deep thinking and intricate calculations. Not so with Manet: he relied on instinct. As soon as he formed an idea of the work, he never let up until he had attained the objective he set himself. What strikes us in each of his pictures is his sureness, deliberation,

213

economy of means, and deep understanding of the resources which the oil medium puts at the painter's command. To confirm this we need only study the head and hands of the girl in *The Balcony* (Louvre) as she buttons her glove.

A Parisian and a man of fashion, Manet could paint popular scenes and types without falling into vulgarity. He was very sensitive to feminine charm, and when his model was a pretty, elegant young woman he was only too happy to paint her; witness *Le Repos* (Vanderbilt Collection, New York), for which Berthe Morisot was the model; *Jeanne* or *Le Printemps* in an American private collection, whose model was a young actress, Mademoiselle Demarsy; and a few pastel portraits of women which he painted at the end of his life, when he was already suffering from his last illness.

Before discussing the revolution which the artists of the Impressionist group brought about, we may mention two landscape artists, Boudin and Jongkind, who bridge the gap between the landscape painters of the Barbizon school and the Impressionist landscape painters Monet, Sisley, and Pissarro. Eugène Boudin (1824–1898) reveals an exquisite sense of light in the delicate grays of his views

JOHAN BARTHOLD JONGKIND · *View of Overschie*
Museum, Douai, France

of Normandy ports and beaches: *The Jetty at Deauville* in the Louvre, *Ships Entering a Harbor* in a Paris private collection. Paul Guigou (1834–1871) painted views of his native Provence (*The La Gineste Road near Marseilles* in the Louvre) with a feeling for values comparable to Corot's and a thick texture that has acquired a marvelous patina with the years.

The great Dutch painter Johan Barthold Jongkind (1819–1891), despite his bohemianism and alcoholism and his periods of amnesia, left behind a number of highly personal landscapes which, unlike Van Gogh's, show no evidence of the disturbed state of his mind. He painted scenes of his native Low Countries (*Street in Antwerp* in the Rijksmuseum, Amsterdam; *En Hollande* in the Louvre) and views of Paris on his visits to France (*Le Pont Marie* in the Louvre). Anticipating the Impressionists with his tiny strokes and shimmering tones, rather than by any emphasis on color, he gave exceptionally accurate renderings of light softened by slight haze, of ports with their rows of red-brick houses, of windmills and ships. He was the real heir of the seventeenth-century Dutch landscape painters, though nobody could ever have accused him of imitating them. Besides his oil paintings, he made a number of

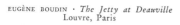

EUGÈNE BOUDIN · *The Jetty at Deauville*
Louvre, Paris

watercolor sketches of French landscapes during the latter part of his life; their flowing lines and fresh colors make them a delight to the eye.

1874: THE BEGINNING OF THE
IMPRESSIONIST MOVEMENT

The term "Impressionists" was coined to describe the group of artists who in 1874 organized an exhibition in the Boulevard des Capucines; it referred to one of Monet's entries, entitled *Impression, Sunrise*, which scandalized many. The chief of these artists were Monet, Pissarro, Sisley, Renoir, Cézanne, and Degas. But the term "Impressionism" also denotes a specific conception of painting which was evolved by Monet, adopted by Sisley and Pissarro, and, for several years, by Manet and Renoir as well. For the last eighty years or more, critics have repeatedly credited the Impressionists with the discovery that far more brilliant effects could be achieved by applying the unmixed pigment in shimmering spots of color. In this view a canvas spattered with pure blues and yellows would produce an "optical mixture" on the viewer's retina, and he should then see a green far more startling than the most brilliant green the artist could find on his palette. This theory, still found in all the histories of art, is unfortunately false. If we examine Impressionist paintings, we see that their painters never used such a method. If we test these methods ourselves, the result will not be a startling green, but merely a jumble of yellow and blue dots.

What, then, was the Impressionists' contribution? To begin with, we must remember that they relied upon practical experience, not abstract theories. Every picture they painted was to them an experiment, from which they drew their own conclusion. They sought to render, as faithfully as possible, the play of light on objects, the outdoor light that changes with the seasons and the time of day. To obtain more luminous and more intense color, they eliminated black and muddy tones from their palettes, attenuated the contrasts between light and dark, and replaced them with contrasts between colors. For instance, when painting foliage in sunlight, they softened the shadows; while yellowish greens rendered the light falling on leaves, blue-greens, pure blues, or even violets rendered the various degrees of shade. At the same time, they adopted freer, more simplified forms and paid a good deal more attention to color than to line. As a result of these innovations, the works of the Impressionists baffled and irritated the public, which had been accustomed to an entirely different kind of painting.

The three artists who most consistently applied the Impressionist method were Claude Monet (1840–1926), Camille Pissarro (1830–1903), and Alfred Sisley (1839–1899). All three were primarily landscape painters. Pissarro worked mainly in Normandy and the Île-de-France; Sisley painted the countryside near Paris; Monet first painted at Argenteuil and Vétheuil, and later in Provence, on the Normandy coast, in Venice, and in London. Monet was the boldest and most original of the group, and in his early pictures he was astonishingly successful in capturing momentary effects of light: for instance in *The Beach at Sainte-Adresse* in the Art Institute of Chicago, in *La Grenouillère* in the Metropolitan Museum of Art, in *The Argenteuil Basin* in the Providence, Rhode Island, School of Design, and in the *Landscape, Vétheuil* in the Louvre. However, by the time he was forty his poetic temperament and his passion for color began to get the upper hand, and color sensations became increasingly stressed in his work. He took to choosing subjects that he could paint at different times of the day, and thus produced his series of paintings of hay-

CLAUDE MONET · *Impression, Sunrise*
Musée Marmottan, Paris

stacks, of a group of poplars, of views of the Thames in London. Examples of this manner are *Rouen Cathedral, Early Morning* (Museum of Fine Arts, Boston), and *London, Houses of Parliament* (Louvre). This development reached its climax with the series of *The Waterlilies* in the Musée de l'Orangerie in Paris, in which the artist confined himself to recording the sky's reflections in the waters of a pond in his garden at Giverny.

Sisley's early works show the influence of Courbet and of Corot, but he soon came under Monet's spell. He is especially remarkable for the subtle accuracy of his vision (*Louveciennes* in the collection of the late Percy Moore Turner, London; *The Flood at Port-Marly* in the Louvre; *Landscape near Louveciennes* in the Durand-Ruel Gallery, New York).

Edgar Degas (1834–1917) is usually linked with the Impressionists because he was their friend and took part in their exhibitions; but by training, artistic outlook, and methods of work he was their opposite. After studying under a pupil of Ingres, he made several trips to Italy, where he had relatives, and there made a thorough study of the fifteenth-century masters. His earliest works are portraits and paintings on historical themes, very tightly drawn and skillfully painted (*Semiramis Building a Town* and *The Bellelli Family*, both in the Louvre), which show the influence of Ingres. Shortly before 1870 he began to paint scenes of horse racing, dancers at the Opera, and cafés offering music and entertainment (*At the Races* and *The Orchestra of the Opera* in the Louvre, *Dancers in Salmon-Pink*, Bührle Collection, Zurich); studies of laundresses at work (*Women Ironing* in the Louvre) and milliners (*The Millinery Shop* in Jacques Seligmann's Collection, New York). Around forty he abandoned oil painting to work in pastel; his drawing became freer and fuller; and he began to pay more attention to color. Around fifty, although his sight was beginning to fail him, he did several pastels of women at their toilet (*After the Bath* in Mme. Durand-Ruel's Collection, Neuilly-sur-Seine; *Woman Drying Her Neck* in the Louvre). In these works his color grew richer and richer, and his technique increasingly bold.

Degas was not merely a painter of the life of his day. Races, ballet girls, laundry women, women combing their hair or having their baths – all these subjects were to him above all problems of color, composition, and form. In his experiments with asymmetrical composition, such as *The Dancing Class* in Harry Payne Bingham's collection, New York, or *The Ballet Class* in the Philadelphia Museum of Art, he seems as daring as Tintoretto.

Whereas the Impressionists wanted to paint only from nature, Degas followed a quite different approach, refusing to give up more traditional ways of working. After carefully studying the subject which he proposed to paint, he executed extremely elaborate drawings from models in his studio, which he then used in his picture, relying on his well-trained memory for the color. In his last pastels of groups of dancers, he achieved a thick texture and unusual color harmonies by continually going over his work and interweaving intense spots of color to produce a tremulous effect.

Throughout his long life, despite the handicap of his bad eyesight, Degas never ceased thinking about his art and exploring new paths. His work is a magnificent example of intelligence, tenacity, and utter devotion to one great passion: painting.

Few artists have absorbed so many different influences as Auguste Renoir (1841–1919); yet he always remained himself. Those of Courbet and Corot can be seen in his early pictures, such as the *Diana Hunting* in the Museu de Arte, São Paulo; that of Diaz in certain landscapes of the same period; that of Delacroix in his *Parisiennes vêtues en Algériennes*. *La Grenouillère* in the Louvre shows the influence of Monet; but the big standing *Baigneuse*, now in the Basel Museum of Art, executed a year later, is not in the least Impressionist. It was only after 1872 that he became

ALFRED SISLEY · *The Loing Canal*
Louvre, Paris

CAMILLE PISSARRO · *Place du Théâtre Français in Paris*
Hermitage, Leningrad

a true Impressionist, as we can see from such landscapes as *The Duck Pond* (Louvre) and *The Boating Party at Chatou* in the Sam Lewisohn Collection, New York. He preferred the human figure to landscape, and it is to this preference that we owe such crystalline jewels as *The Loge* (Courtauld Institute, London), the *Portrait of Jeanne Samary* (Pushkin Museum, Moscow), *Baigneuse* (Sir Kenneth Clark Collection, London) and many other miraculous works expressing Renoir's love of childhood and youth. Around 1884 he gave up the shimmering brush strokes that had marked his Impressionist period, and took

to working in the studio rather than out of doors. For several years he painted tightly drawn nudes and figures in smooth and well-blended colors (*The Bathers* in the Carrol S. Tyson Collection, Philadelphia). From then on up to the end of his life he painted increasingly massive female figures. These are no longer enclosed in rigorous outlines, and the layers of transparent color are applied on top of one another (*Reclining Woman* in the Oskar Reinhart Collection, Winterthur; *The Sleeping Bather* in the Stang Collection, Oslo; *Gabrielle with a Rose* in the Louvre). Finally we must mention his very beautiful Provençal landscapes,

EDGAR DEGAS · *Dancers in Salmon-Pink*
Bührle Collection, Zurich

with their bold color harmonies, and his still lifes, in which fruits take on the glow of precious stones.

Renoir's art sprang from instincts whose deep roots are hidden from us. No theory can be deduced from the few remarks of his which have survived; usually these are witticisms and nothing more. Instinct drove him to paint only subjects that breathed happiness and health: girls, children, flowers, fruit, or harmonious sunlit landscapes. It would be impossible to find the representation of something ugly in any picture by him, anything to suggest sadness or bitterness. Though his life was not without difficulties, both physical and material, neither his money worries nor his illness left the slightest trace in his art. The young people who went to the dance halls of Montmartre must surely have been a rather rough lot, and yet Renoir made them the material for a canvas which sums up all his work, the Louvre's *Moulin de la Galette,* a work permeated with poetry and joy. In

BERTHE MORISOT · *The Cradle*
Louvre, Paris

thus turning his back on ugliness and poverty to paint nothing but happiness and beauty, Renoir broke with the realist trend of his time and harked back to the tradition of Botticelli and Titian, Poussin and Watteau, Tiepolo and Fragonard. Like Miranda in *The Tempest* he could have exclaimed: "How beauteous mankind is!"

Pissarro began by following in the wake of Corot, but he soon became an Impressionist, save for a few years during which he conscientiously applied the Neo-Impressionist methods developed by Seurat and codified by Signac. His landscapes, such as *Louveciennes in Winter* in the Walters Gallery at Baltimore, or *The Edge of the Village* and *Orchard at Pontoise* in the Louvre, have more solidity than Monet's, where the fleeting play of light ends up by dissolving the shapes of trees, fields, and houses. He painted oils and gouaches which, unlike Monet's, are peopled by peasants, as well as views of the Jardin des Tuileries and the Paris

PIERRE AUGUSTE RENOIR · *Jean Renoir*
Private collection, New York

FRÉDÉRIC BAZILLE · *The Artist's Studio*
Louvre, Paris

streets where the delicate grays of the houses and pavements are very well caught.

Frédéric Bazille (1841–1870) studied under Gleyre with Monet, Sisley, and Renoir. He was a promising young painter, remarkable for his vigor and simplicity, but his career was cut short when he was killed in the Franco-Prussian war. Among his works are *View of the Village* in the Musée Fabre at Montpellier, and *Artist's Studio* in the Louvre.

Berthe Morisot (1841–1895) began as a pupil of Corot's but later was influenced by Manet, and learned a good deal from Monet and Renoir. She portrayed children and young women in lucid works which reveal a subtle feeling for color.

Because Cézanne's work was slow in gaining recognition, and because he moved away from Impressionism, it is often forgotten that he was one of the group, and that even if he was younger than Pissarro, he was older than Monet and Renoir. Timid, unsure of himself, Paul Cézanne (1839–1906) largely led a life apart, dividing his time between Paris and his native Aix-en-Provence. He developed slowly. After working without a master in Suisse's studio in Paris, he began to paint in heavy impastos figures, still lifes, and romantic compositions such as *The Abduction* in the late Lord Keynes's Collection or *The Negro Scipio* in the Museu de Arte, São Paulo. At the age of thirty-three, realizing that he was at a dead end, he

221

PIERRE AUGUSTE RENOIR · *Jeanne Samary*
Pushkin Museum, Moscow

PAUL CÉZANNE · *Mont Sainte-Victoire*
Hermitage, Leningrad

went for advice to Pissarro, who set him to work from nature, carefully studying his subject (*The House of the Hanged Man* in the Louvre). For the rest of his life Cézanne painted landscapes, portraits, and still lifes, in and around Paris and in Provence. Gradually his individuality asserted itself and he developed a method all his own. While the Impressionists used color to convey transitory effects of light, Cézanne wanted to return to a more traditional kind of painting, to record the permanent rather than the transitory features of reality, and to render volumes by means of color. Conscious of his deficient artistic training, and having been taught by Pissarro to take nature as his guide, he spent a long time on each of his canvases; the temperate climate and clear light of Provence allowed him to return again and again to the same scene. Whereas a landscape by Monet or Pissarro portrays a given site at a given hour, a landscape by

Cézanne is timeless. It is only by the absence of leaves on the trees that we know that certain of his pictures were painted in the winter (*Landscape near Aix-en-Provence* in the Metropolitan Museum of Art, New York, *Mill on the Couleuve* in the State Museums, Berlin-Dahlem, *Mont Sainte-Victoire* in the Hermitage, Leningrad). Because Cézanne was a pure painter who could see nothing but pictorial problems when faced with a model, he was not a portrait painter, even though he did paint portraits. He was not interested in conveying the personality of his sitter, but only in rendering volumes, just as if he were painting fruit or a stone jug (*Boy in a Red Vest,* formerly in the Goldschmidt Col-

lection; *Madame Cézanne in the Conservatory,* in the Collection of Stephen C. Clark, New York; *Young Man with a Small Hat,* in the Chester Dale Collection, Washington). Among his still lifes, we may mention the one in the New Pinakothek, Munich, the *Still Life with Apples and Oranges* in the Louvre, and *Apples* in the Maurice Wertheim Collection, New York.

There are three sentences by Cézanne which sum up the ideas that underlie his conception of painting: "I wanted to make Impressionism into something solid and durable, like the art in the museum"; "We have to do Poussin over from nature"; "I have discovered that sunlight cannot be reproduced, but must be rep-

ADOLF VON MENZEL · *Recollection of the Théâtre du Gymnase*
State Museums, Berlin-Dahlem

MAX LIEBERMANN · *The Polo Match*
Museum, Hamburg

resented by something else, by color."
Clearly, it was out of respect for tradition that Cézanne wanted to give a quality of permanence to Impressionism. The result of his tenacity and hard work is a kind of painting characterized by color of an amazing fullness and richness. Each single spot of color is beautiful in itself, a delight to the eye, and at the same time an essential, indispensable part of the composition.

THE IMPRESSIONIST INFLUENCE
IN GERMANY

We now come to a highly talented artist, who seems, however, to have failed to make full use of his gifts: Adolf Menzel (1815–1905). He began with small scenes of everyday life remarkable for the accuracy of the draftsmanship and tonal relations, and revealing a very personal vision. *The Room with Balcony* and *Recollection of the Théâtre du Gymnase,* both in the museum at Berlin-Dahlem, bring to mind Degas. Menzel had the makings of a painter of the contemporary scene, but unfortunately his patriotism, or perhaps simply his satisfaction in becoming an official painter, led him astray. He began to produce paintings and illustrations which glorified Frederick the

Great and his reign, and which are of a finicking triviality for all their technical skill.

Two painters of that period returned to the classical tradition, seeking inspiration in Raphael, in the sixteenth-century Venetians, and in ancient art. These were Anselm Feuerbach (1829–1880) and Hans von Marées (1837–1887). We may also mention Böcklin here, since we can scarcely distinguish between the Swiss and German schools in this book. Feuerbach studied in Paris under Couture, who gave him a thorough grounding. Cultivated and intelligent, he seemed to have the makings of a fine painter. Unfortunately, he wanted to create a poetic kind of painting, with an intellectual appeal, while he lacked the necessary visionary gifts to treat his bookish subjects. As a result, his large canvases (*Hafiz* in the Mannheim Municipal Art Gallery, *Iphigenia* in the Stuttgart Museum of Fine Arts, and *Plato's Symposium* in the Karlsruhe Art Gallery), instead of being evocations of the past, are like *tableaux vivants* or arrangements of wax figures. It must be noted that his canvases have blackened badly, probably because of poorly mixed colors.

LOVIS CORINTH · *Vase of Mixed Flowers*
Art Gallery, Bremen

GEORGES SEURAT · *The Bathers*
Tate Gallery, London

Hans von Marées aimed at a formal simplicity comparable to that of classical art, and assigned color a secondary place. He lacked the will power necessary to carry out his ideas, and would work his canvases over and over without ever completing them. For this reason, his best works are his murals in the Naples Aquarium, because the fresco technique made it impossible for him to go on indefinitely changing his mind. Von Marées was evidently the victim of some demon of indecision and disquiet who tempted him to make perpetual fresh starts, and to set himself so high a goal that he used up all his energies en route. This conclusion is suggested by his large canvases *The Ages of Life* and *The Judgment of Paris* in the State Museums, Berlin-Dahlem, and the triptych *Hesperides* in the New Pinakothek, Munich.

Franz von Lenbach (1836–1904) was the complete opposite of Marées. Commissioned to copy old masters, he displayed prodigious skill and acquired an amazing virtuosity in the process. He then turned to painting portraits of the most eminent figures in the Germany of his time, as well as the international set. His portraits were at once flattering and lifelike, and recall those of the sixteenth- and seventeenth-century masters.

The reaction against this theatrical romanticism was led by Max Liebermann (1847–1935), who went to Paris and discovered Impressionism. Gifted with a flexible mind, he shook off the unfortunate early influences to which he had been subjected–Munkacsy and Israëls–and painted outdoor scenes and landscapes in which he sought to render effects of light and movement by fluent drawing rather than to exalt color (*Die Gänserupferinnen* in the State Museums, Berlin-Dahlem, *Die Netzflickerinnen* in the Hamburg Museum, *The Beer Garden* in the Musée d'Art Moderne in Paris).

Like Böcklin and Hans Thoma, Lovis Corinth (1858–1925) set out to put new life into mythological and religious themes, but painted them with so much brutal realism and such extreme virtuosity that his pictures fail to convince. There is a good deal more delicacy and sense of color in portraits of actors painted by Max Slevogt (1868–1932), who also left illustrations that prove him to have been a brilliant and inventive draftsman.

When Fritz von Uhde (1848–1911) showed his pictures of Gospel scenes translated into terms of contemporary life, it was thought that they would lead to a revival of religious art. But for that, the artist would have needed greater gifts than he possessed.

VINCENT VAN GOGH · *Self-Portrait with the Bandaged Ear*
Mr. and Mrs. Leigh B. Block Collection, Chicago

VINCENT VAN GOGH · *Starry Night*
Museum of Modern Art, New York

POINTILLISM

Georges Seurat (1859–1891), who had a systematic mind, set himself the task of giving Impressionism a scientific foundation. He studied the writings of Chevreul, Helmholtz, and Rood, physicists who had investigated the properties of color, and decided that their books provided a basis for painting with the precision of a mathematician. He executed a number of small landscape studies, from which he composed, at the age of twenty-five, a large canvas, *La Baignade* (Tate Gallery, London). This work already reveals a tendency to achieve luminosity and simplification. Seeking to get still more light and truer, more intense and more vibrant colors, he covered his canvas with little dots of color, selected and arranged according to the method he had evolved. Thanks to this method, based on the division of colors into their components and the way the eye blends them, he claimed to obtain color schemes that were much richer and scientifically more exact. Later he used the same method in some small paintings of the Channel ports (*Port-en-Bessin* in the Louvre) and in a few large canvases completed just before his death, notably *A Sunday Afternoon on the Island of La Grande Jatte* in the Art Institute of Chicago.

Seurat's mistake, however, was not that he had recourse to science, but that he failed to understand what it had to say. When physicists conduct experiments in color, they use colored light, whereas painters have to use pigments – in other words, colored matter. This means that the physicists' conclusions are not valid for painting. In fact, it is not the scientific aspect of Seurat's landscapes that makes them so good, but rather his own gifts as a painter: gifts which we find again in his Conté pencil drawings. These reduce the formal complexities of nature to a few large simplified shapes, and

show unusual exactness in their rendering of light and shade.

In basing himself on physicists' theories and thus giving Impressionism a pseudo-scientific character, Seurat was simply carrying the researches of the Impressionists a step further. Three other painters – Cézanne, Gauguin and Van Gogh – deliberately reacted against Impressionism, and should therefore be known as "Anti-Impressionists" rather than Post-Impressionists, as they are usually called. These men gave up trying to set down transient effects of light and stopped working exclusively from nature. They felt that a picture ought not to be simply the product of the artist's instinctive reactions when faced with the subject, but something meditated, thought out, and organized in advance.

POST-IMPRESSIONISM

We have already discussed Cézanne's aims, and his success in carrying them out. As for Vincent van Gogh (1853–1890), his life was such a tragedy as to have become symbolic; moreover, it had a profound effect on his art. Born in a small Dutch village, of which his father was the pastor, Van Gogh early revealed himself of a tormented, shut-in character, condemned to solitude by his inability to make contact easily with those around him. As a young man he worked for a firm of art dealers, but a disappointment in love disturbed him, and at twenty-three he decided to become a minister. Sent to work among the miners of the Borinage in Belgium, he devoted himself to them with admirable self-denial, but was eventually asked to leave. Thereupon, at the age of twenty-six, he realized that painting was his true vocation. His brother Theo then came to his assistance, but he was still obliged to live in great poverty in the little Brabant village of Nuenen, where he painted coarse and crudely executed scenes of peasant life, using nothing but browns and blacks (*The Potato-Eaters*, in the collection of V. W. van Gogh, Amsterdam). When he moved to Antwerp, he discovered Japanese prints and adopted a more colorful palette. From there he moved to Paris, where he was captivated by the work of the Impressionists, and met Gauguin and Seurat. His technique became freer; his colors, which he applied with streaky brush strokes, grew fresher and more vibrant (*View of Montmartre* in the Stedelijk Museum, Amsterdam). Impelled by an intense need for sunshine he next settled at Arles in Provence, a region he looked forward to as resembling Japan, of whose prints he had grown so fond. He found Arles so pleasant that he persuaded Gauguin to come and join him there, but the two men were too unlike in temperament to avoid a clash. After a violent quarrel Van Gogh, who had intended to assault Gauguin, cut off his own right ear and gave it to the porter of a brothel. As a result, he was sent to an insane asylum near Saint-Rémy. There, and later at Auvers-sur-Oise, where his brother had him committed, he suffered from recurrent attacks of insanity. On the evening of July 27, 1890, he shot himself. He died two days later.

Like Gauguin, Van Gogh took some time before he found himself, and his individuality did not assert itself until he went to Arles. His most representative works were all created in the two and a half years that followed. The paintings he had done at Nuenen could be the work of some frenzied Millet, obsessed with coarseness and squalor. In Paris, he had tried to emulate the clarity and freshness of Monet and Seurat. At Arles he began to express the violent feelings aroused in him by his subject matter: landscape, flowers, the human face. He painted what he felt, as much as what he saw; he interpreted nature in his own way, straining his means of expression to render the

full intensity of his emotions. That Van Gogh painted expressions of his own feelings rather than images of what he saw is proved by his firm belief that the Provençal landscape was exactly like that of Japan. Actually, the Arles region is dry, dusty, baked by the sun, and dotted with dark-leaved trees, whereas Japan, with a maritime climate like England's, has thick, bright green vegetation, due to the rain and the mist which are common there.

Painted with the simplest and most personal means – the forms clearly outlined, color emphasized to the limit, the third dimension played down – Van Gogh's canvases grip us by their extremism and by their hallucinatory quality. He was not content to convey what he saw; he was trying to let us into the torments of his soul, as madness gradually gained possession of it; witness his *Self-Portrait* in the Art Institute of Chicago, the *Entrance to the Public Gardens, Arles* in the Phillips Collection, Washington, the *Starry Night* in the Museum of Modern Art, New York, or *The Night Café* in the collection of Stephen C. Clark, New York. In his last works he used spirals and wavy brush strokes to convey the storms raging within him. His madness served him as a double-edged weapon. It released and stimulated his artistic gifts, for without it he would probably have been nothing but the conscientious employee of an art dealer. But if it saved him from a boring, banal existence, it did so only to gain fuller domination over this man who, as he put it in one of his admirable letters, "had a bent for greatness."

To understand the art of Paul Gauguin (1848–1903) and the development which it underwent, it is indispensable to know the chief incidents of his life. As a young man, he was a well-paid employee of a Paris broker, and painted in his leisure time. At the age of thirty-five he gave up his job to devote himself entirely to painting. Life became extremely difficult for him and his family. His Danish wife returned to her own country with the children; Gauguin himself, after working for a time under Pissarro's guidance, went to Brittany. After a visit to Martinique he returned to Brittany, where he met Emile Bernard, a young painter, thanks to whose ideas and works he gained clearer awareness of his own capacities and aims. After that, Gauguin was invited by Van Gogh to join him at Arles. But soon the two artists quarreled, as we have mentioned before. Gauguin, then

forty-three, left for Tahiti, where he stayed two years and then returned to France. After about eighteen months he went back to Tahiti, where he died eight years later.

Gauguin needed time to discover what he wanted to do. His early landscapes done in Brittany show Pissarro's influence; they are in the Impressionist style, and rather unskillful. Then, influenced by Emile Bernard, he began to paint works in which extremely simplified forms were enclosed in heavy outlines. Two of these are typical of his manner before he left for the South Seas: *The Yellow Christ*

PAUL GAUGUIN · *What! Are You Jealous?*
Pushkin Museum, Moscow

HENRI DE TOULOUSE-LAUTREC · *Jane Avril Dancing*
Louvre, Paris

MARY CASSATT · *Young Seamstress*
Louvre, Paris

in the Albright Art Gallery, Buffalo, and *Jacob and the Angel* in the National Galleries of Scotland, Edinburgh. Right up to the time when he left for Tahiti, he was feeling his way, following now Pissarro, now Emile Bernard, now Van Gogh, and even employing conflicting methods in one and the same canvas. By contrast, the moment he began to paint in Tahiti, his hesitations fell away, and he knew what he wanted. Whatever he saw and felt he could now render with astonishing sureness and ease. In these canvases, with their simplified forms and broad, flat areas of bright color, he seems like some exotic Poussin: a Poussin who, instead of drawing inspiration from classical sculpture, has turned to primitive idols in the hope of discovering the secret of their hieratic gravity. His Tahiti canvases are like tapestries, full of purely decorative effects, and in them the artist has not tried to represent the third dimension. They are also like stained-

glass windows, the forms defined with black outlines, and the intense colors chosen not because they reproduce natural appearances, but to serve as the elements of a brilliant mosaic. Tahiti did not turn out to be the paradise Gauguin had looked for, and in his letters he often complained about his living conditions. But his works do not reflect this disappointment: the Tahiti he evoked, with the sureness and mastery which he now possessed at last, was the Tahiti of his dreams. This nostalgia for a paradisiac life among primitive peoples – this feeling that is so strong among civilized men, and that has given us so many pastoral idylls – has never been more compellingly expressed than by Gauguin in such works as *Queen of the Arrois* in W. S. Paley's Collection, Manhasset, or *The Spirit of the Dead Watches* in the A. Conger Goodyear Collection, New York.

Degas's influence was not directly felt in his lifetime: his only disciples were the American Mary Cassatt (1845–1926), and the English painter Walter Sickert, who preferred Degas to the academic traditions of his own country. There was,

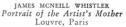

JAMES MCNEILL WHISTLER
Portrait of the Artist's Mother
Louvre, Paris

however, one painter, Henri de Toulouse-Lautrec (1864–1901), who treated analogous subjects and recognized his debt to the older artist.

Scion of a very old Languedoc family, Toulouse-Lautrec was crippled at an early age, and illness and drink shortened his life. A remarkably keen observer, he portrayed with a mixture of cruelty and tenderness the people of the Montmartre milieu – the habitués of cafés, dancers, and prostitutes. He usually painted on plain cardboard, to obtain the mat colors he liked: his fluent and nervous line owes a great deal to the Japanese woodcut, which was fashionable at the time. Despite the nature of his subjects he is never obscene or vulgar; and his work has a natural distinction, truthfully recording the shady world in which he had chosen to live. He did not moralize or denounce vice, for he felt that his task, which he enjoyed, was to describe what he saw in the most lifelike and forceful way. In this he succeeded, and his evidence is all the more convincing because he is a subtle and individual colorist. Good examples of his work are *Jane Avril Dancing* in the Louvre; *Waltzers at the Moulin Rouge* in the Modern Art Gallery in Prague; and *Monsieur Boileau in a Café* in the Cleveland Museum of Art.

OUTSIDE THE SCHOOLS

James McNeill Whistler (1834–1904) was an American, born at Lowell, Massachusetts. As a young man he lived in France, but he made his career in England. In Paris he led a bohemian existence, working little; his earliest canvases (e.g., *At the Piano*) show the influence of Courbet, whom he knew. Later on he developed a passion for Japanese woodcuts and painted small landscapes, most of them night scenes, e.g., *Battersea Bridge* in the Tate Gallery, London, obviously inspired by Japanese art. Al-

ODILON REDON · *The Red Thorns*
Fayet Collection, Arles

though he was friendly with the Pre-Raphaelites when he first went to England, he soon turned against them. Reflecting the ideas he had absorbed in Paris, he scorned literary subjects, and declared that the only thing that mattered was pictorial qualities. His work is uneven, and his technique is occasionally weak. He painted interesting portraits, the most famous of them being the *Portrait of the Artist's Mother* in the Louvre and *Carlyle* in the National Galleries of Scotland. The outstanding feature of his paintings is the artist's highly refined taste.

James Ensor (1860–1949) started out as a vigorous realist, who painted in heavy impastos (*The Lamp Boy* in the Musées Royaux des Beaux-Arts, Brussels). But paintings such as *Russian Music* (Brussels) and *Lady in Distress* (Musée d'Art Moderne, Paris) are more than exact representations of reality. However much the artist tried to exclude every suggestion of literature, his interiors with their soft light and delicate subdued colors have a strange, mysterious, poetic quality. Gradually he developed a free style, as can be seen from the *Woman Eating Oysters* (Musée Royal des Beaux-Arts, Antwerp) with its iridescent harmonies. He began to give free rein to his lively imagination, which combined the macabre and the farcical, the satirical and the fantastic. Ensor now painted human beings only to ridicule them, to reveal their ugliness and stupidity, representing them as skeletons or masks.

Ensor's early interiors anticipated Vuillard and Bonnard. Later, his bold color and free line anticipated Fauvism and Expressionism. He and Hodler are the only non-French artists of their generation to have created a powerful and original art.

Ferdinand Hodler (1853–1918) was born in Bern. At an early age he went to Geneva, where he spent the rest of his life. He had the good fortune of having been discovered and taught by Barthélémy Menn. His early works, which portray the humble people among whom he lived, reveal various influences, a rigorous draftsmanship in his clearly outlined forms,

JAMES ENSOR · *Self-Portrait in a Flowered Hat*
Musées Royaux des Beaux-Arts, Brussels

but no feeling for beauty. Gradually he evolved a very different style: while continuing to render form with rigorous precision, he began to treat historical and symbolical subjects, largely eliminating depth to achieve an essentially decorative painting.

Another artist who followed an independ-

FERDINAND HODLER · *Night*
Art Museum, Bern

ent path was Odilon Redon (1840–1916), whose art owes nothing either to the Impressionists or to the Anti-Impressionists, let alone to academicism. Like Gustave Moreau he shut himself away in a private world of dreams; but unlike Moreau, he did not seek his inspiration in the old masters, and developed a pictorial idiom of his own. Redon had several teachers, but he was dissatisfied by them. Then, deciding that everything could be expressed with black and white, he began to make charcoal drawings, and then lithographs. Taking his subjects from literature or embodying the visions that haunted his imagination, he conjured up fantastic creatures and strangely unreal scenes. Only a small number of writers and young artists appreciated his work. It was not until after he was fifty that he took up color. He painted flowers, and mythological and religious subjects, both in pastel and in oil, e.g., *The Cyclone* (Kröller-Müller State Museum, Otterlo, Holland) and *Anemones in a Vase* (Mrs. Irving H. Vogel Collection, Philadelphia).

VIII

TRENDS IN MODERN PAINTING

The twentieth century marks the advent of a truly new era in painting. To begin with, the visual arts have acquired a universal character. In former periods, individual artists and schools of painting came into contact and influenced each other only sporadically. By chance an artist might find himself confronted with the works of another artist, whose background and talent might be like or unlike his own; or else a government or academy might send an artist to a particular school or master thought to be exemplary. In the twentieth century, however, thanks to ease of communication, superior reproductions, the spread of literacy, and the mass production of books, artistic influences are no longer determined by policy or chance. Art is no longer boxed in by more or less natural frontiers; the oldest and the newest paintings alike are familiar to all. Among the peoples of Europe, exchanges have become the rule. Works reflecting a specific movement are more closely linked to that movement than to the country in which they were produced. Most often we do not refer to a given work as "Norwegian" or "Peruvian" but rather as "Expressionist," "nonfigurative," etc.

That is the first point: art has become an international phenomenon.

At the same time the artists, encouraged and stimulated by the works of their contemporaries and by the publications of writers on art, carry on their explorations with a boldness previously unknown. And that is the second characteristic innovation of this century: daring no longer has any bounds.

Finally, painting has become the object of passionate intellectual debates. Whatever we may think of this development, there has surely never been anything like it, even at the time of the Renaissance. The "social" aspect of the visual arts has changed at least as radically as the climate in which they used to thrive. So the last point is: the increased influence of ideas and social developments on painting.

THE "SCHOOL OF PARIS"

In the years prior to the First World War, Paris was the birthplace of many new schools which, like Fauvism or Cubism, were quick to influence artists all over the world. Young painters eager to familiarize themselves with modern

PABLO PICASSO · *Woman of Majorca*
Pushkin Museum, Moscow ▷

trends flocked to Paris from everywhere. Some of them simply stayed there for a time and then went back home to spread the new gospel. Others became attracted by the artistic life of Montparnasse or Montmartre, settled in Paris, and swelled the ranks of the so-called "École de Paris"—a term that is misleading in that it serves to denote a number of movements and authentic "schools" of painting which are very different from each other.

Certain other developments symptomatic of the new trends aroused little attention at the time. About 1911, the Russian Kandinsky, who had settled in Germany, painted his first nonfigurative works. About 1917, the Dutch painter Mondrian began to apply certain theories he had worked out, which led him to an art entirely abstracted from reality. At the same time a group of German refugees in Zurich founded Dadaism, a literary school whose program was brought to Paris by the Rumanian Tristan Tzara. A few years later, it gave birth to Surrealism, a movement which had repercussions within both literature and art. Finally, about 1918, there appeared the first important works by Paul Klee, who rejected all representational elements, and created a personal world of his own.

During these years so many artists were formulating new theories and advancing new conceptions of painting, that those we have just mentioned made little impression when they appeared. No one could foresee that they would become so influential by the middle of the century, or give rise to a nonfigurative art that would take on such tremendous importance as to gain adherents all over the world.

Let us go back for a moment. In France, Impressionists had gained recognition around 1890, and they had influenced more or less strongly a large number of artists. However, as we have seen, some

of their successors tried either, like Seurat, to carry the Impressionist experiments a stage further, or else to initiate a countermovement based on entirely different principles. Cézanne proposed to depict nature, taking Poussin and the sixteenth-century Venetians as his guides; Gauguin restricted himself to the most brilliant colors, and sought to create an equivalent of nature rather than to reproduce it. Van Gogh used nature simply as a vehicle to express his inner world. By the example of the two last-named, therefore, the painter was now free both in his selection of the elements which may go to make up his picture and in his choice of means. The traditional relationship between the artist and nature, which earlier schools of painting kept within certain fixed limits, was now a much looser one. The first half of the twentieth century saw the factor "artist" gradually assuming greater and greater importance, at the expense of the factor "nature."

Other characteristics appeared at the same time: increasing emphasis on originality, with a concomitant urge to exaggerate, particularly in the area of color. "Do that tree's leaves look green to you?" asked Gauguin one day of one of his disciples in Brittany. "Then paint your canvas with the most beautiful green in your palette." A large number of artists followed Gauguin's advice.

Overindulgence in color was to lead to overindulgence in form, sometimes exaggerated to the point of caricature, out of pursuit of expression and contempt for conventional beauty. The urge to capture the physical beauty of the human species which, from the Greeks to Renoir, had been one of the artist's prime concerns now completely disappeared.

The same period saw a great proliferation of theories. It was not enough to paint pictures; they also had to express a theory that justified them. It was now taken for granted that the chief interest and value of a picture lay in its plastic qualities. The subject became secondary.

The chief influences within painting immediately after 1900 were Cézanne, Gauguin, Van Gogh, Toulouse-Lautrec, and, a little later, African sculpture. The old masters who were most admired were principally the unique figures, such as El Greco, Bosch, and Grünewald.

At the same time, the attitude of the public and the state toward so-called "avant-garde" art changed radically. Before 1914, the public rejected it utterly, and would go to the Indépendants and the Salon d'Automne only to laugh at the exhibits. The State, for its part, favored academic artists.

Thanks to the critics and the theoreticians, the situation was very much changed after 1918. The public showed an increasing taste for the kind of painting that it had spurned only a few years before, and the State began to encourage the artists it had previously ignored.

MAURICE DENIS · *The Muses*
Musée d'Art Moderne, Paris

THE NABIS

In the autumn of 1888 a young painter, Paul Sérusier (1865–1927), on returning

ÉDOUARD VUILLARD · *Breakfast*
Musée d'Art Moderne, Paris

from Brittany showed his friends at the Atelier Julian a small landscape which he had painted under Gauguin's direction. At first, they scoffed at this landscape, which was made up entirely of spots of intense color; but they were gradually won over, and began themselves to apply Gauguin's theories as Sérusier had explained them. For purposes of discussion they banded together and called themselves "Nabis": a Hebrew word meaning "the initiates." The most interesting Nabis were Edouard Vuillard (1868–1940), Pierre Bonnard (1867–1947), Maurice Denis (1870–1943), and Ker-Xavier Roussel (1867–1944). The Swiss artist Félix Vallotton (1865–1927) was not a member of the group, but later associated with these artists, and often exhibited with them. The Hungarian József Rippl-Rónai is also related to this group.

Along with Gauguin, the Nabis discovered Cézanne, Toulouse-Lautrec, and the

PIERRE BONNARD · *The Port of Trouville*
Musée d'Art Moderne, Paris

Japanese prints. Such influences led them in their earliest works to render forms by flowing lines rather than by modeling, to suggest rather than represent the third dimension; and to aim in their paintings primarily at happy arrangements of spots of color.

After painting like this in splashes, as may be seen in a number of large decorative panels in distemper commissioned by private patrons, Vuillard created interiors in which he laid greater stress on the rendering of space and faithfully recorded the changes effected by light in colors, whether artificial or natural light. In other words, Vuillard in his own way was extending the researches of the Impressionists, but employing less brilliant colors. There is an affinity between his interiors and the pastels of Degas which show women at their toilet. Vuillard also produced portraits and views of Paris of incomparable pictorial excellence.

Pierre Bonnard's first works were paintings in which he showed his fondness for Japanese prints and tried to set down the scenes which he saw every day. Next he painted figures in indoor settings, aiming solely at accurate transcriptions of tonal relationships and using a range of extremely subtle grays. Later, he divided his time between the Paris region and Provence, and landscape began to play an increasingly important part in his work. With this he began to use more and more brilliant colors, and seemed to be following the Impressionists in the special attention which he gave to the play of natural and artificial light on objects. But he was an Impressionist who took the utmost liberties with respect to both form and color, and he did not hesitate to stress color sensations when he thought it necessary. Debussy once said of Moussorgsky that he seemed always to be discovering music for the first time. In the same way Bonnard, the least doctrinaire of artists, seems in every canvas to be discovering painting and the natural world all over again. Everything he saw enchanted him, and he hastened to immortalize its beauty. He treated nature like a mistress; a mistress whose whims are not always obeyed, but who cannot be dispensed with, because she is profoundly loved.

Maurice Denis, when still quite young, painted pictures of a studied but charming simplicity in which we find the swirling forms and flat surfaces of Gauguin; subsequently he was influenced by Poussin and by Fra Angelico. He treated religious and mythological scenes, and incidents from everyday life, stripped of all naturalism. This refined and eclectic art seemed to mark out Maurice Denis as the painter who could reconcile tradition with modern tendencies; and it is true that between 1893 and 1916 he executed a number of large murals in this spirit for churches and for private individuals. At the age of forty, however, he realized that for all his intelligence and culture he was repeating himself and producing lifeless conventional works. In an effort to "organize his feelings," as he put it, he had reduced his art to a set of formulas, which had failed to be renewed and rejuvenated by fresh contact with nature.

Born in Lausanne, Félix Vallotton went to Paris at the age of seventeen, and in 1900 claimed French citizenship, to which he was entitled because his ancestors had emigrated to Switzerland for religious reasons. In his early works, this highly conscientious and thoroughly grounded painter sought to be truthful rather than brilliant, and his rigid technique lacked personality. Then, on encountering the art of Bernard and Vuillard, he dabbled in the Japanese style for a time. Eventually, at about the age of forty, he adopted the style which he was to keep for the rest of his life.

He was quite indifferent to the fact that his work was utterly unlike anything done around him. He painted figures, landscapes, and still lifes with a very neat technique, which, though seemingly in conformity with commonplace vision, are profoundly original. As he was not interested either in pleasing the public or in shocking it, his reputation has increased over the years.

The theories on which Seurat had founded Neo-Impressionism were subsequently taken up and spread by his disciple Paul Signac (1863–1935), who up to his death painted views of sea ports, made up of a mosaic of little squares of brilliant color. A few other artists, such as Henri Cross (1856–1910) and Claude Emile Schuffenecker (1851–1934), took up this method of painting, but it fell into disuse after their disappearance from the scene.

A TURNING POINT:
THE STUDIO OF GUSTAVE MOREAU

In the last years of the nineteenth century many young students at the École des Beaux-Arts had chosen to take classes with Gustave Moreau, because they rightly regarded him as the least academic and most broadminded member of the staff.

Several of his pupils subsequently became well known.

Georges Desvallières (1861–1950) took time to discover his proper bent. A fervent Catholic, he proclaimed his faith in paintings characterized by their tortuous line and stirring expression. Charles Guérin (1874–1939) made his mark as early as 1895 with figures, still lifes, and *scènes galantes,* which were influenced by Cézanne. After the First World War, his work grew more ponderous. Albert Marquet (1875–1947) painted several good figurative works in a straightforward naturalistic style; but he was above all a landscape painter who painted ports and river scenes with exceptional faithfulness, eliminating all inessential elements. Georges Rouault, too, was a pupil of Gustave Moreau's, but we shall discuss him later when dealing with French Expressionism.

There is another pupil of Moreau's whose personality is not easily summed up in a few lines: Henri Matisse (1869–1954). This artist continually reformulated the most fundamental problems of painting, and found new solutions for them. Between 1897 and 1905 he joined one contemporary school after another, carrying the ideas of each to their logical conclusion; he was successively an Impressionist, a follower of Cézanne, a Pointillist. In one respect he never changed: he wanted to express himself with the greatest economy of means, keeping only the essential elements of the forms which he distorted, and intensifying his colors. For him, a picture meant nothing more than an arrangement of arabesques and color relationships, with a minimum of representational reference, and no concern with expression as such. There are reasons to believe that around 1917–18

ALBERT MARQUET · *Rotterdam*
Musée d'Art Moderne, Paris

THE FAUVES

KEES VAN DONGEN · *Portrait of Anatole France*
Private collection, New York

At the Salon des Indépendants of 1906, the works of a few painters were grouped together in a room which the critic Vauxcelles christened "the cage of wild beasts" (*la cage aux fauves*). The name "Fauves" stuck, the painters in question being Henri Matisse, Raoul Dufy, Othon Friesz, Kees van Dongen, André Derain, and Maurice de Vlaminck. Vlaminck and André Derain, the two youngest, had set the ball rolling, and their elders had followed. Inspired by Gauguin and Van Gogh, the Fauves wanted to express themselves above all by means of color, using the most brilliant pigments, right from the tube, and putting them alongside one another without intermediate tones to mitigate the shrillness. Drawing was reduced to a mere matter of layout, and the treatment was summary.

The Fauves were never an organized group, clustered round a theory. Each of these very different artists followed a path of his own. They published no manifesto, and seemed to have only one thing

MAURICE DE VLAMINCK · *Poplars*
Musée d'Art Moderne, Paris

Matisse, whose art was carefully calculated and thought out, realized that his pursuit of simplification was impoverishing his painting. In the south of France, he painted a series of luminous, fresh canvases in which he came close to Impressionism: interiors, still lifes, landscapes, odalisques. It is sometimes held that these constitute the finest part of Matisse's work. Around 1935, he again began to cultivate the most extreme simplification, and his style was thereafter characterized by brightly colored flat areas, defined by black lines, and occasionally relieved by white furrows hollowed out in the wet paint.

HENRI MATISSE · *The Dance*
Hermitage, Leningrad

in common: the desire to react against Impressionism.

Within a few years, however, their reaction petered out. By limiting themselves to a perpetual fortissimo of color, the Fauves, as they very well knew, risked becoming monotonous.

We have already described Matisse's development after Fauvism; we shall now deal with that of the other Fauves. Raoul Dufy (1877–1953) for a time pursued experiments which showed him to be flirting now with Matisse, now with the Cubists. After 1918, however, he produced works in which he used a highly personal idiom and, without entirely cutting himself adrift from representation, treated nature rather cavalierly. Adopting

an exceptionally fluent line and bothering little about tonal values, modeling, or perspective, he painted gardens, fashionable beaches, race courses, and Norman and Provençal landscapes, all overflowing with *joie de vivre*. Whatever its subject, every canvas by him seemed to be celebrating some festive occasion, and it was indeed a feast for the eyes, so brilliant were his colors without ever being shrill, and so witty his line. With his nimbleness of technique and freshness of color, and his determination to portray only gay and carefree moments, Dufy seemed like a distant descendant of Boucher and Fragonard.

After abandoning Fauvism, Othon Friesz (1879–1949) at first painted canvases in

244

blue blacks and copper pinks taken over from Cézanne, combining incongruously classical drawing with the naïveté of popular prints. Later his portraits, landscapes, and nudes expressed a love of nature inspired by a warm-hearted romanticism.

The Dutchman Kees van Dongen (born in 1877) appointed himself painter to an elegant but somewhat flashy world of rich people. His big portraits compelled recognition by their qualities, but it was soon realized that some of their originality was superficial; they often suggest poster art rather than painting.

André Derain (1880–1954) went through a long period of hesitation before settling down to a definite style. After his Fauvist

experience he had a phase of Cézanne-like austerity and deliberate awkwardness. Then for a time he tried to combine faceted planes borrowed from the Cubists with a hieraticism derived from the Italians of the twelfth century, who painted in the Byzantine style. After his return from the First World War he surprised the public by repudiating all excess and by going back to a traditional way of seeing. The masters he chose were Corot and Cézanne for landscape, David and Manet for figures, and the seventeenth-century Dutch for still lifes. All this certainly makes a variegated mixture, and even though Derain did leave us one or two soundly constructed and soberly colored paintings, he does not seem to

RAOUL DUFY · *Riders in a Wood*
Musée d'Art Moderne, Paris

ANDRÉ DERAIN · *The Forest of Fontainebleau*
Musée d'Art Moderne, Paris

have completely freed himself from the influence of the old masters.

The career of Maurice de Vlaminck (1876–1958) falls into two stages. First, he was an ultra-aggressive Fauve, one of the wildest beasts in the cage. Then, about 1908, he saw that he could not roar any more loudly than he was already doing, and he moved toward a new kind of landscape, in which simplification is carried to the extreme: the wind bends black twisted trees, blowing across the snow, across muddy cart ruts, past low cottages of mournful aspect. This is the Vlaminck the public knows best; but such works must not make us forget his flower pieces, painted with great delicacy, almost lovingly. Future generations may well prefer them to the rest.

THE CUBISTS

Like "Fauve," the word "Cubist" was first a nickname, originating in a remark made by Matisse at the Salon d'Automne of 1908. The term caught on, but in course of time it proved inaccurate, for the Cubists evolved a conception of painting which made it unnecessary to convey depth, so that the cubes themselves disappeared.

In 1906 a young painter from Catalonia, Pablo Picasso (born in 1881), settled in Montmartre. He had been a child prodigy, who had as early as 1900–01 become known in Paris for paintings portraying Montmartre life, race courses, and prostitutes. In 1901 he gave up this kind of romanticism à la Lautrec, and painted melancholy, half-starved men and women, down-and-out acrobats, and strolling players, using a deliberately restricted color scheme. About 1903 he was painting figures and still lifes in browns and russets, with thick black lines defining the forms. The culmination of these experiments was a large painting which he executed in 1906–07, *Les Demoiselles d'Avignon:* this work was a deliberately impertinent act, which seems to have been dictated by some inner crisis.

A year later, in 1908, the young French painter Georges Braque (1882–1963), who had been one of the Fauves, exhibited with the Kahnweiler Gallery a number of landscapes which had been strongly influenced by Cézanne. The various elements within each picture were simplified to the utmost, and formed an imbricated

PABLO PICASSO · *The Violin*
Musée d'Art Moderne, Paris

pattern like tiles on a roof. We find the same influence of Cézanne in paintings executed by Picasso in 1908–09.

Clearly, just as two men walking along different roads will meet where the roads cross, so Picasso and Braque were brought together by their separate explorations. It is pointless to ask which of the two actually invented Cubism.

Neither Braque nor Picasso started out as Seurat had done, with a long-pondered theory. Like the Impressionists, they simply made their own experiments, and every experiment led to another. Apart from a few aphorisms (or wisecracks) which were published long after, they were careful not to define what it was that led them to create Cubism. For an explanation of Cubism we must therefore address ourselves to the writers who championed their cause – Guillaume Apollinaire, Maurice Raynal, Daniel-Henri (the pen name of Kahnweiler, the art dealer), and Léonce Rosenberg – or else to other painters, such as Juan Gris, Jacques Villon, Albert Gleizes, and Jean Metzinger, who actually formulated theories of Cubism.

According to Apollinaire, art was in the future to set itself "the disinterested task of scientifically examining the whole extent of its own field, with no aesthetic aims in mind," in order, as he put it, to "find its way toward an entirely new art, one which would be in relation to painting, as hitherto conceived, what music is to literature." Or, to turn to Maurice Raynal, "the work of art is not merely an object but a *fact,* concentrated, condensed, rather like an actual *word.*" According to Kahnweiler, the Cubists wanted to convey "the *essence,* not the *appearance* of things." Having achieved complete autonomy, the painter's work would become a "pictorial object." Léonce Rosenberg held that all the senses give us is a "lie," and that the Cubists wanted to "give their forms the dimen-

JUAN GRIS · *Pierrot*
Musée d'Art Moderne, Paris

sions of the *Idea,* not those of the visual."

Now let us turn to the painters themselves. "Cézanne made a bottle into a cylinder," said Juan Gris; "I start with a cylinder in order to create an individual of a specific type. I make a cylinder into a bottle, a particular bottle." For Jacques Villon "the whole of the canvas is divisible into colored pyramids marking different points of the subject, points that are closely enough related for the subject to be reconstituted by dovetailing the pyramids." Finally, Gleizes and Metzinger held that "the idea of figuring the weight of bodies and the time spent enumerat-

247

GEORGES BRAQUE · *The Guitar Player*
Museum of Art, Basel

ing their various aspects is just as legitimate as that of imitating daylight by the clash between orange and blue." They defined Cubism as "a movement which aims at the complete realization of painting."

In short, the Cubists set out to break down forms into their elements and then to reassemble them in an arbitrary way, ignoring how they appear to our eyes or how we imagine them, aiming at the creation of works capable of standing as "pictorial objects" in their own right. Accordingly the Cubists refused either to follow the rules of perspective or to reproduce colors as they appear in three-dimensional space and light. The first step they took was to reduce colors to grays and browns.

At first Cubism was a trend rather than a school, but it was profoundly modified as a result of spontaneous developments and outside influences. Most critics therefore divided it into several periods, and in this they are more accurate than the painters themselves.

From its origin (1907) to 1911, Cubism concentrated on breaking down forms into their component parts and rearranging them according to geometrical patterns. This is the analytical period. But from 1910 on, we find the summarily blocked-in forms yielding to a play of tiny angular planes bounded by straight lines or curves. Even shading serves less to suggest volume than to exploit modeling for geometrical purposes. The austere color scheme is still kept down to grays, browns, and ochers. After 1911, the titles of pictures no longer provide clues to a content which has now become totally hermetic.

Thus, from 1911 to 1914 the Cubist painters, guided by the theoreticians, were trying to put into paint what they had seen within themselves. This is the synthetic period.

It was then that Braque and Picasso began to include stenciled letters and numerals in their pictures, and to paste on the canvas fragments of paper, newspaper, labels, playing-cards, or paper imitations of wood and marble. From this they went on in certain pictures to imitate the grain of wood and the veins of marble, using mixtures of paint and sand. Gradually brilliant colors began to make their appearance, although the basic scheme remained low in key. This is the period that can be characterized as "magical."

Meanwhile the Cubists, whose negation of all rules had helped many artists to find their individual paths, gradually ceased to exist as a group, and extended their influence over a large number of younger painters.

Some, like Dunoyer de Segonzac, Luc Albert Moreau, and Jean Louis Boussingault, took over from Cubism only its emphasis upon conveying essential volumes, and confined themselves to a palette of browns, ochers, and dull greens. Roger de la Fresnaye and André Lhote adopted certain Cubist conventions, but refused to give up representation and to become hermetic. Unlike them, Jean Metzinger (1883–1956) and Albert Gleizes (1881–1955) became thorough converts to Cubism, as did also the Spaniard Juan Gris (1887–1927), who applied its priniciples in a most uncompromising way, and the Polish painter Louis Markous, known as Marcoussis (1883–1941). Fernand Léger translated nature into an arrangement of cylinders. He returned to representational art after 1914, but confined himself to broad black outlines and flat planes of brilliant color.

Roger de la Fresnaye (1885–1925) made a remarkable debut. Without being completely won over to Cubism, he had adopted its simplified forms and its tendency to reduce them to geometrical figures. In the large canvases which he painted before the First World War, there was a happy balance between sensitivity and intelligence, unusual clarity and in-

fallible taste. But La Fresnaye contracted tuberculosis in the trenches and had to go to live at Grasse; badly handicapped by his illness, he could not undertake any prolonged work. For his last seven years his output was uneven, and betrayed his gnawing anxieties.

André Lhote (1885–1962) painted a large number of canvases of pleasing color and design. He wanted to reconcile traditional painting with Cubism, and was equipped to do so by a wide culture and a lively intelligence. Posterity will decide whether he achieved his aim. Jacques Villon, whose real name is Gaston Duchamp (1875–1963), did not begin to paint

JACQUES VILLON · *The Bridge at Beaugency*
Louis Carré Collection, Paris

ANDRÉ DUNOYER DE SEGONZAC · *Bacchus*
Musée d'Art Moderne, Paris

seriously until 1907. Starting from the principles laid down in Leonardo's notebooks, he aimed, according to his biographer Jerome Mellquist, "to divide up his canvas by lines based on certain fixed points, thus splitting it into small surfaces, all of them subordinated to ideal proportions." He used to discuss those "ideal proportions" with his friends. At first he

ROGER DE LA FRESNAYE · *The Fourteenth of July*
Musée d'Art Moderne, Paris

used only dull colors; more recently he has shifted to light, gentle harmonies of pinks, blues, and sulphur yellows.

It is difficult to classify Robert Delaunay (1885–1941). Certain of his experiments are related to those of the Cubists, although he disapproved of them. Guillaume Apollinaire saw him as one of the leaders of "Orphic Cubism." Actually, Robert Delaunay was a forerunner of nonfigura-

ROBERT DELAUNAY · *The Towers
of Laon Cathedral*
Musée d'Art Moderne, Paris

tive painting: starting from a far-reaching simplification of form and glorification of color, he came to paint canvases that were nothing but brilliantly colored arrangements of circles and curves.

Although he made a number of often-quoted pronouncements about Cubism, Juan Gris (1887–1927) was not a doctrinaire. He was above all a painter, and his painting was animated by a search for style and a spark of inspiration that is particularly evident in his sets for the Russian ballet (1922–23). Short as his life was, he was one of the founders of synthetic Cubism. He may be regarded as one of the purest of all the Cubists. "When the French were called to the colors in 1914," Picasso told Kahnweiler, "I took Braque and Derain to the station at Avignon. Since then we have never come together again."

It is curious that Braque and Picasso should have parted company after creating a new school of painting, and after working along the same lines for six years. Whatever the explanation, the day

FERNAND LÉGER · *Still Life with Keys*
Musée d'Art Moderne, Paris

ANDRÉ LHOTE · *Portrait, Front View and Profile*
Musée d'Art Moderne, Paris

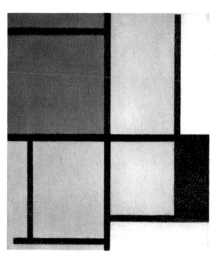

PIET MONDRIAN · *Composition*
Museum of Art, Basel

of pure Cubism was over. Some painters remained faithful to it; others came under its influence who had ignored it before. But after the war both Picasso and Braque underwent extensive personal evolutions. Between 1917 and 1920 Picasso painted a few canvases that were still strictly Cubist, together with others that were not Cubist at all. Around 1920, as though unconsciously influenced by ancient art, he painted several classical-type figures with distorted bodies. From 1923 down to the present day, he has allowed himself complete freedom; whatever figure or object he has depicted, he has first taken apart and then reassembled as he chose. At the same time, he has used brilliant colors and heavy black outlines. He has even applied such methods in the series "interpretating" Delacroix's *Femmes d'Alger* and Courbet's *Demoiselles des bords de la Seine*. The truth is that when we follow his achievement closely, in such an exhaustive monograph as that by the late Antonina Vallentin, we realize that it is impossible to foresee the continual metamorphoses of this Proteus of painting, or even to describe them within the limits of a book like this one. We are incidentally quite justified in applying this mythological epithet to Picasso, for he himself has become a figure of a myth. To the general public today, the whole of modern painting is summed up in his name.

Braque, for his part, between 1917 and 1919 gradually shifted from his prewar Cubism to an entirely new style, revealing himself as a highly subtle colorist. Previously he had kept to a range of subdued colors – browns, dull or yellowy greens, creamy whites, and lemon yellows. After 1929 be began to use brighter tones – violets, vermilions, and blues. Most often, his experiments have taken the form of still lifes; only occasionally has he painted beach scenes or figures in a room, in which the human form is treated with the utmost freedom.

Picasso and Braque were the most influential masters in the years between the two wars. The liberties they took with nature encouraged many young artists to follow their example. As we said before, it was increasingly felt that the painter's essential task was to emancipate himself from natural appearances and give up representation. Some artists, however, refused to break with a centuries-old tradition that had produced so many admirable works.

NEO-PLASTICISM AND SUPREMATISM

In 1917 Piet Mondrian (1872–1944) and Theo van Doesburg (1883–1931) – the latter an architect, sculptor, and writer as well as a painter – founded a group and a magazine both called *De Stijl* (Style). In this publication they expounded the principles of a new art. It was their ambition to create an art as rigorous and impersonal as a science. More radical than the Fauves and the Cubists, they cut the last of the links between art and nature, refusing to draw on the latter in any way, even for an initial impulse. As Mondrian put it: "It is the great strength of Neo-Plastic painting that it has proved in plastic terms the necessity of proof." Mondrian himself discarded all personal elements of style by excluding all colors other than the three primary colors (blue, red, and yellow) plus black and white. He also excluded diagonals and curves. His paintings are made up of rectangular colored areas bounded by heavy black lines. By these means he wanted to create an impersonal and "logical" art – for he saw art as "the concretization of logic" – and so to arrive at an expression of the universal.

Van der Leck and Vantongerloo followed the same principles.

In this survey of artistic movements, we must not leave out Suprematism, even though its history is that of a single painter, Casimir Malevitch (1878–1935), who was its inventor and godfather. Suprematism (for the layman) derives from a strictly applied Cubism, and its pictures are made up of geometric forms, the most famous being that of a white square on a white ground in the Museum of Modern Art in New York. According to Malevitch, the aesthetic should lead to the ethical, and transform humanity by means of art. He developed this idea in his book *Die Gegenstandslose Welt* (World without Objects), which appeared in Germany in 1927. His work had a certain influence; his philosophical theories none.

THE FUTURISTS

If Expressionism is primarily Nordic, Futurism for its part is almost exclusively Italian.

Despite the attempts made by Segantini and the "Macchiaioli" (or "tachistes") to bring fresh life into it, Italian painting had been for too long wrapped in its academic slumbers for an eventual reaction not to be inevitable. When it finally came, it was extremely violent. Such was the origin of Futurism, a movement which is a consequence of Cubism, though it actually claimed to despise it. In 1910, one year after Marinetti's Futurist Mani-

festo had been published in *Le Figaro*, five painters – Giacomo Balla (born in 1874), Umberto Boccioni (1882–1916), Carlo Carrà (born in 1888), Luigi Russolo (1885–1947), and Gino Severini (born in 1893) – published their own manifesto of Futurist art. In their view, painters must disown the past, glorify the most modern features of contemporary life (cars, aeroplanes, machinery, jazz), represent objects enclosed one inside another, and, above all, they must express movement by splitting it up into its successive phases. The Futurist exhibition held in Paris in 1912 was less overwhelmingly successful than its organizers had hoped, and a few years later the Futurists dispersed. In their works they followed their own principles with too much literalness. The most interesting artist of the whole group,

UMBERTO BOCCIONI · *Dynamism of a Cyclist*
Gianni Mattioli Collection, Milan

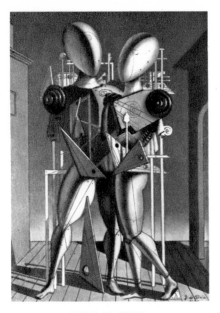

GIORGIO DE CHIRICO
Metaphysic of Man and Woman
Private collection, Chicago

◁ SALVADOR DALI · *A Giraffe on Fire*
Museum of Art, Basel

Gino Severini, has shown some tendency to alter his style. The series of mural paintings he has executed in French-Swiss churches seems today the best part of his work.

THE SURREALISTS

Surrealism sprang from the literary movement known as Dadaism, which was founded in Switzerland around 1917, during the First World War, and which expressed a reaction against the war and against the contemporary world as a whole. It included writers of many different nationalities. The violent explosion which the Dadaists sought to bring about by surprising and shocking the public was also aimed at by the Surrealists, when, about 1924, they set out to reintroduce an element of strangeness and fantasy into art.

By combining disparate objects in contradiction to our rational knowledge of the visible world, Surrealism sought to express a new kind of poetry, capturing, as André Breton put it, "that strange symbolic life which the most everyday objects lead in dreams alone: translating the latent mysteriousness of the commonplace." Here Surrealism took its cue from a passage in *Les Chants de Maldoror,* where Lautréamont speaks of the unexpected meeting on a dissection-table of an umbrella and a sewing-machine; there was also the influence of Freud's stress upon the subconscious.

It is probably among the Surrealists that we should put Marcel Duchamp (born in 1887), a brother of Jacques Villon. This former librarian has had a curious career: his output has been deliberately small, and yet he has had a most powerful influence on the whole modern school. He was a Cubist, and closely associated with the main protagonists of that trend;

yet as early as 1912, with his *Nude Descending the Stairs* (Philadelphia Museum of Art), he had introduced movement into Cubism, which was not quite orthodox. He belonged both to the "Golden Section" group and to the Dadaists. But his clearest association is with the beginnings of Surrealism, above all through his close links with the movement's leaders. He was the organizer of the first Surrealist exhibition in New York (in 1941), and most of his few

HENRI ROUSSEAU (LE DOUANIER) · *War*
Musée d'Art Moderne, Paris

with extreme precision, which sometimes even verges on the *trompe-l'œil*. His perfect technique gives his work the smooth finish of a minor Dutch master.

Giorgio di Chirico (born in 1888) was at first a painter of city scenes and vistas into emptiness, who after 1918 became one of the leaders of "metaphysical painting" in Italy: a school which replaced

MAX ERNST · *Spring in Paris*
Private collection

MAURICE UTRILLO · *Sacré-Coeur de Montmartre*
Private collection

works are in America, where he himself lives.

Though he never worked out a theory or joined the Surrealist group, Pierre Roy (1880–1950), a painter in the lineage of Degas and Cézanne, was one of the originators of this type of pictorial exploration, as writers on Surrealism have come to admit. His laborious pictures of objects or simple scenes, which he endows with a quality of strangeness, are painted the human form with dummies and collections of artificial limbs. Later, he came to paint like Böcklin.

Salvador Dali (born in 1904), though he subsequently broke with the Surrealists, used an extremely smooth and meticulous technique to give the objects represented physical properties contrary to those which they have in real life. Thus, he has painted watches which, balanced on the edge of a table, droop or ooze like an overripe Brie cheese. He also used blots and splashes made by throwing things at the canvas.

Joan Miró (born in 1893) broke loose from his early representational style, and filled his pictures with graphic symbols which, in his view, constitute a highly personal poetry. To these names we might add those of André Masson (born in 1896), Yves Tanguy (born in 1900), and Lucien Coutaud (born in 1904).

The most passionate member of the Surrealist group was Max Ernst, a German painter born in 1891. He had been one of the founders of the Cologne group of Dadaists, but soon moved towards Surrealism and came to be so classified. He applied methods that had been seldom, or inadequately, used before: his collages and frottages are famous and inimitable. His son Jimmy is an abstract painter.

In Belgium, Paul Delvaux (born in 1897) and René Magritte (born in 1898) have been Surrealism's leading representatives. While using deliberately old-fashioned techniques, like Pierre Roy, they have set out to baffle the viewer by making him glimpse the mystery hidden in familar things. We saw something of the same sort of effort with Pierre Roy, but he always represented real objects; the Belgian painters, however, combine these with nude female bodies, seen as if in double exposure, or they will cut open a house or a human body in order to disclose an unexpected "inside." All this is often attractive when set down with a sure hand.

AMEDEO MODIGLIANI · *Seated Nude*
Georges Renand Collection, Paris

MODERN PRIMITIVES

About 1906 a few writers and artists, led by Guillaume Apollinaire, discovered an old man whom they nicknamed *Douanier* ("the Customs Official"). His name was Henri Rousseau (1844–1910), and he painted with a naïve concentration. His works were highly esteemed and subsequently sold for enormous prices, and the search then began for other "naïve" painters. (They were also known as "instinctive painters" or "modern primitives.") Dealers and collectors were soon fighting over the works of a gentleman who sold potato chips on the streets, Emile Boyer (born in 1877), a charwoman, Séraphine Louis (1864–1934) –known as Séraphine de Senlis–André Bauchant (1873–1958), and Camille Bombois (born in 1883). We should arrive at a juster estimate of the Douanier Rousseau if, instead of treating him as a painter comparable to other painters, we saw him as what he really was: a phenomenon on the margin of the art world of his day, an exceptional case. He was certainly a gifted painter, and his ingenuous mind combined with the circumstances in which he lived to ensure that he remained impervious to all that was going on around him. He painted as if he were the only man in the world ever to have done so. His works are interesting on account of his gifts, but in many cases their interest is very limited. In short, because of their exceptional character, their influence could not be a seminal one.

Suzanne Valadon (1865–1938) had been an acrobat, and she was used as a model by Puvis de Chavannes, Renoir, and Toulouse-Lautrec. She disclosed a vigor-

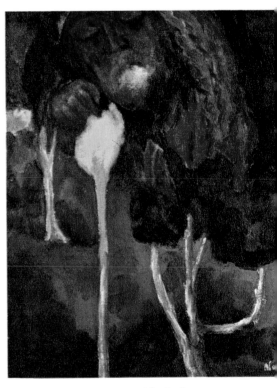

EMIL NOLDE · *The Gardener*
Dr. Bernhard Sprengel Collection, Hannover

EDWARD MUNCH · *Girls on a Bridge*
Wallraf-Richartz Museum, Cologne

ous and original talent in her nudes, landscapes, and still lifes, with their well-contrasted color schemes. Her son Utrillo (1883–1955) gave evidence of an immoderate love of alcohol even in adolescence, and in order to win him away from it she gave him the materials with which to paint. The boy took to this and began to paint landscapes, sometimes from nature, sometimes from views on postcards. He was so gifted that, with the help of odd pieces of advice given him by his mother, he acquired a personal technique which allowed him to express himself with unusual simplicity. Starting from what seemed outwardly the most trivial scenes—Montmartre side-streets, decrepit houses, uninteresting churches—he managed to generate an intense poetry. After a few years his talent fell off; he continued to paint, but the works of his second period are far inferior to those of his first.

Amedeo Modigliani (1884–1920), a highly refined and intelligent artist, was never a "naïve" or "primitive" painter in the current sense of those words. But he was entirely "instinctive," in the sense that everything came to him by instinct. He was a highly original painter, who never belonged to any school. An Italian by birth, he came to Paris in 1906 and quickly attracted attention. It was within himself that he found the inspiration for his work, which falls into two divergent and even opposite groups: on the one hand, big sensual nudes with Ingres-like curves and two-dimensional color; on the other, portraits with a calm and innocent but often most intense expression, painted with great technical refinement. Different as they are, all his canvases have undeniable charm. It would be interesting to know whether, had he

FRANZ MARC · *Roe in a Garden*
Art Gallery, Bremen

lived longer, the artist would have chosen one of the two courses he had already worked out, or have painted in yet other ways. However, Modigliani succumbed to his passion for drugs, and died at the age of thirty-five.

THE EXPRESSIONISTS

"Expressionism," according to Marcel Brion, "makes painting a vehicle for pure emotion, for inner drama, often in the raw state." It is an emotional and self-centered kind of art, which enables the artist to express his emotions by rendering them more intense. It can claim some illustrious masters in the art of the past, including Altdorfer and Matthias Grünewald. For it is an essentially northern phenomenon, and Germany was the country where it developed best.

The 1914–18 war, defeat, inflation, and other extraordinary social and political events all deeply disturbed the German people, and it is not surprising that from 1918 to recent years their art reflected their anxiety and confusion. Even between 1900 and 1914, a kind of foreknowledge had led many Germans to become dissatisfied with their elders' way. They

ERNST LUDWIG KIRCHNER · *Street Scene*
Museum of Modern Art, New York

wanted to exploit the pictorial freedom gained for them by such men as Liebermann, Corinth, and Slevogt, in order to express not only what they saw but also their inner world. They turned accordingly for guidance to such artists as Gauguin, Matisse, Van Gogh, Hodler, and Munch. Munch was a Norwegian who used a very free idiom and bright colors to express his feelings about the basic questions of human existence, and to attack bourgeois conformism.

Christian Rohlfs (1849–1938) painted still lifes and flowers in brilliant colors under the inspiration of Van Gogh. About 1906, Erich Heckel (born in 1883), Ernst Kirchner (1880–1938), Karl Schmidt-Rottluff (born in 1884), and Max Pechstein (1881–1955) founded a group at Dresden called *Die Brücke*, or "the bridge," which Emil Nolde (1867–1937) joined for a short period. Expressionists

ALEXEJ VON JAWLENSKY · *The Asiatic Woman*
Private collection

MAX BECKMANN · *Self-Portrait*
Bavarian National Museum, Munich

in the fullest sense of the term, despising conventional beauty, these painters tried to express their emotions with complete freedom, in works full of shrill colors and extreme distortions.

With these Expressionists, we may class the Czech painter Oskar Kokoschka (born in 1886). At first he painted portraits in a highly tortured technique, then turned to huge panoramas of cities and landscapes, which come close to Impressionism and are not without grandeur. Since the Second World War (when he obtained British citizenship) he has applied his gifts along Symbolist lines.

The art of the *Brücke* painters had an unrelievedly extremist character which, as also with the Fauves, made it difficult for them to develop. It was left to others

WASSILY KANDINSKY · *Improvisation 31*
J. Müller Collection, Solothurn, Switzerland

are shattering the undefiled and ever illusory phenomena of nature, and putting them together again according to our own will.... Matter is something that man may just be able to tolerate, but he is determined not to admit it." To these artists painting became the vehicle for a poetic and philosophical mysticism—it is incidentally significant that they all studied philosophy—and rather than cling to the appearance of things, they wished to penetrate to the core, to communicate not only with animals and vegetables but with inanimate objects as well.

Marc and Macke did not wholly exclude representation from their pictures. But Kandinsky went further, and set out to turn painting into an art as independent of natural appearance as music. His abstract pictures are surfaces covered with lines, points, and signs, by means of which the artist claimed to be interpreting his spiritual states in the same way as a musician does with sounds.

Paul Klee (1879–1940), a late-comer to the Blaue Reiter group, followed similar principles, and in subtly colored works tried to recapture the directness of children and primitive peoples and to express dreams and fantasies.

Kandinsky and Klee were part of the staff at the *Bauhaus* at Dessau, which the architect Gropius had founded at Weimar in 1919, and which moved to Dessau in 1926. It was dissolved in 1933. Other artists of the same school included Lyonel Feininger (1871–1956), whose angular landscapes brought him close to Cubism; Oskar Schlemmer (1888–1943), who reduced human figures and objects to the simplest of forms; Willi Baumeister (1889–1955), who stripped them of their last shreds of personality to transform them into diagrams; and Alexej von Jawlensky (1864–1941).

Two other artists should be mentioned here, although their medium was drawing and engraving rather than painting. Käthe Kollwitz (1867–1945) portrayed the

to explore new avenues. Among these younger artists are those who in 1911 founded a group called the *Blaue Reiter,* in Munich, and tried to express the essence of things by freeing themselves still further from nature. This group included Franz Marc (1880–1916) and August Macke (1887–1914), both of whom were killed in the war, and the Russian Wassily Kandinsky (1866–1944). Here are the group's aims, as expressed on the occasion of their 1912 exhibition in Munich: "Today we are searching behind the veil of superficial external appearances for the hidden things that to us seem to matter more than the discoveries of the Impressionists." Two of Franz Marc's aphorisms shed light on these artists' intentions: "Nowadays we

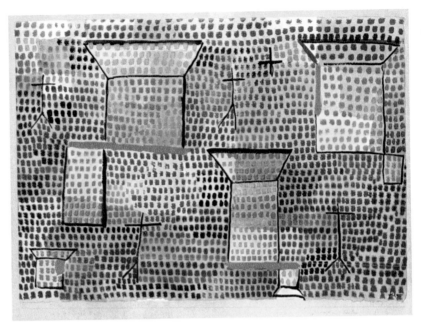

PAUL KLEE · *Columns and Crosses*
Bavarian National Museum, Munich

poverty and anguish of the lower classes in industrial cities with great vigor and conviction. Her art, founded on compassion, is at the opposite extreme from that of Georg Grosz (1893–1959), whose relentlessly ferocious drawings denounced the injustices of the postwar era, and flayed profiteers, militarists, and pleasure-seekers.

The exaggerations of the Brücke and Blaue Reiter painters led to a reaction in the form of a tempered naturalism, which became known as *Neue Sachlichkeit,* or "new matter-of-factness." This tendency was exemplified in Otto Dix, who meticulously recorded what he saw, and had a predilection for physical ugliness; in Karl Hofer (1878–1955), with his heavy naturalism; and in Max Beckmann (1884–1950), who remained an Expressionist despite his realist eye.

It should not be forgotten that after

GEORGES ROUAULT · *Young Worker*
Musée d'Art Moderne, Paris

MARCEL GROMAIRE · *The Tramp*
Musée d'Art Moderne, Paris

utmost. Constant Permeke (1886–1952) found his subjects among peasants and fishermen, to whose heavy bodies he gave a monumental character and simplified forms. Gustave de Smet (1877–1943) painted stylized scenes of everyday life in which he tried to recapture the naïveté of children's drawings. Edgard Tytgat (born in 1879) likewise tries to view the familiar world with a child's unsophisticated eye.

The few French Expressionists have acquired a great reputation: Rouault above all.

After painting intricate compositions at the École des Beaux-Arts, which reflected influences of the fifteenth-century Italian painters and of Rembrandt, Georges Rouault (1871–1958) came out about 1903 with large watercolors in Prussian blue, carmine, and India ink, which were ferocious caricatures of judges, circus performers, and prostitutes. The flowing, elliptical line of these figures, with its amazingly sure touch, brings to mind

CHAIM SOUTINE · *The Page Boy*
Private collection

Hitler seized power all avant-garde artists were regarded as "degenerate" and that the regime made it difficult for them to work. As Hitler himself put it at the opening of the House of German Art: "Cubism, Dadaism, Futurism, Impressionism, and the rest have nothing in common with our German people."

In Holland the new trends in painting appeared about 1910 in the person of Jan Sluyters (1881–1957), whose work is a mixture of realism and Expressionism. Expressionist tendencies gained ground at the expense of realism in the works of H. Kruyder (1881–1935), Leo Gestel (born in 1881), Mathieu Wiegman (born in 1886) and his brother Piet (born in 1885).

In Belgium a group was founded about 1910 which was named after the village where most of its members lived: the School of Laethem-Saint-Martin. They wanted to express the spirit of things by simplifying natural appearances to the such Japanese artists as Korin and Sesshu.

The human race was shown in such repulsive guise in these works that only a few perspicacious viewers were able to discern the great talent displayed in them. Later Rouault went back to the stained-glass technique which he had used in his youth, enclosing his more and more simplified forms in heavy black lines, and painting them in extremely rich colors. His reputation, which until 1918 had been confined to a handful of enthusiasts, grew steadily, and at his death he was held to be one of the greatest artists of our time. There are, however, people who feel that the works of his maturity and old age fall short of the admirable watercolors he painted before 1914.

Some critics regard as forerunners of the French Expressionist movement the group of artists, including La Patellière and Gromaire, that was influenced by Le Fauconnier. But the true representatives of French Expressionism are Gromaire (born in 1892), Soutine (1894–1943), and Chagall (born in 1887).

Amédée de La Patellière (1890–1932) has a place apart. He devoted himself to subjects from country life, which he saw as something more than a mere collection of picturesque motifs. Passionately attached to the age-old ritual of the soil, he was able to express its grandeur and its solemnity. Marcel Gromaire paints firmly drawn compositions illuminated by spots of color – ochers and browns set off by bright vermilions and ultramarines – and their expression is invariably both serene and sensitive. He tries to show us the nobility latent in everyday sights. Marc Chagall paints brightly colored, lively pictures of fantastic subjects; Soutine's colors are whipped together into positive frenzy. Both try by such means to express their inner feelings.

But there are two sides to Chagall's art.

JOAN MIRÓ · *The Wings of the Bird Glide over the Moon to Reach the Stars* Galerie Maeght, Paris

On the one hand, he shows an inborn taste for fantastic subjects, for marvelously colorful dreams. This merely expresses his fundamentally imaginative temperament. But time and again bitter experiences of reality remind him that his first lessons were with a portrait painter, and that under the influence of Cubism he had once inclined toward a form of Surrealism. It is from this other source that he has drawn his paintings inspired by war and political crisis. And this is truly Expressionist.

The Bulgarian painter Julius Pascin (1885–1930) was really called Pincas. His father was a Spanish Jew and his mother an Italian born in Serbia, but he made his reputation mainly in France, or to be precise, in Paris. He settled there after a wandering life that took him to Vienna, Germany, Algeria, and America. It was in Paris that he eventually killed himself. (This enumeration alone illustrates how international modern art has become, and how misleading is the facile

lives. His work as a caricaturist came earlier, but shows the same tendency.

In his effort to convey "life's tragic sense" Francis Gruber (1912–1948) could well seek inspiration in his own short and unhappy life: his birth and childhood in a poor working-class milieu, the struggles of his early years, his delicate health, his premature death. His work belongs entirely to Expressionism: an Expressionism that owes little to modern movements and techniques. Apart from a few systematic physical distortions, his painting goes back to very old traditions: emphasis on line; realism; unobtrusive colors; no exaggerated impastos. His subjects are mostly sad, if not actually sinister, and their effect is still more accentuated by the jagged outlines. A friend of the painters grouped in the "Forces Nouvelles," closely associated with André Marchand, and with his own near-contemporary Georges Rohner, he undoubtedly set off that return to figurative painting whose best-known exponent is now Bernard Buffet.

Although Buffet is at the beginning of his career (having been born in 1928) and is thus in a position to learn and to develop a great deal, his name and work are too well known for us not to dwell on them for a moment. This is not just for his own sake, but because of the way in which his work reflects the various, often contradictory tendencies of our time, and complies with all the requirements of all of them. The part played by publicity in his success should not be exaggerated, though there has certainly been a great deal of it. Left to itself, his genuine talent would not have been enough. But a whole generation of art lovers who had too long been caught in the toils of pure color has rediscovered in him those qualities which they had missed: drawing, subject, style. A younger generation without ideals, without faith, and without hope, weary of the different "messages"

label "École de Paris.") Pascin is most widely known by his delicate sketches, heightened with pale washes, in which he captures the graceful insolence of very young prostitutes. It is these works that connect him with the Expressionist movement. His life and death give evidence of the depth and intensity of his emotions, while his drawings show how sensitive he was to the tragedy of ruined offered to it by masters of verbiage, has found in him the hideous ever present nightmare it knows only too well: distasteful work, vice, disease, and war with all its freshly resuscitated horrors: deportations, torture, and mass exterminations. Following on Gruber's, Buffet's painting represents a return to the past: a line like an engraver's, strict and exact, color that is often absent in his early works and that is always discreet, a continual concern with composition. If the epithet "Expressionist" is to mean anything, to whom could it be better applied than to this painter of the tortured, of sad harlots, and cities reduced to rubble? That is where he stands at the moment. It would be interesting to know where he is heading.

NONFIGURATIVE OR ABSTRACT PAINTERS

The latest school of painting, which owes something to nearly all the preceding schools, and the final upshot of Impressionism, is "nonfigurative" painting: a term which seems more exact than the equally current "abstract painting." It is true that the idea of eliminating all representation of reality—that is, of all outward appearance—is not new, but goes back nearly half a century. Only since the last war, however, has it become widespread. Today nonfigurative painting has adherents all over the world.

In this book, we are trying to be as objective as we can, especially where the painting of the past fifty years is concerned. Thus we do not have to give a verdict on nonfigurative art. All we can do is to note its international character—nobody can tell whether a given nonfigurative painting has been painted in Oslo or Sidney, Paris or Los Angeles—and give a few definitions of this art, put forward by two of its best-known supporters.

According to René Huyghe, the nonfigurative painters "are trying, like the Cubists before them, to make each picture an *object*. To create a work is to create a new reality, as independent as possible of the model." Nonfigurative painters want to "paint pictures that will be plastic objects rather than representations of the real." Marcel Brion, a passionate and intelligent advocate of this kind of art, sees the sources of nonfigurative painting in "weariness ... with realistic, naturalistic representations of things; with accepting nature's forms as they stand.... The abstract picture will shed all similarity with natural forms in order to build up a vocabulary of emotional symbols which will make a direct impact on the viewer's sensitivity without any intermediary. In abstract art the painter is not linked to his object visually, but emotionally." The viewer must not look for "intellectual relationship in a sphere where the only factor is emotional communion." This communion "is developed by abstract art into a bond between souls, by means of forms reduced to mere emotional factors.... A picture is nothing but a *spiritual projection*." Nonfigurative art provides ways of "getting into contact with the soul of the world, of tuning-in on a cryptic revelation of the cosmos." It makes possible "the introduction into painting of a cosmic sense of space and time, a sense of the oneness and infinity of the universe."

THE FUTURE OF PAINTING

Which way will painting develop next? Our survey of its history shows that none of the tendencies it has manifested is in danger of disappearing; and our review of the latest "schools" proves that we can scarcely expect the various currents to merge into one uniform school of painting; the opposite is far more likely.

Figurative painting goes on. Some of its practitioners try to follow the road marked out by the Impressionists; others to stylize nature by choosing the elements that strike them most vividly, and then arousing them according to a personal pattern. Still others practice a neorealism, and thanks to its meticulous technique or its choice of unusual subjects, it is considered acceptable by all those who are interested in pictorial art.

If this last chapter of our book had been arranged on the same principle as the seven others, we should have examined the chief creations of these figurative painters country by country. As things are, however, it seems best to leave this task to individual monographs, of which there is never any shortage, and instead to make clear to the reader the nature of these new "schools" which (let us repeat) are no longer national but universal, and which he continually hears about without being told their origins and history.

Far be it from us to play down the efforts and achievements of the more traditionalist or independent painters. To take France alone, we should remember that these include men like Segonzac and Dufresne and, in the next generation, following them, Roland Oudot, Brianchon, Chapelain-Midy, Brayer, and others. They enjoy the public's esteem; their works fill museums and public buildings; their kind of art is the only one which can, logically speaking, be taught in schools and academies. For how is one to teach movements which deliberately flout most, if not all, the rules?

Our own background and tastes may give us a certain preference for the traditional; but the main thing for both supporters and opponents of the most "advanced" art (and especially of "non-figurative" painting) is to be properly informed. They have no use for personal opinions. What they need is an objective account, and definitions as accurate as possible. This is what we have tried to give without taking sides. We have impartially noted the various tendencies, examining the artists' work and classifying it in a way that seems to us to correspond with the facts. This we have done as often as possible by letting the artists speak for themselves, or by quoting reliable authorities. Most important of all, this book includes reproductions of their works.

What then do we conclude?

On the one hand, those still loyal to the schools which stemmed directly from Impressionism or began as a reaction against it are still doing serious, worthwhile work. On the other hand, abstract painting, which is a direct but younger descendant of the Impressionist revolution, is also pursuing its difficult task. If we discount those artists – and the innumerable "amateur artists" – who wrongly imagine that abstract art is going to provide them with easy answers, then at least two tendencies seem to be discernible in it. The one leads back towards Impressionism; the other yields to the temptation of ornamentalism. We must wait hopefully for one or two "styles" to crystallize in this field, for otherwise this art movement will inevitably break up into ever smaller splinter groups and perhaps even disappear.

At all events we can be sure that painting itself will never disappear. Never has there been so much talk about painters; never has art been the object of such passionate speculation, both intellectual and financial. Painting, which gives so much pleasure to the eye and to the spirit, has never been so much alive or so many-sided as today.

The future will make its own choice.

LIST OF ILLUSTRATIONS

INDEX OF NAMES

Principal references are shown in italics